John Lancaster Spalding

Essays and Reviews

John Lancaster Spalding

Essays and Reviews

ISBN/EAN: 9783741158063

Manufactured in Europe, USA, Canada, Australia, Japa

Cover: Foto ©Andreas Hilbeck / pixelio.de

Manufactured and distributed by brebook publishing software
(www.brebook.com)

John Lancaster Spalding

Essays and Reviews

ESSAYS

AND

REVIEWS.

BY

RT. REV. J. L. SPALDING, D.D.,

Bishop of Peoria.

NEW YORK:

THE CATHOLIC PUBLICATION SOCIETY,

9 BARCLAY STREET.

—

1877.

PREFACE.

HE papers contained in this volume have appeared, with one or two exceptions, substantially as they are here published, in the *Catholic World* during the last eighteen months. The essay entitled "Religion and Art" has been rewritten from a sketch made several years ago. Some of the subjects which are here discussed, hurriedly and imperfectly enough, have at least the merit of dealing with questions of present interest; and throughout the entire volume that which has chiefly engaged my thought is religion, which, however it be considered, remains, and must for ever remain, the chief and most essential element in the history and civilization of mankind, as it alone gives to human nature a higher than animal value and a more than mortal destiny.

NEW YORK, May 1, 1877.

CONTENTS.

ESSAYS AND REVIEWS.

—•••—

THE CATHOLIC CHURCH IN THE UNITED STATES, 1776–1876.

THE conditions of social life which have been developed in the European colonies of North America, though to a certain extent the result of the physical surroundings of the early settlers, are chiefly the freer growth of principles which have been active for centuries in the Christian nations of the Old World. The elements of society here, unhindered by custom, law, or privilege, grouped themselves quickly and spontaneously into the forms to which they are tending in Europe also, but slowly and through conflict and struggle. The great and most significant fact, that it was found impossible in the New World to create privileged classes, clearly pointed in the direction in which European civilization was moving. Another fact not less noteworthy was the failure of every attempt to establish religion in this country.

Though there is but little to please the fancy or fire the imagination in American character or institutions, it is nevertheless to this country that the eyes of the thoughtful and observant from every part of the world are turned. The catholicity of Christian civilization has generalized political problems and social movements. Civilization, like religion, has ceased to be national ; and the bearing of a people's life upon the welfare of the human race has come to be of greater moment than its effect upon the national character. It is to this that the universal interest which centres in the United States must be attributed.

We are a commonplace and mediocre people ; practical, without high ideals, lofty aspirations, or excellent standards of worth and character. In philosophy, in science, in literature, in art, in culture, we are inferior to the nations of Europe. No mind transcendentally great has appeared among us ; not one who is heir to all the ages and citizen of the world. Our ablest thinkers are merely the disciples of some foreign master. Our most gifted poets belong to the careful kind, who with effort and the file give polish and smoothness, but not the *mens divinior*, to their verse ; and who, when they attempt a loftier flight, grow dull and monotonous as a Western prairie or Rocky Mountain table-land. Our most popular heroes—Washington and Lincoln—are but common men, and the higher is he who is least the product of our democratic institutions.

Our commercial enterprise and mechanical achievements are worthy of admiration, but not so far above those of other nations as to attract special attention.

If to-day, then, the American people draw the eyes of the whole world upon themselves, it is not because they have performed marvellous deeds, opened up new realms of thought, or created higher types of character, but because their social and political condition is that to which Europe, whether for good or evil, seems to be irresistibly approaching. Beyond doubt, the tendency of modern civilization is to give to the people greater power and a larger sphere of action. Every attempt to arrest this movement but serves to make its force the more manifest. This spirit of the age is seen in the general spread of education, in the widening of the popular suffrage, in the separation of church and state, and in the dying out of aristocracies. We simply note facts, without stopping to examine principles or to weigh consequences. Those who resist a revolution are persuaded that it will work nothing but evil, while those who help it on hope from it every good ; and the event most generally shows both to have been in error. Our present purpose does not lead us to speculate as to the manner in which the general welfare is to be affected by the great social transformations by which the character of civilized nations is being so profoundly modified ; but we will suppose that the reign of aristocracies and of privilege is past, and that in the future the people are to govern ; and we ask, What will be the influence of the new society upon the old faith ?

The essential life of the Catholic Church is independent of her worldly condition; and though we are bound to believe that she is to remain amongst men until the end, we are yet not forbidden to hold that at times she may to human eyes seem almost to have ceased to be; that as in the past Christ was entombed, the *deletum nomen Christianum* was proclaimed, in the future also the heavens may grow dark, God's countenance seemingly be withdrawn, and the voice of despair cry out that all have bent the knee to Baal.

" But yet the Son of Man, when he cometh, shall he find, think you, faith on earth ? " We may hope, we may despond; let us, then, dispassionately consider the facts.

First, we will put aside the assumption that it is possible to organize this modern society so as to crush the church by persecution or violence. In a social state, which can be strong only by being just, attempts of this kind, if successful, would inevitably lead to anarchy and chaos, out of which the church would again come forth with or before the civil order. We cannot, then, look forward to a prolonged and open conflict between the church and the civilized governments of the world without giving up all hope in the permanency and effectiveness of the social phase upon which we have entered. In the end the European states, like the American, must be convinced that, if they would live, they must also let live; since a *modus vivendi* between church and state is absolutely essential to the permanence of society as now constituted.

The question, then, is narrowed to the free and peaceable life of the church in contact with the popular governments which are already constituted or are struggling for existence ; and it is in their bearing upon this all-important subject that the world-wide significance of the lessons to be learned from a careful study of the history of the Catholic Church in the United States becomes apparent. For a hundred years this church has lived in the new society, and all the circumstances of her position have been admirably suited to test her power to meet the difficulties offered by a democratic social organization. The problem to be solved was whether or not a vigorous but yet orderly and obedient Catholic faith and life could flourish in this country, where what are called the principles of modern civilization have found their most complete expression.

If we would understand the history of our country, we must not lose sight of the religious character of the men by whom it was explored and colonized. Religious zeal led the Puritans to New England, the Catholics to Maryland, and the Quakers to Pennsylvania ; and among the Spaniards and the French there were many who, like Columbus and Champlain, deemed the salvation of a soul of greater moment than the conquest of an empire. We might, indeed, without going beyond our present subject, speak of the heroic and gentle lives of the apostolic men who, from Maine to California, from Florida to the Northern Lakes, toiled among the Indians, and not in vain, that they might win

them from savage ways and lift them up to higher
modes of life.   The Catholics of the United States
can never forget that the labors of these men belong to the history of the church on this continent ;
that the lives they offered up, the blood they shed,
plead for us before God ; and that if their work is
disappearing, it sinks into the grave only with the
dying race which they more than all others have
loved and served.   But in this age men are little
inclined to dwell upon memories, however glorious.
We live in the present and in the future, and, in
spite of much cheap sentiment and wordy philan-
thropy, we have but weak sympathy with decaying
races.   We are interested in what is or is to be, not
in what has been ; and perhaps it is well that this
is so.   We have but feeble power to think or act or
love, and it should not be wasted.   If Americans
to-day are busy with thoughts of a hundred years
ago, it is not that they love those old times and
their simple ways, but that by contrast they may,
in boastful self-complacency, glory in the present.
They look back, not to regret the fast-receding
shore, but to congratulate themselves that they
have left it already so far behind.   It is enough,
then, to have alluded to the labors of the Catholic
missionaries among the North American Indians,
since those labors have had and can have but small
influence upon the history of the church in the
United States.   To understand this history we
need only study that of the Europeans and their
descendants on this continent.

The early colonists of the present territory of the

United States were as unlike in their religious as in their national characters.   English Puritans founded the colonies of New England ; New York was settled by the Dutch ; Delaware and New Jersey by the Dutch and the Swedes; Pennsylvania by Quakers from England, who were followed by a German colony.   Virginia was the home of the English who adhered to the Established Church of the mother country, and North Carolina became the refuge of the Nonconformists from Virginia ; in South Carolina a considerable number of Huguenots found an asylum ; and in Maryland the first settlers were chiefly English Catholics.   Nearly all these colonies owed their foundation to the religious troubles of Europe.   The Puritans, the Catholics, and the Quakers were more eager to find a home in which they could freely worship God than to amass wealth.

The religious spirit of New England, whose influence in this country, before and since the Revolution, has been preponderant, was as narrow and proscriptive as it was intense, and a gloomy fanaticism lay at the basis of its entire political and social system.   The Puritan colonies were not so much bodies politic as churches in the wilderness. To the commission appointed to draw up a body of laws to serve as a declaration of rights, Cotton Mather declared that God's people should be governed by no other laws than those which He himself had given to Moses ; and one of the first acts of the Massachusetts colony was the expulsion of John and Samuel Browne with their followers, be-

cause they refused to conform to the religious practices of the Pilgrims. If dissenting Protestants
were not tolerated in New England, Catholics certainly could not hope for mercy; and, in fact, they
were denied religious liberty even in Rhode Island,
which had been founded by the victims of Puritan
persecution as a refuge for the oppressed and a
protest against fanaticism.   Though Mr. Bancroft,
whose partisan zeal whenever there is question of
New England is unmistakable, denies that this
unjust discrimination was the act of the people of
Rhode Island, it served, at any rate, so effectually
to exclude Catholics that when the war of independence broke out not one was to be found within
the limits of the colony.

Puritanism, more than any other form of Protestantism, drew its very life from a hatred of all that is
Catholic.   The office and authority of bishops, the
repetition of the Lord's Prayer, the sign of the
cross, the chant of the psalms, the observance of
saints' days, the use of musical instruments in
church, and the vestments worn by the ministers
of religion were all odious to the Puritans because
they were associated with Catholic worship; and
in their eyes the chief crime of the Church of England was that she still retained some of the doctrines and usages of that of Rome.   Religion and
freedom, though their conception of both was partial and false, were the predominant passions of the
Puritans ; and since they looked upon the Catholic
Church as the fatal enemy alike of religion and of
freedom, their fanaticism, not less than their enthu-

siastic love of independence, filled them with the deepest hatred for Catholics.   They had the virtues and the vices of the lower and more ignorant classes of Englishmen, from which for the most part they had sprung.   If they were frugal, content with little, ready to bear hardship and to suffer want, not easily cast down, they were also narrow, superstitious, angular, and unlovely ; and these characteristics were hardened by a cold, gloomy, and unsympathetic religious faith.   The credulity which led them to hang witches made them ready to believe in the diabolism of priests ; while the narrowness of their intellectual range rendered them incapable of perceiving the grandeur and excellence of an organization which alone, in the history of the world, has become universal without becoming weak, and which, if it be considered as only human, is still man's most wonderful work.   With the æsthetic beauty of the Catholic religion they could have no sympathy, since they were deprived of the sense by which alone it can be appreciated.   Though they fasted, appointed days of thanksgiving, and, through a false asceticism, changed the Lord's day into the Jewish Sabbath, the fasts and saints' days of Catholics were in their eyes the superstitions of idolaters ; and while they assumed the right to declare what is true Christian doctrine and to enforce its acceptance, they indignantly rejected the spiritual authority of the church, though historically traceable to Christ's commission to the apostles.

The measures, therefore, which the colonies of New England took to prevent the establishment

of the Catholic Church on their soil, were merely
the expression of the horror and dread of what they
conceived its influence and tendency to be. In
1631, just eleven years after the landing of the
Mayflower, Sir Christopher Gardiner, on mere suspicion of being a papist, was seized and sent out
of the Colony of Massachusetts Bay, and in the
same year the General Court wrote a letter denouncing the minister at Watertown for giving expression to the opinion that the Church of Rome is
a true church.   Three years later Roger Williams,
whose tolerant temper has been an exhaustless
theme of praise, joined with the Puritans in declaring the cross a " relic of Antichrist, a popish symbol
savoring of superstition and not to be countenanced
by Christian men "; and, in proof of the sincerity
of their zeal, these godly men cut the cross from
out the English flag.   Priests were forbidden, under
pain of imprisonment and even death, to enter the
colonies ; and the neighboring Catholic settlements
of Canada were regarded with sentiments of such
bigoted hatred as to blind the Puritans to their own
most evident political and commercial interests.
So unrelenting was their fanaticism that one of the
grievances which they most strongly urged against
George III. was that he tolerated popery in Canada.
In the New England colonies, down to 1776, the
Catholic Church had no existence, and the same
may be said of the other colonies, with the exception of Maryland and of a few families scattered
through parts of Pennsylvania.   In Maryland itself,
where the principles of religious liberty, which now

form a part of the organic law of the land, had
been first proclaimed by the Catholic colonists, the
persecution of the church early became an important
feature in the colonial legislation.   In successive
enactments the Catholics were forbidden to teach
school, to hold civil office, and to have public worship ; and were, moreover, taxed for the support
of the Established Church.   The religious character
of Virginia, though less intense and earnest than
that of New England, can hardly be said to have
been less anti-Catholic; and it is therefore not surprising that we should find the cruel penal code of
the mother country in full vigor in this colony.

It would have been difficult to find anywhere
communities more thoroughly Protestant than these
thirteen British colonies one hundred years ago.
The little body of Catholics in Maryland, in all
about 25,000, who, in spite of persecution, had retained their faith, had sunk into a kind of religious
apathy ; and as their public worship had long been
forbidden and they were not permitted to have
schools, to indifference was added ignorance of the
doctrines of the church.   A few priests, once members of the suppressed Society of Jesus, lingered
amongst them, though they generally found it
necessary to live upon their own lands or with their
kindred, and with difficulty kept alive the flickering
flame of faith.   Without religious energy, zeal, or
organization, the Maryland Catholics were gradually being absorbed into mere worldliness or into
the more vigorous Protestant sects; and, in fact,
many of the descendants of the original settlers had

already lost the faith. In this way the character of the old Catholic colony had been wholly changed; so that Maryland surpassed all the other colonies in the odious proscriptiveness of her legislation, levying the same tax for the introduction into her territory of a Catholic Irishman as for the importation of a negro slave. The existence of the Catholic families there, and of the small and scattered settlements in Pennsylvania, if recognized at all by the general public, was looked upon as an anomaly, an anachronism, which, from the nature of things, must soon disappear. There is no exaggeration, then, in saying that the Revolution found the British provinces of North America thoroughly Protestant, with a hatred of the church which nothing but the general contempt for Catholics tended to mitigate; while the seeming failure of the Catholic settlement in Maryland, one hundred and fifty years after the landing of Lord Baltimore, gave no promise of a brighter future for the faith.

In the presence of the impending conflict with England political questions became supreme, and the Convention of 1774, in its appeal to the country, entreated all classes of citizens to put away religious disputes and animosities, which could only withhold them from uniting in the defence of their common rights and liberties. Though this appeal was probably meant to smooth the way for a more cordial union between New England and the Southern colonies, which were even then as unlike as Puritan and Cavalier, it was also an evidence of the public feeling, showing that with the American

people religious questions were fast coming to be
merely of secondary importance. At any rate it
was responded to cheerfully and generously by the
Catholics, who, without stopping to think of the
wrongs they had suffered, threw themselves heartily into the contest for national independence.
The signer of the Declaration who risked most was
a Catholic, and a Catholic priest was a member of
the delegation sent to Canada to bring about an
alliance, or at least to secure the neutrality of that
province.

The conduct of the Catholics in the war made,
no doubt, a favorable impression, and the very important aid given to the American cause by Catholic France had still further influence in softening
the asperities of Protestant prejudice ; but, unless
we are mistaken, we must seek elsewhere for the
explanation of the clause of the federal Constitution which provides that "no religious test shall
ever be required as a qualification for any office or
public trust under the United States" ; as well as
of the First Amendment, to the effect that " Congress shall make no law respecting an establishment
of religion or prohibiting the free exercise thereof."
These acts were merely part of a general policy,
which restricted as far as possible the functions of
the federal government, and left to the several
States as much of their separate sovereignty as was
consistent with the existence of the national Union.

This is evident from the fact that the federal
Constitution placed no restriction upon the legislation of the different States in matters of religion,

leaving them free to pursue the intolerant and per-
secuting policy of the colonial era ; and, indeed,
laws for the support of public worship lingered in
Connecticut till 1816 and in Massachusetts till 1833,
and anti-Catholic religious tests were introduced
into several of the State constitutions. In New
York, as late as 1806, a test-oath excluded Catholics
from office ; and in North Carolina, down to 1836,
only those who were willing to swear to belief in
the truth of Protestantism were permitted to hope
for political preferment. New Jersey erased the
anti-Catholic clause from her constitution only in
1844 ; and even to-day, unless we err, the written
law of New Hampshire retains the test-oath.*

The law which denied to the general government all right of interference in religious matters
was a political necessity. Any attempt to introduce into Congress religious discussions would
have surely rent asunder the still feeble bands
by which New England and the Southern States
were held together. The reasons of policy which
forbade the federal government to meddle with
slavery applied with tenfold force to questions of
religion.

The First Amendment to the Constitution, of
which we Americans are so fond of boasting, was
not, therefore, an assertion of the principle of toleration or of the separation of church and state ;
it was merely the expression of the will of the
confederating States to retain their pre-existing

---

* Since this was written, New Hampshire has abrogated the law which excluded Catholics from office.

rights of control over religion, which, indeed, théy could not have delegated to the general government without imperilling the very existence of the Union.   Nearly all the leading statesmen of that day recognized the necessity of some kind of union of church and state, and their views were embodied in the different State constitutions.

The year before the first battle of the Revolution no less than eighteen Baptists were confined in one jail in Massachusetts for refusing to pay ministerial rates ; and yet John Adams declared " that a change in the solar system might be expected as soon as a change in the ecclesiastical system of Massachusetts"; and at a much later period Judge Story was able to affirm that " it yet remained a problem to be solved in human affairs whether any free government can be permanent where the public worship of God and the support of religion constitute no part of the policy or duty of the state."

There is no foundation, we think, for the opinion which we have sometimes heard expressed, that the First Amendment to the Constitution was intended as an act of tardy justice to the Catholics of the United States, in gratitude for their conduct during the war and for the aid of Catholic France.   It in fact made no change in the position of the Catholics, whom it left to the mercy of the different States, precisely as they had been in the colonial era.   Various causes were, however, at work which, by modifying the attitude of the States towards religion, tended also to give greater freedom to the

Catholic Church. The first of these was the rise of what may be called the secular theory of government, whose great exponent, Thomas Jefferson, had received his political opinions from the French philosophers of the eighteenth century. The state, according to this theory, is a purely political organism, and is not in any way concerned with religion ; and this soon came to be the prevailing sentiment in the Democratic party, whose acknowledged leader Jefferson was, which may explain why the great mass of the Catholics in this country have always voted with this party. Another cause that tended to bring about a separation of church and state was the rapidly-increasing number of sects, which rendered religious legislation more and more difficult, especially as several of these were opposed to any recognition of religion by the civil power. And to this we may add the growing religious indifference which caused large numbers of Americans to fall away from, or to be brought up outside of, all ecclesiastical organization. The desire, too, to encourage immigration—which sprang from interested motives, and also from a feeling, very powerful in the United States half a century ago, that this country is the refuge of all who are oppressed by the European tyrannies—predisposed Americans to look favorably upon the largest toleration of religious belief and practice. There is no question, then, but the Catholics of this country owe the freedom which they now enjoy to the operation of general laws, the necessary results of given social conditions, and not at all to the good-

will or tolerant temper of American Protestants.
Let us, however, be grateful for the boon, whence-
soever derived. At the close of the war which
secured our national independence and created the
republic the Catholic Church found herself, for all
practical purposes, unfettered and free to enter
upon a field which to her, we may say, was new.
At that time there were in the whole country not
more than forty thousand Catholics and twenty-
five priests. In all the land there was not a convent
or a religious community. There was not a Catholic school ; there was no bishop ; the sacraments of
confirmation and of Holy Orders had never been
administered. The church was without organization, having for several years had no intercourse
with its immediate head, the vicar-apostolic of
London ; it was without property, with the exception of some land in Maryland, which, through
a variety of contrivances, had been saved from the
rapacity of the colonial persecutors ; and, surrounded by a bigoted Protestant population, ignorant of all the Catholic glories of the past, it was
also without honor. But faith and hope, which
with liberty ought to make all things possible, had
not fled, and soon the budding promise of the
future harvest lifted its timid head beneath the
genial sun of a brighter heaven. The priests of
Maryland and Pennsylvania addressed a letter to
Pius VI., praying him to appoint a prefect-aposto-
lic to preside over the church in the United States ;
and as the Holy See was already deliberating upon
a step of this kind, Father Carroll was made supe-

3

rior of the American clergy, with power to administer the sacrament of confirmation. This was in 1784.

The priests, who at this time, for fear of wounding Protestant susceptibilities, thought it inexpedient to ask for a bishop, were now, after longer deliberation, persuaded that in this they had erred, and they therefore named a committee to present a petition to Rome, praying for the erection of an episcopal see in the United States. The Holy Father having signified his willingness to accede to this proposition, and it having been ascertained, too, that the government of this country would make no objection, they at once fixed upon Baltimore as the most suitable location for the new see, and presented the name of Father Carroll as the most worthy to be its first occupant. The papal bulls were dated November 6, 1789, and upon their reception Father Carroll sailed for England, where he was consecrated on the 15th of August, the Feast of the Assumption, 1790.

Events were just then taking place in France which were of great moment to the young church on the other side of the Atlantic Ocean. The French Revolution was getting ready to guillotine priests and to turn churches into barracks; and M. Emery, the Superior-General of the Order of Saint Sulpice, who was as far-seeing as he was fearless, entered into correspondence with Bishop Carroll, in England, with a view to open an ecclesiastical seminary in the United States. The offer was gladly accepted, and the year following (1791) M.

Nagot organized the Theological Seminary of Baltimore, and in the same year the first Catholic college in the United States was opened at Georgetown, in the District of Columbia. In 1790 Father Charles Neale brought from Antwerp a community of Carmelite nuns, who established themselves near Port Tobacco, in Southern Maryland. This was the first convent of religious women founded in the United States, the house of Ursuline nuns in New Orleans having come into existence while Louisiana was still a French colony. A few years later a number of religious ladies adopted the rule of the Order of the Visitation and organized a convent in Georgetown; and in 1809 Mother Seton founded near Emmittsburg, in Maryland, the first community of Sisters of Charity in this country, just one year after Father Dubois, the future Bishop of New York, had opened Mt. St. Mary's College. In 1805 Bishop Carroll reorganized the Society of Jesus, and in 1806 the Dominicans founded their first convent in the United States, at St. Rose, in Kentucky. Two years later episcopal sees were established at New York, Boston, Philadelphia, and Bardstown, with an archiepiscopal centre at Baltimore.

In this way the church was preparing, as far as the slender means at her command would permit, to receive and care for the vast multitudes of Catholics who began to seek refuge in the United States from the persecutions and oppressions of the British and other European governments. But her resources were not equal to the urgency and magnitude of the occasion, and her history during the half-century immediately following the close of the Revolutionary war, though full of examples of courage, zeal, and energy, shows her in the throes of a struggle which, whether it were for life or death, seemed doubtful.

Like an invading army, her children poured in a ceaseless stream into the enemy's country, and, arrived upon the scene of action, they found themselves without leaders, without provisions, without means of defence or weapons of heavenly warfare. Far from their spiritual guides, in a strange land, without churches or schools, the very air of this new world seemed fatal to the faith of the early Catholic immigrants; and when, yielding to the rigors of the climate or the hardships of frontier life, they died in great numbers, their orphan children fell into the hands of Protestants and were lost to the church. Their descendants to-day are scattered from Maine to Florida, from New York to California.

Bishop England, though inclined to exaggerate the losses of the church in this country, was certainly not mistaken in holding that during the period of which we speak, though there was an increase of congregations, there was yet a great falling away of Catholics from the faith in the United States.

. Unfortunately, the want of priests and churches cannot with truth be said to have been the greatest evil, especially in the early years of the organization of the hierarchy. A spirit of insubordination existed both in the clergy and the laity. " Every day," wrote Bishop Carroll, " furnishes me with new reflections, and almost every day produces new events to alarm my conscience and excite fresh solicitude at the prospect before me. You cannot conceive the trouble which I suffer already, and the still greater which I foresee from the medley of clerical characters, coming from different quarters and of various educations, and seeking employment here. I cannot avoid employing some of them, and soon they begin to create disturbances." There were troubles and scandals in nearly all the larger cities, which in some instances were fomented by the priests themselves. The trustee system was a fruitful cause of disturbance, threatening at times to bring the greatest evils upon the church; especially as there seemed to be reason to fear lest the dissensions between the clergy and the laity might serve as a pretext for the intermeddling of the civil authority in ecclesiastical affairs. Except in the two or three colleges of which we have spoken, there was no Catholic education to be had ; and for a long time the few elementary schools which were opened were of a very wretched kind. Indeed, we may say that it is only within the last quarter of a century that many of the bishops and priests of this country have come to realize the all-importance of Catholic education.

Another unavoidable evil was the mingling of various nationalities in the same church, giving rise to jealousies, and frequently to dissensions ; and to this we may add that the very people to whom

above all others the church in this country is indebted for its progress met with peculiar difficulties
in the fulfilment of their God-given mission. This
fact did not escape the keen eye of the first bishop
of Charleston.

"England," he says, "has unfortunately too well
succeeded in linking contumely to their name [the
Irish] in all her colonies; and though the United
States have cast away the yoke under which she
held them, many other causes have combined to
continue against the Irish Catholic more or less to
the present day the sneer of the supercilious, the
contempt of the conceited, and the dull prosing of
those who imagine themselves wise. That which
more than a century of fashion has made habitual
is not to be overcome in a year; and to any Irish
Catholic who has dwelt in this country during one-
fourth of the period of my sojourn it will be painfully evident that, although the evil is slowly dimin-
ishing, its influence is not confined to the American
nor to the anti-Catholic. When a race is once
degraded, however unjustly, it is a weakness of our
nature that, however we may be identified with
them upon some points, we are desirous of showing
that the similitude is not complete. You may be
an Irishman, but not a Catholic; you may be Catholic, but not Irish. It is clear you are not an
Irish Catholic in either case! But when the great
majority of Catholics in the United States were
either Irish or of Irish descent, the force of the
prejudice against the Irish Catholic bore against
the Catholic religion, and the influence of this pre-

judice has been far more mischievous than is generally believed." *

We must not omit to add that many of the early
missionaries spoke English very imperfectly and
were but little acquainted with the habits and cus-
toms of the people among whom they were called
to labor ; while the five or six bishops of the country, separated by great distances from their priests,
rarely saw them, and consequently were in a great
measure unable to control or direct them in the
exercise of the sacred ministry.   The French missionaries, who in their own country had seen the
most frightful crimes committed in the name of
liberty and of republicanism, found it difficult to
sympathize heartily with our democratic institutions; and from Ireland very few priests came,
because the French Revolution had broken up the
Continental Irish seminaries from which she drew
her own supplies.

The purchase of Louisiana from France in 1803
added little or nothing to the strength of the church
in the United States, since, owing to the wretched
French ecclesiastical colonial policy, which did not
permit the appointment of bishops, the Catholic
population of that province, a large portion of whom
were negro slaves, had been almost wholly neg-
lected.   What the state of the church was in Florida
at the time of its cession to the United States may
be inferred from the fact that in the whole province
there was but one efficient priest, who at once withdrew to Cuba, and afterwards to Ireland, his native

---

* Bishop England's works, vol. iii. p. 233.

country. In the early years of the present century Protestant feeling in this country was much more earnest and self-confident than at present—in the simple days of camp-meetings and jerking revivals and childlike faith in the pope as Antichrist, and in priests and nuns as Satan's chosen agents ; when the preachers had the whole world of anti-popery commonplace wherein to disport themselves without fear of contradiction. The universal feeling of pity for those who doubted the supreme wisdom of our political institutions was bestowed with not less boundless liberality upon all who failed to perceive that American Protestantism was the fine essence and final outcome of all that is best and purest in religion. Catholic opinion, on the other hand, was feeble, unorganized, and thrown back upon itself by the overwhelming force of a public sentiment strong, fresh, and defiant. We were, moreover, still under the ban of English literature that for three hundred years had been busy travestying the history and doctrines of the church, to defend which was made a crime. There were but few Catholic books, and those to be had generally failed to catch the phases of religious thought through which American Protestants were passing. It was more than thirty years after the erection of the see of Baltimore that the Charleston *Miscellany*, which Archbishop Hughes called the first really Catholic newspaper ever published in this country, was founded ; and fifty years after the consecration of Bishop Carroll there were but six Catholic journals in the United States.

Much else might be said in illustration of the difficulties with which the church has had to contend, and of the obstacles which she has had to overcome, in order to win the position which she now occupies in the great American republic. Enough, however, has been said to show that it would be difficult to imagine surroundings which, while allowing her freedom of action, would be better suited to test her strength and vitality.

The 15th of next August eighty-six years will have passed since the consecration of Bishop Carroll, and to this period the organized efforts of the church to secure a position in this country are confined. The work then begun has not for a moment been intermitted. In the midst of losses, defeats, persecutions, anxieties, doubts, revilings, calumnies, the struggle has been still carried on. Each year with its sorrows brought also its joys. The progress, if at times imperceptible, was yet real. When in the early synods and councils of Baltimore were gathered the strong and true-hearted bishops and priests who have now gone to their rest, there was doubtless more of sadness than of exultation in their words as they spoke of their scattered and poorly-provided flocks, of the want of priests, of churches, of schools, of asylums, of the hardships of missionary life, and of labors that seemed in vain. Still, they sowed in faith, knowing that God it is who gives the increase. Like weary travellers who seem to make no headway, by looking back they saw how much they had advanced. New churches were built, new congregations were formed,

4

new dioceses were organized.   On some mountain-
side or in deep wooded vale a cloister, a convent, a
college, a seminary arose, one hardly knew how,
and yet another and another, until these retreats of
learning and virtue dotted the land.   The elements
of discord and disturbance within the church grew
less and less active, the relations between priest
and people became more intimate and cordial, the
tone of Catholic feeling improved, ecclesiastical
discipline was strengthened, and the self-respect
of the Catholic body increased.

The danger, which at one time may have seemed
imminent, of the estrangement of the laity from the
clergy, disappeared little by little, and to-day in no
country in the world are priest and people more
strongly united than here.   With the more thorough
organization of dioceses and congregations parochial schools became practicable, and the great progress made in Catholic elementary education is one
of the most significant and reassuring facts connected with the history of the church in the United
States.   The number of pupils in our parochial
schools was, in 1873, 380,000, and to-day it is probably not much short of half a million, which, however, is even less than half of the Catholic school
population of the entire country.   But the work
of building schools is still progressing, and the conviction of the indispensable necessity of religious
education is growing with both priests and people ;
so that we may confidently hope that the time is
not very remote when in this country Catholic children will be brought up only in Catholic schools.

By establishing protectories, industrial schools, and asylums we are growing year after year better able to provide for our orphan children.

The want of priests, which has hitherto been one of the chief obstacles to the progress of the church, is now felt only in exceptional cases or in new or thinly-settled dioceses. A hundred years ago there were not more than twenty-five priests in the United States ; in 1800 there were supposed to be forty ; in 1830 the number had risen to two hundred and thirty-two, and in 1848 to eight hundred and ninety. In ten years, from 1862 to 1872, the number of priests was more than doubled, having grown from two thousand three hundred and seventeen to four thousand eight hundred and nine. The lack of vocations to the priesthood among native Americans was formerly a subject of anxiety and also of frequent discussion among Catholics in this country ; but now it is generally admitted, we think, that if proper care is taken in the education and training of our youths, a sufficient number of them will be found willing to devote themselves to the holy ministry.

In 1875 there were, according to the official statistics of the various dioceses, five thousand and seventy-four priests, twelve hundred and seventy-three ecclesiastical students, and six thousand five hundred and twenty-eight churches and chapels in the United States. There were also, at the same time, thirty-three theological seminaries, sixty-three colleges, five hundred and fifty-seven academies and select schools, sixteen hundred and forty-five parochial schools, two hundred and fourteen asylums, and ninety-six hospitals under the authority and control of the Catholic hierarchy of this country.

One hundred years ago there was not a Catholic ecclesiastical student, or theological seminary, or college, or academy, or parochial school, or asylum, or hospital from Maine to Georgia.

Father Badin, the first person who ever received Holy Orders in the United States, was ordained in the old cathedral of Baltimore on the 25th of May, 1793, just eighty-three years ago. It is now eighty-six years since Bishop Carroll was consecrated, and down to 1808 he remained the only Catholic bishop in the American Church, whose hierarchy is composed at present of one cardinal, ten archbishops, forty-six bishops, and eight vicars-apostolic.

In 1790 there was not a convent in the United States ; in 1800 there were but two ; to-day there are more than three hundred and fifty for women, and there are probably one hundred and thirty for men.

•We may be permitted to refer also to the increase of the wealth of the church in this country, especially since this seems to be the cause of great uneasiness to the faithful and unselfish representatives of the sovereign people. The value of the property owned by the church in this country, as given in the census reports, was, in 1850, $9,256,-758 ; in 1860, $26,774,119; and in 1870, $60,985,565. The ratio of increase from 1850 to 1860 was 189 per cent., and from 1860 to 1870 128 per cent. ; while the aggregate wealth of the whole country during these same periods increased in the former decade only 125 per cent. and in the latter only 86 per cent.   In 1850 the value of the church property of the Baptists, the Episcopalians, the Methodists, and the Presbyterians was greater than that of the Catholics, but in 1870 we had taken the second rank in point of wealth, and to-day we think there is no doubt but that we hold the first.

" Whatever causes," says Mr. Abbott, in his recent article on " The Catholic Peril in America," " may have contributed to this significant result, it is certain that among the chief of them must be reckoned exemption from just taxation, extraordinary shrewdness of financial management, and fraudulent collusion with dishonest politicians."

Those who know more of the history of the church in this country than can be learned from statistical reports, or articles in reviews, or cyclopædias are aware that there are no possessions in the United States more honestly acquired, or bought with money more hardly earned, than those of the Catholic Church ; and that her present wealth, instead of being due to special financial shrewdness, has in many instances been got in spite of great and frequent financial blundering ; while the bishops and priests of America, with here and there an exception, have neither had nor sought to have any political influence, nor would they, if disposed to meddle with partisan politics, meet with any encouragement from the Catholic people.   Their position with regard to the question of education is

the result of purely conscientious and religious
motives ; and while claiming for Catholics the
right to give to their children the benefit of religious
training, they have everywhere and repeatedly
given the most convincing proofs of their sincere
desire to concede to all others the fullest liberty in
this as in other matters ; and though they cannot
approve of that feature in the common-school system which excludes all teaching of doctrinal religion, they have never thought of pretending that
those to whom it does commend itself should not
be permitted to try the experiment of a purely
secular education, provided they respect in others
the freedom of conscience which is now a part of
the organic law of the land.

With very few exceptions, Catholics have, throughout the whole country, been rigidly excluded from
all the higher political offices ; though now, unfortunately, this can hardly be considered a grievance
since the general corruption and unworthiness of
public life have caused the more respectable class
of American citizens to shrink from the coarseness
and vulgarity of our partisan contests. On the
other hand, those nominal Catholics who acquire
influence in what is called "ward politics" are
generally very much like other politicians, eager to
serve God and the country whenever it puts money
in their purse. What political reasons may have
determined the great body of Catholic voters in
this country to prefer the Democratic to the Whig,
and later to the Republican, party, we know not ;
but we are very sure that nothing could be more

unfounded than to imagine that the welfare or progress of the church can in any way be connected with the success of Democratic partisanism. As a religious body we have nothing to hope from either or any party. We ask nothing but the liberty which with us is considered the inalienable heritage of all men ; and for the rest, we know that a politician doing a good deed is more to be shunned than an enemy plotting evil.

The property of the Catholic Church in the United States has not been exempted from taxation, except under general laws which applied equally to that of all other religious denominations ; and though we can imagine nothing more barbarous, more hurtful to the progress of the national architecture and to the general æsthetic culture of the people, than a change in the policy which has hitherto prevailed, not in this country alone, but in all the civilized states of the world, nevertheless, if those who hold that religion has no social value succeed in revolutionizing legislation on this subject, the Catholics will not be less prepared than their neighbors to abide the issue.

A more interesting study than the wealth of the church is the growth of the Catholic population in the United States, though, in the absence of reliable or complete statistics on this subject, we are not able to give an entirely satisfactory or exact statement of the facts. The " number of sittings," to use the phrase of the official reports, given in the United States Census, is of scarcely any assistance in determining the religious statistics of the country. The number of Protestant church sittings, for instance, was in 1870 19,674,548, whereas the membership of all the Protestant sects of the country was only about 7,000,000; and it is well known that, while in most Protestant churches many seats are usually unoccupied during religious service, in the Catholic churches the same seat is frequently filled by three, or four, or even five different persons, who take it in succession at the various Masses.

Ninety-one years ago Father Carroll set down the Catholic population of the United States at twenty-five thousand, and he may have fallen short of the real number by about ten thousand. In 1808, when episcopal sees were placed at Boston, New York, Philadelphia, and Bardstown, the Catholic population had increased to about one hundred and fifty thousand. In 1832 Bishop England estimated the Catholics of the United States at half a million; but in 1836, after having given the subject greater attention, he thought there could not be less than a million and a quarter. Both these estimates, however, were mere surmises; for Bishop England, who always exaggerated the losses of the church in this country, not finding it possible to get the data for a well-founded opinion as to the Catholic population, was left to conjecture or to arguments based upon premises which, to say the least, were themselves unproven. The editors of the *Metropolitan Catholic Almanac* for 1848, basing their calculations upon the very satisfactory returns which they had received from the thirty dioceses then existing in the United States, set down our Catholic population at 1,190,700, and this is probably the nearest approach which we can make to the number of Catholics in this country at the time the great Irish famine gave a new impulse to emigration to America. From 1848 down to the present day the increase of the Catholic population has been very rapid, it having risen in a period of twenty-eight years from a little over a million to nearly seven millions. The third revised edition of Schem's *Statistics of the World for* 1875 gives 6,000,000 as the Catholic population of the United States, and the *American Annual Cyclopædia* for 1875 reckons it as more than 6,000,000; and from a careful consideration of the data, which, however, are still imperfect, we think it is at present probably not less than 7,000,000. This remarkable growth of the church during the last thirty years must be attributed to various causes, by far the most important of which is beyond all doubt the vast immigration from Ireland; to which, indeed, we must also chiefly ascribe the progress of the church during this century in all other countries throughout the world in which the English language is spoken. No other people could have done for the Catholic faith in the United States what the Irish people have done. Their unalterable attachment to their priests, their deep Catholic instincts, which no combination of circumstances has ever been able to bring into conflict with their love of country; the unworldly and spiritual temper of the national character; their indifference to ridicule and con-

tempt; and their unfailing generosity—all fitted
them for the work which was to be done here, and
enabled them, in spite of the strong prejudices
against their race which Americans had inherited
from England, to accomplish what would not have
been accomplished by Italian, French, or German
Catholics.   Another cause of the more rapid
growth of the church during the last quarter of a
century may be found in the more thorough organization of dioceses, congregations, and schools, by
which we are better able to shield our people from
unhealthy influences, and thus year after year to dim-
inish our losses; while the increasing number of converts to the faith helps to swell the Catholic ranks.
Of 22,209 persons who were confirmed in the diocese of Baltimore from 1864 to 1868, 2,752, or more
than 12 per cent., were converts; and our converts
are generally from the more intelligent classes of
Americans.   The efforts to arrest the progress of
the church, which now for nearly half a century
have assumed a kind of periodicity, may be placed among the causes which have added to her
strength.   These attempts are made in open violation of the religious and political principles which
are the special boast of all Americans, and the only
arguments which can be adduced to justify them
are drawn from fear or hatred.   Whenever we have
been made the victims of lawlessness or fraud, as
in the burning of the Charlestown convent and the
churches of Philadelphia, or in the spreading " Awful Disclosures " throughout the land, the sympathies of generous and honest men have been at-

tracted to us. And when Protestant bigotry has made an alliance with a political party in order to compass our ruin, it has merely succeeded in forcing the opposing party to take up throughout the whole country the defence of the Catholics. Thus during the brief day of the " Know-nothing " conspiracy large numbers of Protestants, for the first time since the Reformation, were led to examine into the history of the church, with a view to defend her against the traditional objections of Protestantism itself. In fact, in a country which looks with equally tolerant complacency upon every form of belief or unbelief from Atheism to Voodooism, from the Joss-House of the Chinaman to the Mormon Tabernacle and breeding caravansary of freelove, to imagine that there can be either decent or reasonable motives for exciting to persecution of the Catholic Church is sheer madness ; nor can we think it less absurd to suppose that the good sense and justice of the American people will allow them to commit themselves to a policy as inconsistent as it would be outrageous.

However this may be, there can be no doubt but the repeated and unprovoked attacks made upon the Catholics of the United States by fanatics and demagogues have helped to increase their union and earnestness ; and this leads us away from the growth of the church in her external organization to the consideration of the development of her spiritual and intellectual life. And here we are at once struck by the similarity between her progress and that of the country itself, which has been diffusive at the expense of concentration and thoroughness. Nevertheless, no attentive observer can fail to be struck by the intense and earnest religious spirit by which the great body of the Catholics of the United States are animated, as well as the readiness with which they co-operate with their priests in promoting the interests of religion. Nowhere do we find greater eagerness for instruction in the truths of the faith, or greater willingness to make sacrifices in order to give to the young a religious education, than among the Catholics of this country. Our priests are, as a body, laborious, self-sacrificing, and disinterested, and are honestly struggling to make themselves worthy of the great mission which God has given them in America.

Our position in this country hitherto has turned the thoughts of our best minds to polemical and controversial writing, which, though useful and even necessary, has only a temporary value, since it is addressed primarily to objections and phases of belief which owe their special significance to transitory conditions of society and opinion. Controversies between Catholics and Protestants which forty years ago attracted general attention and produced considerable impression, would now pass unnoticed ; for the simple reason that Americans, in the confusion of sects and religious opinions, have come to realize that Protestantism has no doctrinal basis, and is left to trust exclusively to religious sentiment. Dogmatic Protestantism is of the past, and the most popular preachers are those who appeal most skilfully to the religious in-

stincts without requiring the acceptance of any religious beliefs. Most of our best writers have been
men whose arduous labors left them but little time
for study or literary composition, and their works
frequently bear the marks of hasty performance ;
but they will nevertheless not suffer from comparison with the religious writings of American Protestants. The ablest man who has devoted himself
to the discussion of religion and philosophy, or probably any other subject, in the United States during
the last hundred years is Dr. Brownson, all of whose
best thoughts have been given to the elucidation
of Catholic truth ; and though there was something
wanting to make him either a great philosopher or
a great theologian, or even a perfect master of
style, we know of no other American of whom this
may not also be justly said ; unless, perhaps, we
may consider Prescott, Hawthorne, or Irving worthy
of the last of these titles. And though we Catholics have no man who is able to take up the pen
which has just fallen from the hand of Dr. Brownson, none who have the power which once belonged
to England and Hughes, we are in this not more un-
fortunate than our country, which no longer finds
men like Adams or Jefferson to represent not un-
worthily its supreme dignity ; nor any like Web-
ster, Clay, or Calhoun, whose minds were as lofty
as their honor was pure, to lend the authority of
wisdom and eloquence to the deliberations of a
great people.

During the hundred years of our independent
life the external development of the church, like

that of the nation, has been so rapid that all individual energies have to a greater or less degree
been drawn to help on this growth. Another century, bringing other circumstances, with them will
bring the opportunity and the duty of other work.
A more thorough organization must be given to our
educational system ; Catholic universities must be
created which in time will grow to be intellectual
centres in which the best minds of the church in
this country may receive the culture and training
that will enable them to work in harmony for the
furtherance of Catholic ends ; a more vigorous and
independent press, one not weakened by want or
depraved by human respect or regard for persons,
must be brought into existence. We must prepare ourselves to enter more fully into the public
life of the country ; to throw the light of Catholic
thought upon each new phase of opinion or belief
as it rises ; to grapple more effectively with the
great moral evils which threaten at once the life of
the nation and of the church. All this and much
else we have to do, if our God-given mission is to
be fulfilled.

And now we will crave the indulgence of our
readers while we conclude with a brief reference to
what we conceive to be the office which the Catholic Church is destined to fulfil in behalf of the American state and civilization.

De Tocqueville, in his thoughtful and singularly
judicious treatise on American institutions, makes
the following very just remarks :

" I think the Catholic religion has been falsely

looked upon as the enemy of democracy. On the
contrary, Catholicism, among the various sects of
Christians, seems to me to be one of the most favorable to the equality of social conditions. The religious community in the Catholic Church is composed of but two elements—the priest and the
people. The priest alone is lifted above his flock,
and all below him are equals. In matters of doctrine the Catholic faith places all human capacities
upon the same level; it subjects the wise and the
ignorant, the man of genius and the vulgar crowd,
to the details of the same creed ; it imposes the
same observances upon the rich and the poor ; it
inflicts the same austerities upon the powerful and
the weak ; it enters into no compromise with mortal
man, but, reducing the whole human race to the
same standard, it confounds all the distinctions of
society at the foot of the same altar, even as they
are confounded in the sight of God. If Catholicism
predisposes the faithful to obedience, it certainly
does not prepare them for inequality ; but the contrary may be said of Protestantism, which generally tends to make men independent more than to
render them equal. . . . But no sooner is the priesthood entirely separated from the government, as is
the case in the United States, than it is found that
no class of men are naturally more disposed than
the Catholics to transfuse the doctrine of the equality of conditions into political institutions." *

The generous sentiments which two centuries
and a half ago led the Catholics of Maryland to

* *Democracy in America*, vol. i. p. 305.

become the pioneers s.'religious liberty in the New World, are still warm in the hearts of the Catholic people of the United States. We have even here been the victims of persecution, and it is not impossible that similar trials may await us in the future ; but we have the most profound conviction that, even though we should grow to be nine-tenths of the population of this country, we shall never prove false to the principle of religious liberty, which, to the Catholics of the United States, at least, is sacred and inviolable. For our own part, we should turn with unutterable loathing from the man who could think that any other course could ever be either just or honorable.

The Catholics of this republic are deeply impressed with the inviolability of the rights of the individual. We believe that the man is more than the citizen ; that when the state tramples upon the divine liberty of the most wretched beggar, the consciences of all are violated : that it is its duty to govern as little as possible, and rather to suffer a greater good to go undone than to do even a slight wrong in order to accomplish it. For this reason we believe that when the state assumed the right to control education, it took the first step away from the true American and Christian theory of government back towards the old pagan doctrine of state-absolutism. Though we uphold the rights of the individual, we are not the less strong in our advocacy of the claims of authority. In fact, the almost unbounded individual liberty which our American social and political order allows would fatally lead to anarchy, if not checked by some great and sacred authority ; and this safeguard can be found only in the Catholic Church, which is the greatest school of respect the world has ever seen. The church, by her power to inspire faith, reverence, and obedience, will introduce into our national life and character elements of refinement and culture which will temper the harshness and recklessness of our republican manners. By her conservative and unitive force she will weld into stronger union the heterogeneous populations and widely-separated parts of our vast country. The Catholics were the only religious body in the United States not torn asunder by sectional strife during our civil war, and we are persuaded that, as our numbers grow and our influence increases, we are destined to become more and more the strong bond to hold in indissoluble union the great American family of States. The divisions and dissensions of Protestantism have a tendency to prepare the public mind to contemplate without alarm or indignation like divisions and dissensions in the state ; and all who love the country and desire that it remain one and united for ages must look with pleasure upon the growth of a religion which, while maintaining the unity of its own world-wide kingdom, inspires those who are guided by its teachings with a horror of political contention and discord.

5

THE PERSECUTION OF THE CHURCH IN THE GERMAN EMPIRE.*

THE Catholics are suffering to-day, in the very heart of Europe, a persecution which, if less bloody, is not less cruel or unjust, than that which afflicted the Christian Church in the beginning of the fourth century, under the reign of the brutal old emperor, Diocletian. The prisons of Germany are filled with confessors of the faith, who, in the midst of every indignity and outrage, bear themselves with a constancy and heroism not unworthy of the early martyrs. And it is strange, too, that this struggle should be only a renewal of the old conflict between Christ and Cæsar, between the Son of Man and the prince of this world. In fact, anti-Christian Europe is using every exertion to re-create society on the model of Grecian and Roman paganism. This tendency is manifest in all the various realms of thought and action.

We perceive it—and we speak now more particularly of Germany—in literature, in science, in the manner of dealing with all the great problems which concern man in his relations with both the visible

* Written in 1875.

and the unseen world : and it looms up before us, in palpable form and gigantic proportions, in the whole attitude of the state toward the church. There has never lived on this earth a more thorough pagan than Goethe, the great idol of German literature, to whom the very sign of the cross was so hateful that in his notorious Venetian Epigram he put it side by side with garlic and vermin. The thought of self-sacrifice and self-denial was so odious to his lustful and all-indulgent nature that he turned from its great emblem with uncontrollable disgust, and openly proclaimed himself a " decidirter Nichtchrist." " Das Ewig Weibliche "—sensualism and sexualism—was the god of his heart, in whose praise alone he attuned his lyre. And Schiller, in his *Gods of Greece*, complained sorrowingly that all the fair world of gods and goddesses should have vanished, that one (the God of the Christian) might be enriched ; and with tender longing he prayed that "nature's sweet morn " might again return.

Both the religion and the philosophy of paganism were based upon the deification of nature, and were consequently pantheistic. Now, this pagan pantheism recrudescent is the one permanent type amid the endless variations of modern German sophistry. It underlies the theorizing of Schelling, Fichte, and Hegel, as well as that of Feuerbach, Büchner, and Strauss. They all assume the nonexistence of a personal God, and transfer his attributes to nature, which is, in their eyes, the mother of all, the sole existence, and the supreme good. This pantheism, which confuses all things in extri-

cable chaos, spirit with matter, thought with sensa-
tion, the infinite with the finite, destroying the
very elements of reason, and taking from language
its essential meaning, has infected all non-Catholic
thinking in Germany. When we descend from the
misty heights of speculation, we find pantheistic
paganism in the idolatry of science and culture,
which have taken the place of dogma and morality.
It is held to be an axiom that man is simply a product of nature, who knows herself in him as she
feels herself in the animal.

The formulas in which the thought is clothed are
of minor importance. In the ultimate analysis we
find in all the conflicting schools of German infidelity this sentiment, however widely its expression
may vary : that nature is supreme, and there is no
God beside. The cosmos, instead of a personal
God, is the ultimate fact beyond which science pro-
fesses to be unable to proceed ; and therefore the
duality of ends, aims, and results which underlies
the Christian conception of the universe must
necessarily disappear. There is no longer God and
the world, spirit and matter, good and evil, heaven
and hell ; there is not even man and the brute.
There is only the cosmos, which is one; and from
this it necessarily follows that the distinction between the spiritual and the temporal power is unreal and should cease to be recognized.

Now, here we have discovered the very germ
from which the whole Prussian persecution has
sprung. In the last analysis it rests upon the assumption that the spiritual power has no right to

exist, since the truths upon which it was supposed
to be based—as God, the soul, and a future life—
are proven to be myths. Hence the state is the
only autonomy, and to claim authority not derived
from it is treason. Thus the struggle now going on
in Prussia is for life or death. It rages around the
very central citadel of the soul and of all religion.
The Catholics of Germany are to-day contending
for what the Christians of the first centuries died—
the right to live. To understand this better it will
be well to consider for a moment the attributes of
the state in pagan Greece and Rome.

Hellenic religion, in its distinctive forms, had its
origin in the deification of nature and of man as
her crowning work, and both were identified with
the state. Hence religion was hero-worship; the
good man was the good citizen, the saint was the
successful warrior who struck terror into the enemies of his country, and thus the religious feeling
was confounded with the patriotic spirit. To be a
true citizen of the state, it was necessary to profess the national religion; and to be loyal to the
state was to be true to its protecting gods. The
highest act of religion was to beat back the invader
or to die gloriously on the battle-field. Indeed, in
paganism we find no idea of a non-national religion.
The pagan state, whether imperial, monarchical, or
republican, was essentially tyrannical, wholly incompatible with freedom as understood in Christian
society. To be free was to be, soul and body, the
slave of the state. Plato gives to his ideal Republic
unlimited power to control the will of the indivi-

dual, to direct all his thoughts and actions, to model and shape his whole life. He merges the family and its privileges into the state and its rights, gives the government absolute authority in the education of its subjects, and even places the propagation of the race under state supervision.

The pagan state was also essentially military, recognizing no rights except those which it had not the power to violate. Now, the preaching of Christ was in direct contradiction to this whole theory of government. He declared that God and the soul have rights as well as Cæsar, and proclaimed the higher law which affirms that man has a destiny superior to that of being a citizen of any state, however glorious; which imposes upon him duties that transcend the sphere of all human authority. Thus religion became the supreme law of life, and the recognition of the indefeasible rights of conscience gave to man citizenship in a kingdom not of this world. It, in consequence, became his duty as well as his privilege to obey first the laws of this supernatural kingdom, and to insist upon this divine obligation, even though the whole world should oppose him.

This teaching of Christ at once lifted religion above the control of the state, and, cutting loose the bonds of servitude which had made it national and narrow, declared it catholic, of the whole earth and for all men. He sent his apostles, not to the Jew, or the Greek, or the Gentile, but to all the nations, and in his church he recognized no distinction of race or social condition—the slave was like the freeman, the beggar like the king.

This doctrine, the most beneficent and humanitarian that the world has ever heard, brought forth from the oblivion of ages the all-forgotten truth of the brotherhood of the race, and raised man to a level on which paganism was not able even to contemplate him; proclaiming that man, for being simply man, irrespective of race, nationality, or condition, is worthy of honor and reverence. Now, it was precisely this catholic and non-national character of the religion of Christ which brought it into conflict with the pagan state. The Christians, it was held, could not be loyal citizens of the empire, because they did not profess the religion of the empire, and refused to sacrifice to the divinity of Cæsar. They were traitors, because in those things which concerned faith they were resolved not to recognize on the part of the state any right to interfere ; and therefore were they cast into prison, thrown to the wild beasts in the Amphitheatre, and devoured under the approving eyes of the worshippers of the emperor's divinity. This history is repeating itself in Prussia to-day.

Many causes have, within the present century, helped to strengthen the national feeling in Germany. The terrible outrages and humiliations inflicted upon her by the pitiless soldiers of the first Napoleon made it evident that the common safety required that the bonds of brotherhood among the peoples of the different German states should be drawn tighter. The development of a national

literature also helped to foster a longing for national
unity.   In the seventeenth, and even down to
nearly the end of the eighteenth, century, French
influence, extending from the courts of princes to
the closets of the learned, gave tone to both literature and politics.

Leibnitz wrote in French or Latin, and Frederick the Great strove to forget his own tongue, that
he might learn to speak French with idioma-
tic purity—an accomplishment which he never acquired.

As there was no German literature, the national
feeling lacked one of its most powerful stimulants.
But in the latter half of the eighteenth century, and
during the first half of the nineteenth, a literature
rich, profound, thoroughly German, the creation of
some of the highest names in the world of letters,
came into existence, and was both a cause and an
effect of the national awakening.   Goethe especially did much, by the absolute ascendency which he
acquired in the literature of his country, to unify
and harmonize the national mind.

Still, a thousand interests and jealousies, local
and dynastic, old prescriptive rights, and a constitutional slowness and sluggishness in the Germanic
temperament, stood in the way of a united fatherland, and had to be got rid of or overcome by force
before the dream of the nationalists could become a
reality.

Prussia, founded by rapine, built up and strengthened by war and conquest, has always been a heartless, self-seeking state.   The youngest of the great

European states, and for a long time one of the most inconsiderable, she has gradually grown to be the first military power of the world. Already, in the time of Frederick the Great, she was the formidable rival of Austria in the contest for the hegemony of the other German states. This struggle ended, in 1866, in the utter defeat of Austria on the field of Sadowa. Hanover, Saxony, Hesse-Cassel, and other minor principalities were at once absorbed by Prussia, who, besides greatly increasing her strength, thus became the champion of German unity. But German unity was a menace to France, who could not possibly maintain her preponderance in European affairs in the presence of a united Germany. Hence the irrepressible conflict between France and Prussia, which ended in the catastrophe of Sedan.

The King of Prussia became the Emperor of Germany, and German national pride and enthusiasm reached a degree bordering on frenzy.

By a remarkable coincidence the Franco-Prussian war broke out at the very moment when the dogma of Papal infallibility was defined, and immediately after the capitulation of Sedan, Victor Emanuel took possession of Rome. The Pope was without temporal power—a prisoner indeed. The feeling against the newly-defined dogma was especially strong in Germany, where the systematic warfare carried on by the *Janus* party against the Vatican Council had warped the public mind. France, the eldest daughter of the church, was lying, bleeding and crushed, at the feet of the conqueror. The

6 ·

time seemed to have arrived when the bond which united the Catholics of Germany with the Pope, and through him with the church universal, might easily be broken.

The defection of Döllinger and other rationalistic professors, as well as the attitude of many of the German bishops in the council, and the views which they had expressed with regard to the probable results of a definition of the infallibility of the Pope, tended to confirm those who controlled the policy of the new empire in the opinion that there would be no great difficulty in forming the Catholics of Germany into a kind of national religious body wholly subject to the state, even in matters of faith. If we add to this the fact that the infidels of our day have a kind of superstition which leads them to think that all religious faith has grown weak, and that those who believe are for the most part hypocritical, insincere, and by no means anxious to suffer for conscience' sake, we shall be able to understand how Bismarck, who is utterly indifferent to all religion, and who believes in nothing except the omnipotence of the state, should have persuaded himself to destroy the religious freedom which had come to be considered the common property of Christendom. Already, in the month of August immediately following the close of the war with France, we find the Northern German press, which obsequiously obeys his orders, beginning to throw out hints that Rome had always been the enemy of Germany; that her claims were incompatible with the rights of the state and hurtful to the national development; and that, in presence of the newly-defined dogma of Papal infallibility, the necessity of resisting her ever-increasing encroachments upon the domain of the civil authority had become imperative. The watchword given by the official press was everywhere re-echoed by the organs of both infidel and Protestant opinion, and it at once became evident that the German Empire intended to make war on the Catholic Church.

There was yet another end to be subserved by the persecution of the church. Bismarck made no secret of his fears of a democratic movement in Germany after the excitement of the French campaign had died away, and he hoped to avert this danger by inflaming the religious prejudices of the infidel and Protestant population.

On the 8th of July, 1871, the Catholic department in the Ministry of Public Worship was abolished, and the government openly lent its influence to the Old Catholic movement.

The Prussian constitution makes religious instruction in the gymnasia obligatory, and in schools in which Catholic doctrines are taught the government admits that only persons who have received the approbation of the bishop of the diocese are to be appointed to perform this duty. Dr. Wollmann, who had for a long time held the office of teacher of religion in the Catholic gymnasium of Braunsberg, apostatized after the Vatican Council, and was, in consequence, suspended from the exercise of the priestly office by his bishop, who declared that, since Wollmann had left the church, he could no longer be considered a suitable religious instructor of Catholic youth. Von Mühler, the Minister of Public Worship, refused to remove Wollmann ; and since religious instruction is compulsory, the pupils who could not in conscience attend his classes were forced to leave the school.

This act of Von Mühler was in open violation of the Prussian constitution, which expressly recognized in the Catholic Church the right of directing the religious instruction of its members.

To require that Catholics should send their children to the lessons of an excommunicated priest was to trample upon the most sacred rights of conscience. By declaring, as in this case, that those who rejected the dogma of infallibility were true Catholics, the German government plainly showed that it intended to assume the competency of deciding in all matters of faith, and consequently to wholly ignore the existence of any religious authority distinct from that of the state.

Bismarck's next step was not less arbitrary or tyrannical. He proposed to the Federal Council and Reichstag a law against what was termed the abuse of the pulpit, by which the office of preaching should be placed under the supervision of the police.

This law, which was passed by a feeble majority, was simply a renewal of the attempt to suppress Christianity made by the Jewish Council in Jerusalem when the apostles dared to preach in the name of Jesus, without asking permission of the rulers of the people : " But that it may be no further spread among the people, let us threaten them, that they speak no more in this name to any man. And calling them, they charged them not to speak at all, nor teach in the name of Jesus " (Acts iv. 17, 18).

The injustice of this law was plainly shown by the Saxon member of the Federal Council, who pointed out the fact that, whilst liberty of speech was denied to Catholic priests, socialists and infidels were permitted every day to attack the very foundations of all government and civilization.

This, however, is but the necessary consequence of the theory of the *state-God.* To preach in the name of any other God is treason ; whereas atheism is the correlative of the omnipotence of the government. That the present tendency in Germany is to put the nation in the place of God is expressly recognized by the *Allgemeine Evang. Luth. Kirchenzeitung*, which is the organ of orthodox Lutheranism. These are its words : " For the dogmatic teaching of Christianity they hope to substitute the national element. The national idea will form the germ of the new religion of the empire. We have already seen the emblems which foreshadow the manner in which this new worship is to be organized. Instead of the Christian festivals, they will celebrate the national memories, and will call to the churches the masses to whom the road is no longer known. Have we not seen, on the anniversary of Sedan, the *eidolon* of the emperor placed upon the altar, whilst the pulpit was surrounded with the busts of the heroes of the war?

" During eight days they wove crowns of oak-

leaves and the church was filled; whilst out of ten
thousand parishioners, scarcely a dozen can be got
together to listen to the word of God.   Such is the
religion of the future church of the empire.   Little
more is needed to revive the ancient worship of the
Roman emperors; and if the history of Germany is
to be reduced to this duel between the church of
the emperor and that of the Pope, we must see
on which side the Lutherans will stand."

The next attack on the church was made under
cover of an enactment on the inspection of public
schools.   A project of law was presented to the
House of Deputies, excluding all priests from the
inspection of schools, and at the same time oblig-
ing them to undertake this office whenever asked
to do so by the state authorities.   This latter clause
was, however, so openly unjust that it was rejected
by the House.   But the law, even as it stands, is
a virtual denial that Catholic schools have any right
to exist at all, and is an evidence that the German
Empire intends to destroy Christian faith by establishing an atheistic system of popular education.

And now war was declared against the Jesuits.
The Congress of the Old Catholics, which met at
Munich in September, 1871, had passed violent re-
solutions against the order; and later the Old Catholic Committee at Cologne presented a petition
of similar import to the imperial Parliament.

The debate was opened in the month of May,
1872.   A project of law, restricting the liberties of
religious orders, and especially directed against the
Society of Jesus, was brought before the Federal

Council and accepted by a large majority. When it came before the imperial Parliament, amendments were added rendering it still more harsh and tyrannical. The order was to be shut out from the empire, its houses to be closed, foreign Jesuits were to be expelled, and the German members of the society were to be confined to certain districts; and the execution of these measures was to be entrusted to the Federal Council.

On the 4th of July the law received the approval of the emperor, and on the 5th it was promulgated.

Thus in the most arbitrary manner, without any legal proceedings, hundreds of German citizens, against whom there was not the slightest proof of guilt, were deprived of their rights and expelled from their country. Besides, the measure was based upon the most ignorant misconception of the real condition of the church, and was therefore necessarily ineffective. The religious orders and the secular priesthood do not represent opposite tendencies in the church; their aims are identical, and, in our day at least, the secular priests are as zealous, as active, and as efficient as the members of the religious orders.

What end, then, was to be gained by expelling the Jesuits, whilst devoted and zealous priests were left to minister to the Catholic people, whose faith had been roused by this scandalous persecution of men whom they knew to be guilty of no crime except that of loving Jesus Christ and his church ? The blow struck at the Jesuits was, in truth, aimed at the church, and this the bishops, priests, and entire Catholic people of Germany at once recognized. They saw now, since even the possibility of doubting was no longer left to them, that the German Empire had declared war on the church; and Bismarck, seeing that his half-way measures had deceived no one, resolved to adopt a policy of open violence. With this view a new minister of Public Worship was appointed in the person of Dr. Falk, who drew up the plan of the famous Four Church Laws to which he has given his name, and which was adopted on the 11th of May, 1873.

In virtue of these laws—which it is unnecessary to transcribe in full—the state arrogates the right of appointing to all ecclesiastical offices, since the government claims authority to approve or annul all nominations made by the bishops; and the President of the Province (*Oberpraesident*) is bound to interdict the exercise of any religious function to ecclesiastics appointed without his consent. The bishop who makes an appointment to the cure of souls without the consent of the civil authority is fined from two hundred to one thousand thalers; and the priest who, appointed in this way, exercises spiritual functions, is visited with a proportionate penalty. This is an attempt to change the very nature of the church; it is a denial of its right to exist at all.

The third of these laws creates the "Royal Court of Justice for Ecclesiastical Affairs," which claims and possesses by act of Parliament the right to reform all disciplinary decisions made by the bishops in relation to the ecclesiastics under their jurisdiction. This same court has by law the right to depose any ecclesiastic whose conduct the government may see fit to consider *incompatible with public order.*

The Pope is interdicted from the exercise of disciplinary power within the territory of the Prussian monarchy.

The state takes control of the education of the young men destined to the priesthood. It requires them to pass the *arbiturienten-examen* in a German gymnasium, and then to devote three years to the study of theology in a German university, during which time they are not to be permitted to live in an episcopal seminary; and thereafter they are to pass a public examination before the state officials. All educational establishments for the clergy, especially all kinds of seminaries, are placed under the superintendence of the government, and those which are withheld from this supervision are to be closed. The education of priests, the fitness of candidates for holy orders, appointments to the cure of souls, the infliction of ecclesiastical censures, the soundness of the faith of the clergy, are, in the new German Empire, matters to be regulated by the police.

This is not a struggle between Catholicity and Protestantism; it is a battle between the Atheist State and the Kingdom of God. The Protestant Church in Germany does not alarm Bismarck, because it is feeble and has no independent organization, since its ministers are appointed and ruled by the emperor, and it is also well understood that very few of them have any faith in positive religion.

But the orthodox Protestants of Germany thoroughly understand that the attempt to crush the Catholic Church is meant to be a fatal blow at the vital principle of all religion. This is recognized by the *Allgemeine Evang. Luth. Kirchenzeitung* in the article from which we have already quoted. "It is a common remark," says this organ of orthodox Lutheranism, "that the blows struck at the Church of Rome will tell with redoubled force against the evangelical church. But what is meant to injure, only helps the Roman Church. There she stands, more compact than ever, and the world is amazed at beholding her strength. Once the word of the Monk of Wittenberg made her tremble, but to-day the blows of power make her stronger. Let us beware of illusion; it is certain that in the Protestant North of Germany there has grown up a public opinion on the Church of Rome which provokes the respect even of the liberals. We have enough to do, they say, to fight the socialists; it is time to leave the Catholic bishops in peace."

In the spring of 1870, whilst the discussion concerning the opportuneness of defining the infallibility of the Pope was attracting the attention of every one, and when the distant mutterings of the Franco-Prussian war were not yet audible, the leading organs of the Party of Progress in Berlin sought to weigh the probable results of a definition, by the Vatican Council, of the much-talked-of dogma. In case the Pope should be declared infallible, the

Volkszeitung, of Berlin, affirmed that many would favor the interference of the government to prevent all further intercourse between the bishops of Prussia and the Roman Pontiff, which would result in the creation of a national church wholly independent of Rome.

But this organ of the Party of Progress openly avowed that there was not the slightest probability that the state could, by any means at its command, succeed in separating the Catholic Church in Prussia from communion with the See of Peter; nor was there, it confessed with perfect candor, a single bishop in Germany who would desire such a separation.

And yet, as we have shown, the task which the German Empire has set itself is precisely the one which is here pronounced impossible. We will return now to the history of the tyrannical enactments and violent measures by which the worshippers of the God-State hope to destroy the faith of thirteen millions of Catholics. The project of the Falk laws was brought before the Landtag on the 9th of January, 1873, and on the 30th of the same month the Catholic episcopate of the kingdom of Prussia entered a solemn protest against this iniquitous attempt to violate the most sacred rights of conscience and religion.

In the name of the natural law, of the historical and legitimately-acquired rights of the church in Germany, of the treaties concluded by the crown of Prussia with the Holy See, and, in fine, in the name of the express recognition of these rights by the constitution, they protest against measures which are a manifest violation of the doctrine, the constitution, and the discipline of the church.

It is of the duty and right of each bishop, they declare, to teach the Catholic doctrine and administer the sacraments within his own diocese ; it is also of his duty and right to educate, commission, and appoint the priests who are his co-operators and representatives in the sacred ministry ; and it is of his duty and right to exhort and encourage them in the fulfilment of their charge, and, when they obstinately refuse to obey the doctrine and laws of the church, to depose them from office, and to forbid them the exercise of all ecclesiastical functions ; all of which rights are violated by the proposed laws.   As to the Royal Court for Ecclesiastical Affairs, they affirm that they can never recognize its competency, and that they can see in it only an attempt to reduce the divinely-constituted church to a non-Catholic and national institution.

The memorial concludes with the following noble and solemn words :

" Concord between church and state is the safeguard of the spiritual and the temporal power; the indispensable condition of the welfare of all human society. The bishops, the priests, the Catholic people, are not the enemies of the state ; they are not intolerant, unjust, or without charity towards those of a different faith.   They ask nothing so earnestly as to be allowed to live in peace with all men ; but they demand that they themselves be permitted to live according to their faith, of the divinity and truth of which they are most thoroughly convinced. They require that the integrity of religion and their church and the liberty of their conscience be left inviolate, and they are resolved to defend their lawful freedom, and even the smallest right of the church, with all energy and without fear.

" From our inmost souls, in the interest of the state as much as of the church, we conjure and implore the authorities to abandon the disastrous policy which they have taken up, and to give back to the Catholic Church, and to the millions of the faithful of that church who are in Prussia and in the empire, peace, religious liberty, and security in the possession of their rights, and not to impose upon us laws obedience to which is incompatible, for every bishop and for every priest and for all Catholics, with the fulfilment of duty—laws, consequently, which violate conscience, are morally impossible, and which, if carried into execution by force, will bring untold misery upon our faithful Catholic people and our German fatherland."

The organs of the government declared that the Memorial was an *ultimatum*, " a declaration of war "; that " it was impossible to keep the peace with these bishops ; and that they should be reduced as soon as possible to a state in which they could do no harm." Accordingly, the discussion of the Falk laws was hurried up, and they were adopted in May by a majority of two-thirds.

In the meantime, the government continued to follow up its harsh measures against the religious orders, going so far as to close the churches of royal

patronage in Poland, in order to prevent their consecration to the Sacred Heart of Jesus. It even
forbade the children of the schools to assist at the
devotions of the Sacred Heart. The Catholic ca-
sinos were closed ; the Congregations of the Blessed
Virgin, the Society of the Holy Childhood, and
other religious associations were suppressed. The
church in Cologne, which had been devoted to the
use of the Catholic soldiers of the Prussian army, was
turned over to the Old Catholics.

By the beginning of 1873 nearly all the Jesuits
had withdrawn from the territory of the German
Empire, and taken refuge in France, England, Austria, Belgium, Brazil, the Indies, and the United
States. Those who still remained were interned
and placed under the supervision of the police.
The government next proceeded to take steps to
suppress those religious orders which it considered
as *affiliated* to the Jesuits. A mission which the
Redemptorists were giving at Wehlen, near Treves,
was broken up by the police. Another mission
which they were about to open at Oberjosbach
(Nassau) was interdicted ; whilst almost at the
same time several Redemptorists were decorated
" for services rendered to the fatherland during the
war." A community of Lazarists at Kulm was dis-
solved, and convents of the Ladies of the Sacred
Heart, of the Sisters of Notre Dame, of the Sisters
of Charity, and of the Sisters of St. Charles were
closed.

Von Gerlach, the President of the Court of Appeals of Magdeburg, himself a Protestant, has in-

formed us, in a pamphlet which he published about
this time, of the effect of these persecutions upon
the Catholics of Germany.

"As for the Catholic Church," he wrote, "persecutions strengthen her. In fact, her moral power
is increased under pressure. The Catholic Church
is to-day more zealous, more compact, more united,
more confident of herself, more energetic, and better organized, than she was at the commencement
of 1871. The Roman Catholics have good reason
to be thankful that their church has gained in faith,
in the spirit of sacrifice and prayer, in devoutness
in worship, and in all Christian virtues.

"It is even evident that the interior force of the
religious orders, especially that of the Jesuits, has
been proportionately augmented. Around these
proscribed men gather all those who love them to
protect and help them."

The courageous conduct of the German bishops
in taking a firm and decided stand against the persecutors of the church met with the almost unanimous approval of both priests and people. Dr.
Döllinger and his sect were forgotten. If there had
ever been any life in the impossible thing, it went
out in the first breath of the storm that was breaking over the church. All the cathedral chapters
gave in their adhesion to their respective bishops,
and their example was followed by the pastors, rec-
tors, and vicars of the eleven Prussian dioceses.
They repelled with horror, to use the words of the
clergy of Fulda, the attempt to separate the members from the head, and to give to the priesthood

tutors in the person of a state official. Even the
twenty-nine deacons of the Seminary of Gnesen entered their protest, recalling in their address to
Archbishop Ledochowski the beautiful words of St.
Laurence to Pope Sixtus as he was led to martyrdom : *Quo sine filio, pater ?*

The Catholic nobility, in their meeting at Münster in January, 1873, openly proclaimed their fidelity to the church and their firm resolve to defend
her rights and liberties; and the Catholic people
began to organize throughout the Empire.

"The Association of the Catholic Germans,"
which now counts its members by hundreds of
thousands, was formed, with the motto, *Neither
rebel nor apostate.* Its *Wanderversammlungen* (mi-
gratory reunions) spring up everywhere, and become
centres of Catholic life. This association is based
upon the constitutional law, its acts are public, the
means it employs are legitimate, and the end it
aims at is distinctly formulated in its statutes.

In this manner the Catholics of Germany prepared themselves, not to commit acts of violence or to
transgress the law, but to offer a passive resistance
to tyranny and oppression, to uphold liberty of conscience against state omnipotence, and to suffer
every evil rather than betray their souls' faith.

The Imperial government, on the other hand,
showed no intention of withdrawing its arbitrary
measures, but through its organs openly declared
that " the execution of the clerical laws would form
a clergy as submissive and tractable as the Prussian
army"; whilst Herr Falk proclaimed in the Reich-

stag " that the government was resolved to make use of every means which the law placed within its power ; and if the present laws were not sufficient, others would be framed to ensure their execution."

The ukase, signed by Bismarck on the 20th of May, 1873, suppressed the convents of the Redemptorists, of the Fathers of the Holy Ghost, of the Lazarists, and of the Ladies of the Sacred Heart; and the members of these orders were commanded to abandon their houses before the end of the following November. The Ladies of the Sacred Heart were accused of desiring to acquire " universal spiritual dominion."

The bishops were called on to submit for the approval of the government, in accordance with the tenor of the May laws, the plan of studies and the disciplinary rules of their diocesan seminaries; which, of course, they declined to do, though they foresaw that their action would bring about the closing of these institutions. Herr Falk, the Minister of Worship, ordered an examination into the revenues of the different parishes, without even asking the co-operation of the bishops; and the civil authorities were warned of their duty to notify the government of all changes which were made in the body of the clergy. The police received orders to interfere, at certain points, with Catholic pilgrimages, which, in other instances, were positively interdicted.

The annual allowance of twelve hundred thalers to Mgr. Ledochowski, Archbishop of Posen, was withdrawn, his seminary was closed, and all teach-

7

ers were forbidden to ask his permission to give religious instruction. In November, 1873, the archbishop's furniture was seized ; even his paintings
were carried off. The people, gathering in crowds,
shouted after the officials : "Thief! thief!" On
the 23d of the same month Mgr. Ledochowski
was condemned to pay a fine of five thousand four
hundred thalers, or, in default, to an imprisonment
of two years, for having made nine appointments
to ecclesiastical offices contrary to the laws of
May.

Before the end of December, the fines imposed
upon the archbishop had reached twenty-one thousand thalers. In January, 1874, he was cited before
a delegate judge of the Royal Court for Ecclesiastical Affairs, but refused to appear, since he could
not, in conscience, recognize the competency of a
civil tribunal to pass sentence on the manner in
which he had exercised his pastoral functions. He
moreover averred that, in case the threat to drag
him into court should be carried out, it was his
firm resolve to say nothing.

Several priests of the Diocese of Posen had al
ready been incarcerated for failure to pay the fines
of the government, and on the 3d of February,
1874, at five o'clock in the morning, the archbishop
was himself arrested and carried off to prison in
Ostrowo, a town of about seven thousand inhabitants, chiefly Protestants and Jews.

The bishops of Prussia at once drew up a letter
to the clergy and the Catholic people of their dioceses, in which they declared that "the only crime

of Archbishop Ledochowski was that of having chosen to suffer everything rather than betray the liberty of the church of God and deny Catholic truth, sealed by the precious blood of the Saviour.'

The canons of the Chapter of Posen were ordered by the government to elect a capitular-vicar; and as they declined to give their approval to the cruel and unjust imprisonment of their archbishop, a state official was appointed to take charge of the affairs of the diocese.

Both the priests and people of Prussian Poland remain firm, and give noble examples of steadfastness in the faith.

The history of the persecution in one diocese is, with a few unimportant differences, that of all. More than a year ago the annual allowance of three thousand four hundred and seventy thalers made to the Theological Seminary of Cologne was withdrawn. Archbishop Melchers and his vicargeneral were cited before a civil tribunal for the excommunication of two apostates. The Lazarists were driven from the preparatory seminaries of Neuss and Münstereifel.

On the 22d of November, 1873, the archbishop was condemned to pay a fine of twenty-five hundred thalers for five appointments made in violation of the May laws; and almost every week thereafter new fines were imposed, until finally his furniture was seized on the 3d of February, 1874, and in a very short time the venerable prelate was incarcerated, not even his lawyer being allowed to visit him. His prison-cell was thought to be too

comfortable, and he was soon changed to a wretched hole under the very roof of the jail. A great
number of pastors and vicars of his diocese were
deprived of their positions, and some of them
imprisoned.

On the 20th of November, 1873, the priests of
twenty-eight towns and villages of the Diocese of
Treves were interdicted by the government, and
the bishop fined thirty-six hundred thalers. The
Theological Seminary was closed, "not to be re-
opened until the bishop and rector should accept
in good faith the laws of May, 1873 "; and all
seminarians who should be found there on the 12th
of January, 1874, were to be forcibly ejected.

The 15th of this same month the professors were
forbidden to instruct the students of theology,
under penalty of a fine of fifteen thalers or five
days' imprisonment for each offence ; and this pro-
hibition is to remain in vigor until the bishop
accepts the Falk laws. On the 21st of January an
inventory of the furniture of the episcopal palace
was taken. The goods were sold at public auction
on the 6th of February; in a few days Bishop
Èberhard was thrown into prison ; and before the
end of August, 1874, sixty of his priests were con-
fessing the faith in the dungeons of Treves and
Coblentz.

The old Dominican convent in Treves had been
converted into a prison, and it is there that the
bishop and some thirty of his priests were incarcerated. The prison discipline is rigid and harsh
in the extreme, These confessors of Christ are

forced out of their beds at five o'clock in the morning, and from this until they retire at nine in the evening they must either walk to and fro in their cells, or sit upon stools, as chairs are not allowed. If during the day they wish to lie down for a moment, an official at once informs them that this is not permitted ; if they lean against the wall, the table, or the bed, they again receive the same warning. A jailer accompanies them whenever necessity forces them to leave their cells. All letters to and from the prison are read by the officials, and, in case the slightest pretext can be found, are destroyed. None save those who have voluntarily given themselves up, and who, after a first imprisonment, have not received an ovation from the people, are allowed to say Mass. The bishop is permitted to celebrate the Holy Sacrifice, but no one is suffered to be present except the server and the indispensable government official.

The food seems scarcely sufficient to sustain life. We have received from a most trustworthy person, who during the past summer examined into this whole matter on the spot, the bill of fare of the priests confined in the prison of Treves, which we here submit to our readers:

	Breakfast.	*Dinner.*	*Supper.*
Sunday	Porridge	Peas	Soup and Bread.
Monday	Coffee	Beans	Soup and Bread.
Tuesday	Porridge	Potatoes	Soup and Bread.
Wednesday	Soup	Rye Meal	Soup and Bread.
Thursday	Soup	Peas	Porridge.
Friday	Coffee	Rice	Soup.
Saturday	Porridge	Cabbage	Soup.

Three times in the week each of the prisoners
receives a small piece of meat, and this is the only
change ever made in the bill of fare which we have
just given. What we have called " porridge " is
known at Treves under the name of *Schlicht*, and is
a kind of flour-paste. When we reflect that there
are in Germany to-day not less than a thousand
priests who are suffering this slow and cruel martyrdom, we shall be able to realize that the present
pagan persecution may in all truth be compared to
those which, in the first ages of Christianity, gave
to the church her legions of martyrs and confessors.
It is not necessary that we should enter into a
detailed account of the persecution in the other
dioceses of Germany. The same scenes are everywhere enacted—fines, citations, seizure of effects,
interdicts, and imprisonments, on the part of the
government ; whilst the Catholics, standing in unshaken fidelity to God and conscience, suffer in
patience every outrage that their enemies can inflict, rather than betray the sacred cause of the
religion of Christ. The May laws of 1873 did not
prove sufficiently harsh or tyrannical to satisfy the
Prussian infidels; and they were consequently sup-
plemented by clauses which passed both houses of
the Reichstag in May, 1874. In virtue of these
amendments, the state can decree the sequestration
of the goods of an ecclesiastical post not occupied
in the manner prescribed by the Falk laws. In this
case these goods are to be administered by a royal
commissary.

The Royal Court for Ecclesiastical Affairs receives

the power to depose bishops ; and, this deposition being once pronounced, they are forbidden to exercise any ecclesiastical functions in their respective dioceses, which by this very fact are placed under interdict. When the bishop is deposed by the Royal Court, the cathedral chapter is summoned to proceed to elect his successor ; and in case it fails to comply with this injunction within ten days, all goods belonging to the episcopal see, as well as those of the chapter of the diocese, and of the parishes, are sequestrated and administered by the government.

This miserable legislation gives to the state the entire spiritual power, and ignores alike the rights of God and those of the free Christian conscience. Still, it is only the legitimate and logical expression of the views and aims of the modern heathenism which is organizing throughout Europe for the destruction of the religion of Christ.

The May laws of 1873 required the bishops to convert all the incumbents having charge of churches into permanent and irremovable parish priests ; and in consequence the position of twelve hundred and forty-one incumbents in the Rhine Province became illegal on the 11th of May, 1874. A general interdict was therefore expected, and even a process to compel the bishop to comply with this clause was looked for ; but Herr Falk seems to have been frightened by his own legislation, since already, on the 8th of May, he announced in the Reichstag that only those priests whom "the government considered dangerous" would be

notified of the proceedings taken against the bishops, and that no others would be held to come under the operation of the law.   In this manner the
Prussian Minister of Worship avoided the odium of
a general interdict; whilst by a slower process he
hopes eventually to bring about this result.   The
moment the incumbent of a church receives official
notification that his bishop has been put under restraint, he is by the very fact forbidden to perform
any ecclesiastical function, and his post is considered vacant.   The *Landrath* then declares this *vacancy*,
and invites the parishioners to prepare for the
election of a successor to their former pastor.

That this election may take place, it suffices that
ten men, who are of age and in the full possession of
their civil rights, put in an appearance, and the person chosen by them and approved of by the civil
authority is recognized as the lawful incumbent.

The evident aim of this law is to create a schism
in every parish in the German Empire, which, by
fomenting divisions amongst the Catholics, would
greatly aid the government in its efforts to destroy
the church.   But this is only one of innumerable
instances in which the persecutors have been wholly
mistaken.

They counted first upon the weakness of the
Catholic bishops ; confidently expecting that one or
the other of them would place himself at the head
of the Old Catholics, and thus, whilst causing great
scandal in the church, give to that still-born sect at
least a semblance of respectability.   But not one of
the German prelates wavered.   They go to prison,

like the apostles, rejoicing that they are found worthy to suffer for Christ, and declare that they are willing to shed their blood for the holy cause. Their enemies are not more ready to inflict than they to bear wrong and outrage for the love of Jesus. Then, there was no doubt in the minds of the Prussian infidels that large numbers of the clergy would take advantage of the bribes offered by government to apostates to throw off the authority of the bishops, and to constitute themselves into a schismatical body. On the contrary, the persecution has only drawn tighter the bonds which unite the priests with their chief pastors. In all Germany there have not been found more than thirty rationalistic professors and suspended priests who were willing to take sides with Döllinger in his rebellion ; and the juridically-proven immorality of Bishop Reinkens will no doubt give us a true insight into the characters of most of the men who have elected him their ecclesiastical superior.

When the persecutors found that both bishops and priests were immovable in their devotion to the church, they appealed to the Catholic people, and, by the laws of May, 1874, placed it in their power to create a schism, by giving them the right to elect their own pastors, with the promise that government would turn the churches over to them. But this attempt to show that the bishops and priests of Germany have not the sympathy and confidence of the laity has met with signal rebuke.

The elections for the Prussian Landtag in November, 1873, and those for the Reichstag in Janu-

8

)

ary, 1874, had not merely a political significance;
their bearing upon the present and future welfare of
the church in the German Empire is of the greatest
importance. Opportunity was given to the Catholic people to make a public confession of faith ; to
declare, in words which could not be misunderstood,
whether or not they were resolved to stand firm
in the struggle into which their leaders had been
forced.

In the November elections, in spite of every effort of the government, the Catholics increased
their representatives in the Landtag from fifty-two
to eighty-nine ; and in the Reichstag their members
have grown from sixty-three to considerably more
than one hundred.

The entire Rhenish Province elected Catholics.
Cologne, Düsseldorf, Treves, Coblentz, Aix-la-Chapelle, Crefeld, Bonn, Neuss, Düren, Essen, Mal-
medy, Mülheim, all the cities of the Lower Rhine,
made their vote an act of faith. Windthorst, the
leader of the Catholic party, was elected at Mep-
pen (Hanover) over Falk, the author of the May
laws, by a majority of nearly fifteen thousand.
The entire vote for Falk was only three hundred
and forty-seven.

The result of the elections undoubtedly startled
the government, and possibly shook Bismarck's confidence in the power of persecution to destroy .
Catholic faith ; but the struggle had grown too
fierce to allow him to think of withdrawing.

· On the contrary, the firmness of the Catholic
people incited the persecutors to still harsher mea-

sures; but nothing that they have done or can do will succeed in breaking the combined passive opposition of the clergy and the laity.

In the Vatican Council, the most determined resistance to the definition of the infallibility of the Pope was made by the German bishops, who felt no hesitation in openly declaring with what anxiety they regarded the probable effects of such a definition upon the Catholics of their own country. Divisions, apostasies, schisms, seemed imminent ; and it is not easy now to determine what might have been the result had not God's providence interfered.

In the first place, at the very moment when the definition was made, the terrible conflict between France and Prussia broke forth, and raged so fiercely that the loud earth was struck dumb, and men held their breath till it should be ended. In the meantime, the angry feelings aroused by the discussions in the Vatican Council had, in great measure, been calmed, and it was possible to take a fairer and more dispassionate view of the whole subject.

Then the attempt of the government to destroy the Catholic Church in Germany, by tearing it away from its allegiance to the Pope, and debasing it to a mere function of the state, roused those who might have been disposed to waver, and brought about a universal reawakening of faith. It is the fate of the enemies of God's people to bless when they mean to curse. In fact, when Catholics begin to suffer, they begin to triumph ; and hence even those who hate us have of nothing so great horror as of making martyrs and confessors of us. They know the history of martyrdom—that in the whole earth and in all ages it means victory.

The church, which sprang from the conflict of the God-Man with death, like him, in her greatest humiliation shows forth her highest power.

Her march through the world and through the ages is not along pleasant roads and through peaceful prospects, or, if so, only at times and rarely. If she move in pomp amid the acclamations of peoples, her triumphal procession ends in sorrow. The bark of Peter must be storm-tossed ; and when the angry waves would swallow it, the divine voice speaks the magic word, and the quiet deep bears it secure on its peaceful bosom.

The road wherein the progress of the church is most certain is the blood-stained way of the cross. When she is all bruised, and there is no comeliness left in her; when her eyes are red with weeping, and the world, beholding her agony, mocks and jeers and laughs her to scorn, then is she strongest ; for her strength comes from humility, from suffering, from the cross. When she is humbled, God exalts her ; when he permits her enemies to entomb her in ignominy, he is near at hand to crown her with the immortal glory of a new life. The word of Christ is: "You shall live in the world in the midst of persecutions ; but take heart: I have conquered the world."

Within the memory of those who are still young, it was the fashion with our enemies to proclaim that the church was decrepit, that she was dying, that of her own weight she would fall to pieces in the new society that was growing up around her : to-day we hear that she is everywhere waxing too strong, and men appeal against her to tyranny and to brute force.

The most powerful and the most thoroughly organized of the modern nations, the great *Cultur-Staat* of this most enlightened age, has confessed that it is unable to check the growth of the church by legitimate means, and it has therefore had recourse to the most arbitrary legislation and to the harshest measures of compulsion and violence. This, of course, is an explicit avowal of its own impotence. We find also that the two nations which have manifested the most supercilious indifference to the Catholic Church, as being something which did not and could not concern them, now applaud this Prussian tyranny, in spite of the pretence of the love of freedom and fair play. The sympathy of the English press, and to a great extent of the American press, in this struggle, is with the absolute and liberty-destroying government of Prussia. The favorite motto of " civil and religious liberty all the world over" has been wholly lost sight of, and Englishmen and Americans give moral aid to a state which wantonly tramples upon both.

This, too, was a cherished watchword : The church is the friend of absolutism, the enemy of freedom.

But to-day we behold the Catholic Church, single-handed, fighting again the same battles of liberty

which she fought and won in the early centuries
of Christianity. Now, as then, she opposes absolutism in the state; denies, as she then denied,
that Cæsar can lawfully lay claim to "the things
of God"; and protests, in the name of the outraged
dignity of human nature, that there is a freedom
which transcends the sphere of all earthly authority.
Her children, when nothing else remains to be done,
utter the divine words: *Non possumus*—we cannot;
we must obey God rather than men.

Referring to this struggle, Bismarck has said, in
a memorable speech, that "it is the ancient contest
for power, which is as old as the human race itself—
the contest for power between king and priest."
This is necessarily the view which he takes, since
he believes in nothing but force. But the dualism
here is not in the combatants alone; it is in the
objects for which they contend.

It is indeed the ancient contest between good
and evil, between the spirit and the flesh, between
the Christ and the rulers of this world, which makes
life a warfare and the earth a battle-field, and which
must continue until the end. Never has it been
fiercer than in our day, and the battle is yet hardly
begun. But very few indeed understand the nature of the struggle, or are at all aware of the real
principles and interests which are at stake. Few
men can see further than an hour or beyond the
little circle that bounds their private interests; but
each day it is becoming more evident that all must
take sides; that not to be for Christ is to be against
him.

Twice in the last eighteen hundred years the church has been the ark of the nations: she survived the destruction of paganism; she converted and civilized barbarism. Some historian will tell, in another age, how, when Christian society, grown luxurious and corrupt, without God and without future hope, was sinking back into the flesh-worship and the death of ancient paganism, she, gathering around her the remnant of her children, and fearlessly facing the storm and the wrath of those who had ceased to know her, kept her own pure and undefiled till the dawn of the brighter day, to become the leaven of the social state that is to be.

COMPARATIVE INFLUENCE OF CATHOLICISM AND PROTESTANTISM ON NATIONAL PROSPERITY. *

WEALTH.

"IT is wonderful," wrote Proudhon, "how in all our political questions we always stumble on theology." Mr. Gladstone will doubtless concur in this sentiment; for he cannot take a step without stumbling on the Catholic Church. She is everywhere, and everywhere she is to him a cause of alarm. So potent is her influence growing to be, so cunningly laid are the plans by which her policy is directed, so perfect is the organization and discipline of her forces, so insidious are her methods of procedure, as he would have us believe, that it is full time all Christendom were warned of the approaching danger. She is in his eyes an ever-present menace to the civilization of the world.

He at least bears testimony to her power and vitality. She is not a relic of a past age; she lives,

* *Protestantism and Catholicism in their bearing upon the Liberty and Prosperity of Nations.* A study of social economy. By Emile de Laveleye. With an introductory letter by the Rt. Hon. W. E. Gladstone, M.P. London, 1875.

and, what is more, it does not seem that she is willing to die. If we consider the various efforts by which men are seeking to weaken and destroy the church, we shall find in them no mean evidence of her divine strength. And first of all, in an age intellectually most active, she is the subject of universal criticism, and is cited before every tribunal of human knowledge to be tried on an hundred different and often contradictory counts. Her historical relations with the world, extending over eighteen hundred years and co-extensive with Christendom, are minutely examined into by men who, shutting their eyes to the benefits which she has conferred upon the human race, are eager to discover charges against her. She is made responsible for the crimes of those who called themselves Catholics, though she was the first to condemn their evil deeds. The barbarism, the ignorance, and the cruelty of the middle ages are set to her count, when, in fact, she was the chief source of civilization, of enlightenment, and of mercy during that period. When she opposes the tyranny of kings, she is called the enemy of the state; when she seeks to restrain the lawlessness of the people, she is proclaimed the friend of tyrants. Not in politics alone, but in all the sciences, men in our day stumble on the Catholic Church.

We are told that she is the one great spiritual organization which is able to resist, and must as a matter of life and death resist, the progress of science and modern civilization. Men profess to find innumerable points of collision between her dogmas and the conclusions of science, and are surprised when she claims to understand her own teachings better than they, and is not prepared to abandon all belief in God, the soul, and future life because physical research has given us a wider knowledge of the phenomena of matter. Now we hear objections to her moral teaching—that it is too severe, that she imposes burdens upon men's shoulders too heavy for human nature to bear, that she encourages asceticism, celibacy, and all manner of self-denial opposed to the spirit of the age and of progress; then, on the contrary, that her morality is lax, that she flatters the passions of men, panders to their sensual appetites, and grants, for gain, permission to commit every excess.

At one time we are told that her priests are indolent, immoral, ignorant, without faith; at another, that they are ceaselessly active, astute, learned, and wholly intent upon bringing all men to their own way of thinking. Now we are informed that her children cannot be loyal subjects of any government; and immediately after we hear that they are so subservient, so passively obedient, that they willingly submit to any master. And here we come more immediately upon our subject; for whereas Mr. Gladstone has declared that the loyalty of Catholics is not to be trusted, M. de Laveleye asserts that " despotic government is the congenial government of Catholic populations."

The pamphlet from which we quote these words, and which we propose now to examine, has been presented to the English-reading public by special

request of Mr. Gladstone, and has been farther
honored by him with a prefatory letter. The
author, it is true, takes a fling at the Church of
England, and plainly intimates that in his opinion
it is little better than the Catholic Church; but the
ex-premier could not forego the opportunity of
striking his enemy, though he should pierce his
dearest friend in giving the blow. He takes the
precaution, indeed, to disclaim any concurrence in
M. de Laveleye's " rather unfavorable estimate of
the Church of England in comparison with the
other reformed communions." The question discussed in the pamphlet before us, as its title
implies, is the relative influence of Catholicism and
Protestantism on the liberty and prosperity of
nations; and the conclusion which is drawn is that
the Reformation is favorable to freedom and progress, and that the Catholic Church is a hindrance
to both.

This has long been a favorite theme with Protestants—the weapon with which they think themselves best able to do good battle in their cause;
and doubtless it is employed, in most favorable
circumstances, in an age like ours, in which material progress is so marked a feature that its influence
may be traced in everything, and in nothing more
than in the thoughts and philosophies of the men
of our day. It is worthy of remark that Protestantism, professing to be a purer and more spiritual
worship, should have tended to turn men's minds
almost exclusively to the worldly and temporal
view of religion; so that it has become the fashion

to praise Christianity, not because it makes men humble, pure, self-denying, content with little, but rather because its influence is supposed to be of almost an opposite nature. Much stress is laid upon the physical, social, and mental superiority of Christian nations to those that are still pagan, and the inference implied, if not always expressly stated, is that these temporal advantages are due to the influence of Christianity, and prove its truth and divine origin. Without stopping to consider the question whether the material and social superiority of Christian nations is to be attributed to their religious faith, we may ask whether, admitting that this is the case, it may with propriety be adduced in proof of the truth of the religion of Christ ?

In the case of individuals no one, certainly, would think of arguing that prosperity proves a right faith, or even consistent practice. To hold that wealth and success are evidences of religious life, whatever it may be, is certainly not Christian doctrine. Does the teaching of Christ permit the rich to lay the unction to their souls that they are God's favored children ? Were they his friends ? Did they flock round him ? Did they drink in his words gladly ? If men who claim to be his disciples have deified worldly success, and made temporal prosperity a sufficient test of the truth of his religion, they cannot plead any word of his in excuse.

He certainly never paid court to the great, or stooped to flatter the rich. Was it not he who said, " Woe be to you rich : ye have received your reward"? and again, "It is harder for a rich man to enter the kingdom of heaven than for a camel to pass through the eye of a needle"? Did he not take Lazarus to his bosom when Dives was in hell?

" Blessed are ye," he said, " when men shall revile you, and persecute you, and shall say all manner of evil against you falsely for my sake. Rejoice and be exceeding glad; for great is your reward in heaven : for so persecuted they the prophets which were before you."

The preaching of Christ was wholly unworldly. He sternly repressed the earthly ambitions of his disciples, and declared that, as the world hated him, it would also hate those who believed in him. They would be outcasts for his name's sake ; if this life were all, they of all men would be most miserable. Indeed, he rarely speaks of human happiness in the customary sense ; he passes over what might be said in favor of this life, and brings out in bold relief its vanity and unsatisfactoriness. He draws no pictures of domestic bliss, and says but little of even innocent pleasures or those temporal blessings which are so sweet to all ; and as he taught that worldly prosperity is no evidence of God's favor, he was careful to correct the error of those who looked upon misfortune as a proof of guilt, as in the case of the man born blind and of those upon whom a tower had fallen.

Christ was poor, his apostles were poor, his disciples were poor, nearly all the Christians of the first ages were poor; and yet every day we hear men talk as though they considered poverty and Christianity incompatible. This is manifestly the opinion of M. de Laveleye. His argument may be stated in this way: England and Scotland are rich, Ireland is poor. The Protestant cantons of Switzerland are rich, the Catholic are poor. " In the United States," says De Tocqueville, " the greater part of the Catholics are poor." In fact, wherever the two religions exist together, the Protestants are more active, more industrious, and consequently richer than the Catholics.

This is the substance of what is spread over a dozen pages of the pamphlet. The conclusion is not difficult to draw. Protestants are richer than Catholics, and therefore better Christians.

" No man can serve two masters," said Christ: "you cannot serve God and Mammon." On the contrary, says M. de Laveleye, the success with which you worship Mammon is the best proof that you serve God truly. Of course it would be foreign to M. de Laveleye's purpose to stop to inquire whether the poverty of Ireland be due to the Catholic faith of her people or to the rapacity and misgovernment of England; whether that of the Catholic cantons of Switzerland might not be accounted for by the fact that they are mountainous, with an inhospitable climate and a barren soil; and whether even M. de Tocqueville's assertion that the greater part of the Catholics of the United States are poor might not be satisfactorily explained by stating that the greater part of them are emigrants who have recently landed upon these shores without a superabundance of this world's goods.

He had also good reasons, while treating this part of his subject, for not looking nearer home. He had in Belgium, under his very eye, one of the most thrifty, industrious, and prosperous peoples of Europe, and at the same time one of the most Catholic. Why did he not compare the wealth of Belgium with that of Sweden or Denmark? Why did he not say a word about Catholic France, whose wealth and thrift cannot be denied. He does, indeed, make mention of two French manufacturing towns, in which, he states, on the authority of M. Audiganne, the capitalists are for the most part Protestants, whilst the operatives are Catholics; though what this has to do with any debatable question between Catholicism and Protestantism is not easily seen.

The assertion * that " wherever the two religions co-exist in the same country the Protestants are more active, more industrious, more economical, and consequently richer than the Catholics," is not borne out by facts. A single example will suffice to show how rash M. de Laveleye has been in making so wide an affirmation. The Catholics of the Rhine Province are universally acknowledged to be among the most thrifty and enterprising popu- lations of Prussia, and are far richer than, for in- stance, the Protestants of Pomerania.

It would not be difficult, by adopting M. de Laveleye's mode of reasoning, to turn his whole argument on this point against his own position. Whether or not national wealth, we might say, is

* P. 14.

evidence of orthodox Christian faith, there can be
no doubt but that the Christian religion is favorable to even the temporal interests of the lowest and
most degraded classes of society.   Its doctrines on
the brotherhood of the race and the equality of all
before God first inspired worthy notions of the dignity of man.   Then the sympathy which is created
for the poor, the suffering, and the oppressed naturally set men to work to devise means for the relief
of human misery.   It is to its influence that we
must ascribe the abolition of slavery, the elevation
of woman, and the thousand ministries which in
Christian lands attend on the wretched and the
weak.

We must infer that those nations in which this
influence is most powerful—which, in other words,
are most truly Christian—will have, in proportion
to their population, the smallest class of human
beings cursed by the worst plague known to modern
civilization, bearing with it, as it does, a threefold
degradation, moral, physical, and social.   We of
course refer to pauperism.

Now, in England, from whose wealth M. de
Laveleye would infer the superiority of her religion,
we find that this pauper class, compared with the
whole population, is as 1 to 23 ; whereas in Ireland,
which is poor—and, according to this theory, for
that reason under the ban of a false religion—there
is but 1 pauper to 90 inhabitants ; in other
words, pauperism is four times more common in
England than in Ireland.   Now, whether we refer
this fact to England's wealth or to England's reli-

gion—and in M. de Laveleye's opinion they are correlative—our conclusion must be either that the influence of the Christian religion, which necessarily tends to promote the temporal well-being of the most degraded classes of society, is less felt in England than in Ireland, or else that national wealth is hurtful to the interests of these same classes, and consequently opposed to the true Christian spirit ; and in either case we have Catholic Ireland more fairly Christian than Protestant England. We would not have our readers think for a moment that we are seriously of the opinion that our argument proves anything at all. We give it merely as a specimen of the way in which the reasoning of this pamphlet may be turned against its own conclusions, though, in fact, we have done the work too respectably.

We cannot forget, if M. de Laveleye does, that, of all sciences, the social—if, indeed, it may be said as yet to exist at all—is the most complex and the most difficult to master. The phenomena which it presents for observation are so various, so manifold, and so vast, our means of observation are so limited, our methods so unsatisfactory, and our prejudices so fatal, that only the thoughtless or the rash will tread without suspicion or doubt upon ground so uncertain and so little explored.

M. de Laveleye himself furnishes us an example of how easily we may go astray, even when the way seems plain.

"Sectarian passions," he writes,* "or anti-re-

* P. 11.

ligious prejudice have been too often imported into the study of these questions. It is time that we should apply to it the method of observation and the scientific impartiality of the physiologist and the naturalist. When the facts are once established, irrefragable conclusions will follow. It is admitted that the Scotch and Irish are of the same origin. Both have become subject to the English yoke. Until the sixteenth century Ireland was much more civilized than Scotland. During the first part of the middle ages the Emerald Isle was a focus of civilization, while Scotland was still a den of barbarians. Since the Scotch have embraced the Reformation, they have outrun even the English. . . . Ireland, on the other hand, devoted to ultramontanism, is poor, miserable, agitated by the spirit of rebellion, and seems incapable of raising herself by her own strength." The conclusion which is drawn from all this, joined with such other facts as the late victories of Prussia over Austria and France, is that " Protestantism is more favorable than Catholicism to the development of nations."

We may as well pause to examine this passage, which, both with regard to the statement of facts and to the interpretation put upon them, fairly represents the style and method of the pamphlet before us.

" It is admitted that the Scotch and Irish are of the same origin." This is true, as here stated, only in the sense that both are descended of Adam ; and hence it would have been as much to the point to affirm that all the nations of the earth are of the same origin. The Scots were, indeed, an Irish tribe ; but when they invaded Caledonia, they found it in the possession of the Picts, of whom whether they were of Celtic or Teutonic race is still undecided. The inhabitants of the Scotch low-lands are chiefly of Anglo-Saxon blood, and it is almost exclusively among them that the progress of which our author speaks is noticeable. The Highlanders, who are of Celtic race, had made but little advancement in wealth and civilization so late as the beginning of the last century. There is consequently no meaning or point in this comparison between the Scotch and Irish, since it is based upon a manifestly false assumption.

" Until the sixteenth century," continues M. de Laveleye, " Ireland was much more civilized than Scotland. During the first part of the middle ages the Emerald Isle was a focus of civilization, while Scotland was still a den of barbarians." Now, it was precisely in those ages in which Ireland was " a focus of civilization " that the Catholic faith of her people shone brightest. It was then that convents sprang up over the whole island ; that the sweet songs of sacred psalmody, which so touched the soul of Columba, were heard in her groves and vales ; that the sword was sheathed, and all her people were smitten with the high love of holy life and were eager to drink at the fountains of know-ledge. It was then that she sent her apostles to Scotland, to England, to France, to Germany, to Switzerland, and to far-off Sicily ; nor did she remit her efforts in behalf of civilization until the invading Danes forced her children to defend at once their country and their faith.

But let us follow M. de Laveleye: "Since the Scotch have embraced the reformed religion, they have outrun even the English. . . . Ireland, on the other hand, devoted to ultramontanism, is poor, miserable, agitated by the spirit of rebellion, and seems incapable of raising herself by her own strength."

We cannot think that Mr. Gladstone had read this passage when he requested the author to have his pamphlet translated into English; for we cannot believe that he is prepared to lay the misfortunes of Ireland to the influence of the Catholic faith upon her people, and not to the cruelty and mis-government of England.

The Irish Catholics are reproached with their poverty, when for two hundred years the English government made it a crime for them to own anything. They are taunted with their misery, when for two centuries they lived under a code which placed them outside the pale of humanity; of which Lord Brougham said that it was so ingeniously contrived that an Irish Catholic could not lift up his hand without breaking it; which Edmund Burke denounced as the most proper machine ever invented by the wit of man to disgrace a realm and degrade a people; and of which Montesquieu wrote that it must have been contrived by devils, ought to have been written in blood and registered in hell!

Ireland is found fault with because she is agitated

by the spirit of rebellion, when even to think of the wrongs she has suffered makes the blood to boil. Is it astonishing that she should be poor when England, with set purpose, destroyed her commerce and ruined her manufacturing interests, fostering at the same time a policy fatal to agriculture, the aim of which, it would seem, was to force the Irish to emigrate, that the whole island might be turned into a grazing ground for the supply of the English markets?

"What a contrast," further remarks M. de Laveleye,* "even in Ireland, between the exclusively Catholic Connaught, and Ulster, where Protestantism prevails!"

Mr. Gladstone certainly cannot be surprised at this contrast, nor will he seek its explanation in the baneful influence of the Catholic Church. He at least knows the history of Cromwell's invasion of Ireland; he has read of the massacres of Drogheda and Wexford; he knows the fate of the eighty thousand Catholic Irishmen whom Cromwell drove into the ports of Munster, and shipped like cattle to the sugar plantations of the Barbadoes, there to be sold as slaves; nor is he ignorant of what was in store for those Irish Catholics who were still left; of how they were driven out of Ulster, Munster, and Leinster across the Shannon into Connaught— that is, into the bogs and wild wastes of the most desolate part of Ireland—there to die of hunger or cold, or to survive as best they might. Five-sixths of the Catholics had perished; the remainder were driv-

* P. 12.

en into barren Connaught; the Protestants settled on the rich lands of Ulster, Munster, and Leinster; and now here comes good M. de Laveleye to find that Connaught is poor because it is Catholic, and Ulster is rich because it is Protestant. But we must not forget Scotland.

"Since the Scotch," says M. de Laveleye, " have embraced the reformed religion, they have outrun even the English."

We shall take no pains to discover whether or in what respect or how far the Scotch surpass the English. The meaning of the words which we have just quoted is evidently this: The progress which the Scotch have made during the last three centuries, in wealth and the other elements of material greatness, must be ascribed to the influence of the Protestant religion.

To avoid even the suspicion of unfairness in discussing this part of the subject, we shall quote the words of an author who devoted much time and research to the study of the character and tendencies of Scotch Presbyterianism, and whose deeply-rooted dislike of the Catholic Church is well known :

" To be poor," says Buckle,* describing the doctrines of the Scotch divines of the seventeenth century—" to be poor, dirty, and hungry; to pass through life in misery and to leave it with fear; to be plagued with boils and sores and diseases of every kind ; to be always sighing and groaning; to have the face streaming with tears and the chest heaving with sobs ; in a word, to suffer constant affliction

* *History of Civilisation*, vol. ii. p. 314.

and to be tormented in all possible ways—to un-
dergo these things was a proof of goodness just as
the contrary was a proof of evil. It mattered not
what a man liked, the mere fact of his liking it
made it sinful. Whatever was natural was wrong.
The clergy deprived the people of their holidays,
their amusements, their shows, their games, and
their sports; they repressed every appearance of
joy, they forbade all merriment, they stopped all
festivities, they choked up every avenue by which
pleasure could enter, and they spread over the
country an universal gloom. Then truly did darkness sit on the land. Men in their daily actions
and in their very looks became troubled, melancholy, and ascetic. Their countenance soured and
was downcast. Not only their opinions, but their
gait, their demeanor, their voice, their general aspect, were influenced by that deadly blight which
nipped all that was genial and warm. The way of
life fell into the sere and yellow leaf; its tints
gradually deepened; its bloom faded and passed
off; its spring, its freshness, and its beauty were
gone; joy and love either disappeared or were
forced to hide themselves in obscure corners, until
at length the fairest and most endearing parts of
our nature, being constantly repressed, ceased to
bear fruit and seemed to be withered into perpetual
sterility. Thus it was that the national character
of the Scotch was in the seventeenth century dwarf-
ed and mutilated. . . . They [the Scotch divines]
sought to destroy not only human pleasures, but
human affections. They held that our affections are

necessarily connected with our lusts, and that we
must therefore wean ourselves from them as earthly
vanities.   A Christian had no business with love or
sympathy.   He had his own soul to attend to, and
that was enough for him.   Let him look to himself.   On Sunday, in particular, he must never
think of benefiting others ; and the Scotch clergy
did not hesitate to teach the people that on that
day it was sinful to save a vessel in distress, and
that it was a proof of religion to leave ship and
crew to perish.   They might go : none but their
wives and children would suffer, and that was nothing in comparison with breaking the Sabbath.
So, too, did the clergy teach that on no occasion
must food or shelter be given to a starving man, unless his opinions were orthodox.   What need for
him to live ?   Indeed, they taught that it was a sin
to tolerate his notions at all, and that the proper
course was to visit him with sharp and immediate
punishment.   Going yet farther, they broke the domestic ties and set parents against their offspring.
They taught the father to smite the unbelieving
child, and to slay his own boy sooner than to allow
him to propagate error.   As if this were not enough,
they tried to extirpate another affection, even more
sacred and more devoted still.   They laid their
rude and merciless hands on the holiest passion of
which our nature is capable—the love of a mother
for her son. . . .   To hear of such things is
enough to make one's blood surge again, and raise a
tempest in our inmost nature.   But to have seen
them, to have lived in the midst of them, and yet

not to have rebelled against them, is to us utterly inconceivable, and proves in how complete a thraldom the Scotch were held, and how thoroughly their minds as well as their bodies were enslaved."

The seventeenth century, which was the golden age of French literature, and also of the Catholic Church in France, threw almost total darkness over Scotland, which during that period was most completely under the power of Protestantism. The clergy governed the nation; they were the only men of real influence; and yet there was no philosophy, no science, no poetry, no literature worth reading. "From the Restoration," says Laing, "down to the Union the only author of any eminence whom Scotland produced was Burnet.'

If the thrift and industry of the Scotch are due to Protestantism, to what shall we ascribe the enterprise and commerce of the Catholic republics of Venice and Genoa during the middle ages?

If England's wealth to-day comes from the Reformation, how shall we account for that of Spain in the sixteenth and seventeenth centuries? And if the decline of Spain has been brought about by the Catholic faith, to what cause shall we assign that of Holland, who in the seventeenth century ruled the seas and did the carrying trade of Europe?

M. de Laveleye's way of accounting for the prosperity of nations is certainly simple, but we doubt whether it would satisfy any respectable school-boy. Unfortunately for such as he, there is no rule of

9

three by which social problems may be solved.
Race, climate, soil, political organization, and many
other causes, working through every-varying combinations, must all be considered if we would understand the history of material progress.   As labor
is the most fruitful cause of wealth, there is a necessary relation between national wealth and national habits, which are the outcome of a thousand influences, one of the most powerful of which undoubtedly is religious faith.   But who does not
know that climate influences labor, not only by
enervating or invigorating the laborer, but also
by the effect it produces on the regularity of his
habits?   If the Italian loves the *dolce far niente,*
while the New-Englander makes haste to grow rich
as though some demon whom gold could bribe pur-
sued him, shall we find the secret of their peculiar
characters in their religious faith or in the climate
in which they live, or shall we not rather seek it in
a combination of causes, physical and moral ?   We
have assuredly no thought of denying the intimate
connection which exists between faith and character or between a nation's religion and its civilization.   We are willing even to affirm that not only
the general superiority of Christian nations, but
their superior wealth also, is in great measure attri-
butable to their religion.   And now, bidding adieu
to M. de Laveleye for a while, we propose to discuss this subject, to which we have already alluded,
somewhat more fully.

Christianity certainly does not measure either the
greatness or the happiness of a people by its wealth,

nor does it take as its ideal that state of society in which "the millionaire is the one sole god" and commerce is all in all; in which "only the ledger lives, and only not all men lie."

Whether we consider individuals or associations of men, the Catholic Church does not hold and cannot hold that material interests are the highest. To be noble, to be true, to be humble, to be pure, is, in her view, better than to be rich. Man is more than money, which is good only in so far as it serves to develop his higher nature.

"The whole aim of man is to be happy," says Bossuet. "Place happiness where it ought to be, and it is the source of all good; but the source of all evil is to place it where it ought not to be."

"It is evident," says St. Thomas, "that the happiness of man cannot lie in riches. Wealth is sought after only as a support of human life. It cannot be the end of man; on the contrary, man is its end. . . . The longing, moreover, for the highest good is infinite. The more it is possessed, the more it is loved and the more all else is despised; for the more it is possessed, the better is it known. With riches this is not the case. No sooner are they ours than they are despised, or used as means to some other end; and this, as it shows their imperfect nature, is proof that in them the highest good is not to be found."

If wealth is not the highest good of individuals, is it of nations? What is the ideal of society? The study of the laws which govern national life must necessarily begin with this question, which

all who have dealt with the subject, from Plato to
Comte and Mill, have sought to answer.   It is manifest that each one's attempt to solve this problem
will be based upon his views on the previous question :   What is the ideal of man ?   This, in turn, will
be answered according to each one's notions of the
ideal of God ; and here we have the secret of the
phenomenon which so surprised Proudhon—the
necessary connection between religion and society,
theology and politics.

Is there a God, personal, distinct from nature?
Or is nature the only god, and science her prophet ?
It is just here at this central point that men are
dividing ; it is here we must place ourselves, if we
would view the two great armies that in all Christendom are gathering for a supreme conflict.

There is a form of infidelity in our day—and it
is the one into which all unbelief must ultimately
resolve itself—which starts with this assumption :
Whether or not there is a God must for ever remain unknown to man.   It reasons in this way :
This whole subject belongs within the region, not
only of the unknown, but of the unknowable.   It is
an insoluble riddle, and the philosophies and theo-
logies which have sought to unravel it, if only idle,
might deserve nothing more than contempt; but
they have been the bane of human thought, have
soured all the sweetness of life, and therefore ought
to be visited with the execration of mankind.   Since
religion is a subject about which nothing can be
known, what is so absurd as to spend time upon it ?
What so absurd as to divert the thoughts of men

from subjects in which thinking is fruitful to those
in which it must for ever remain barren of all except evil results? What so absurd as to set them
working for a future life, of which we can never
know whether it exists at all, when we might at
least teach them how to make the present one
worth having? The paradise of the future, which
the prophetic eye of science can already descry, is
in the world, not *beyond* it ; and to seek to hasten
its approach is the highest and only worthy object
in life. As we take it, this is the creed of modern
unbelief, to which as yet few will openly subscribe,
but toward which all its hundred conflicting schools
of thought are moving. Few men indeed are able
to perceive the logical outcome of their opinions,
and still fewer have the courage to confess what
they more than half suspect.

This superstition is a return to the nature-worship of paganism, but under a different aspect. Of
old, nature was worshipped as revealed to sense,
and now as revealed to thought ; then as beautiful,
now as true or useful. The first was artistic, and
form was its symbol ; the last is scientific, and law
is its expression. The religion of humanity is a
phase of this worship ; for in it man is considered,
not as the child of God, but as the product of
nature.

And now what has this to do with the ideal of
society or the wealth of nations? At the basis of
all social organization lies morality, as it is by conduct that both individuals and nations are saved or
lost. The history of the human race shows that

religion and morality are intimately related. That there have been good atheists does not affect the truth of this proposition any more than that there have been bad Christians. Men are usually better or worse than their principles ; practice and profession rarely accord ; and this is remarked because it ought not to exist.

Conduct, to be rational, should be motived, and consequently referable to certain general principles by which it is justified. To be particular, a man who believes in God, the Creator, a Father as just as he is good, has fundamental motives of action which are wanting to the atheist. The one should seek to approve himself to his heavenly Father ; the other cannot go farther than conform to the laws of nature. To the one this life, as compared with that which is to be, is of value only as it relates to it ; to the other it is all in all. And since the ultimate end of society is the welfare of the associated, the one will regard this end from a transcendental point of view, taking in time and eternity ; the other will consider it merely with reference to man's present state. Their notions of life, of its ends, aims, and proper surroundings, will be radically different.

Suppose for a moment that religious beliefs are mere dreams, fancies of sick brains ; is it not at once manifest that human life is a much poorer and sorrier thing than it is commonly thought to be ? As the light of heaven fades away, do not all things grow dark, leaving us in the shadow of death, despairing or debauched, sullen or frantic ? The poet's dream, the mother's fond hope, the heart's deep yearning, the mind's flight towards the infinite—all become flat, meaningless, and unprofitable. Men are simply animals chained to this clod, too happy if the heaven-seeking eye permitted them to see it alone. Trouble, danger, and physical pain are the only evils, and virtue is the sharp-sighted prudence which enables us to avoid them. Self-denial is not only useless, it is irrational. Our appetites are good and ought to be indulged. Nothing, of its own nature, is sinful; excess alone is wrong; all indulgence, provided it hurt no one, is good—nay, it is necessary. Whoever denies any one of his appetites the food it craves cripples himself, is maimed and incomplete. "He may be a monk; he may be a saint; but a man he is not."

When these views are transferred to questions of political economy and social organization, they lead to materialistic and utilitarian theories. Society must be organized on the basis of positivism; the problem of the future is how to give to the greatest number of individuals the best opportunities of indulgence, the greatest amount of comfort, with the least amount of pain. This is the greatest-happiness principle of Bentham and Mill. Culture, of course, intellectual and æsthetic, as affording the purest pleasure, must form a feature of this society; but its distinctive characteristic is wealth, which is both the means and the opportunity of indulgence.

"We constantly hear of the evils of wealth," says Buckle, "and of the sinfulness of loving money; although it is certain that, after the love of knowledge, there is no one passion which has done so much good to mankind as the love of money."

" If we open our eyes," says Strauss,* " and are honest enough to avow what they show us, we must acknowledge that the entire activity and aspiration of the civilized nations of our time is based on views of life which run directly counter to those entertained by Christ.   The ratio of value between the here and the hereafter is exactly reversed ; and this is by no means the result of the merely luxurious and so-called materialistic tendencies of our age, nor even of its marvellous progress in technical and industrial improvements. . . .⌠All that is best and happiest which has been achieved by us has been attainable only on the basis of a conception which regarded this present world as by no means despicable, but rather as man's proper field of labor, as the sum total of the aims to which his efforts should be directed.⌡ If, from the force of habit, a certain proportion of workers in this field still carry the belief in an hereafter along with them, it is nevertheless a mere shadow, which attends their footsteps without exercising any determining influence on their actions."

This is the cosmic religion, which is preached as " the new faith, the religion of the future."   This world is all in all—let us make the most of it ; or, as the pagans of old put it : " Let us eat and drink, for to-morrow we die."

In its essence it is sensualism ; in its manifesta-

---

* *The Old Faith and the New.* p. 86.

tions it will be refined or coarse, according to the dispositions of the persons by whom it is accepted. Now its worship will be accompanied with music and song and dance ; at other times it will sink to those orgies in which man becomes only an unnatural animal.

Let us now turn to the Christian religion, and consider its teachings in their bearing upon the subject we are discussing. They are the very opposite of those which we have just read, and proceed from principles which are in direct contradiction to the cosmic philosophy. God is the highest, the Creator of all things, which are of value only as they relate to him and are in. harmony with the laws of his being. The earth is but the threshold of heaven or of hell, as the case may be. This life is a preparation for a future one, which is eternal ; and all human interests, whether individual or social, to be rightly understood, must be viewed in their relation to this truth. [Man is essentially a moral being, and duty, which is often in conflict with pleasure, is his supreme law. He is under the action of antagonistic forces ; seeing the better and approving it, he is drawn to love the worse and to do it. Thus self-denial becomes the condition of virtue, and warfare with himself his only assurance of victory.]

" But he said to all : If any one wishes to come after me, let him deny himself, take up his cross every day, and follow me."

Wealth, which is the world's great slave and idol, and universal procurator of the senses, though in itself not evil, is yet a hindrance to the highest spiritual life. " If thou wouldst be perfect, go sell what thou hast, and give it to the poor, and thou shalt have treasure in heaven : and come and follow me."

As duty is the supreme law of the individual, it follows that we must seek the ideal of society in the moral order, to which all other social interests should be made subservient, or else they will beget only an unbounded and lawless activity. Even education is valuable only in so far as it gives man a deeper sense of his responsibility to God, and enables him more thoroughly to understand and perform his duty.

The social problem as between Christianity and modern paganism may be stated in this way : is it the end of society to grow strong in virtue through self-denial, or to increase indefinitely the means and opportunity of indulgence ? On which side is progress, on which decline ?

We cannot now go farther into this subject, but before leaving it we wish to quote the words of Fitzjames Stephen, who will hardly be called a Christian, on modern progress.

" I suspect," he says,* " that in many ways it has been a progress from strength to weakness ; that people are more sensitive, less enterprising and ambitious, less earnestly desirous to get what they want, and more afraid of pain, both for themselves and others, than they used to be. If this should

---

Liberty, Equality, Fraternity, p. 220.

be so, it appears to me that all other gains, whether in wealth, knowledge, or humanity, afford no equivalent. Strength, in all its forms, is life and manhood. To be less strong is to be less a man, whatever else you may be. This suspicion prevents me, for one, from feeling any enthusiasm about progress, but I do not undertake to say it is well founded. . . . I do not myself see that our mechanical inventions have increased the general vigor of men's characters, though they have no doubt increased enormously our control over nature. The greater part of our humanity appears to me to be a mere increase of nervous sensibility, in which I feel no satisfaction at all."

The general superiority, and even the greater wealth, of Christian nations as compared with others we would attribute, in great part at least, to the influence of their religious faith, to which they owe their sentiments on the dignity and sacredness of human nature in itself, apart from surroundings ; on the substantial equality of all men before God, which tends to produce as its counterpart the equality of all before the law, thus leading to the abolition of slavery, the elevation of woman, and the protection of childhood. To it also they owe their ideas on the family, which, in its constitutive Christian elements, lies at the very foundation of our civilization. To Christianity they owe the principles of universal charity and compassion, which have revolutionized the relations of social life ; and, finally, to it they are indebted for the rehabilitation of labor, the chief source of wealth, which the pagan nations looked upon as degrading.

"I cannot say," writes Herodotus, "whether the Greeks get their contempt for labor from the Egyptians; for I find the same prejudice among the Thracians, the Scythians, the Persians, and the Lydians."

"The Germans," says Tacitus, "cannot bear to remain quiet, but they love to be idle; they hold it base and unworthy of them to acquire by their sweat what they can purchase with their blood." In the same way the Gauls looked upon labor with contempt.

We shall have to take up M. de Laveleye's pamphlet again; for the present we lay it aside with the following remark: If we should grant, to the fullest, all that is here said about the greater wealth and material prosperity of Protestant as compared with Catholic nations, what are we thence to conclude? Shall we say that the greed of gain which is so marked a feature in the populations of England and the United States is at once the result and proof of true Christian faith? May it not be barely possible that the value of material progress is exaggerated? Is there not danger lest, when man shall have made matter the willing slave of all his passions, he should find that he has become the creature of this slave? However this may be, might not a Catholic find some consolation in the words of Holy Writ?

"And the angel that spoke in me, said to me: Cry thou, saying, Thus saith the Lord of hosts: I

am zealous for Jerusalem and Sion with a great zeal.
*And I am angry with a great anger with the nations
that are rich;* for I was angry a little, but they
helped forward the evil."

COMPARATIVE INFLUENCE OF CATHO-LICISM AND PROTESTANTISM ON NATIONAL PROSPERITY.

II. EDUCATION.

ONE of the most mischievous prejudices of our day is the popular theory that the cure for all evils is to be sought in the intellectual education of the masses. Those nations, we are told by every declaimer, in which the education of the people is most universal, are the most moral, the richest, the strongest, the freest, and their prosperity rests upon the most solid and lasting foundation. Make ignorance a crime, teach all to read and write, and war will smooth its rugged front, armies will be disbanded, corruption will disappear, and mankind will have found the secret of uninterrupted progress, the final outcome of which will surpass even our fondest dreams.

This fallacy, which has not even the merit of being plausible, is, of course, made to do service in M. de Laveleye's pamphlet on the comparative bearing of Protestantism and Catholicism on the prosperity of nations.

"It is now universally admitted," he informs us,* "that the diffusion of enlightenment is the first condition of progress. . . . The general spread of education is also indispensable to the exercise of constitutional liberty. . . . In short, education is the basis of national liberty and prosperity."

He then declares that in this matter of popular education Protestant countries are far in advance of those that are Catholic ; that this is necessarily so, since "the Reformed religion rests on a book—the Bible ; the Protestant, therefore, must know how to read. Catholic worship, on the contrary, rests upon sacraments and certain practices—such as confession, Masses, sermons—which do not necessarily involve reading. It is, therefore, unnecessary to know how to read ; indeed, it is dangerous, for it inevitably shakes the principle of passive obedience on which the whole Catholic edifice reposes : reading is the road that leads to heresy."

We will first consider the theory, and then take up the facts.

"The diffusion of enlightenment is the first condition of progress. Education is indispensable to the exercise of constitutional liberty. Education is the basis of national liberty and prosperity."

Enlightenment is, of course, of the mind, and means the development, more or less perfect, of the intellectual faculties ; and education, since it is here considered as synonymous with enlightenment, must be taken in this narrow sense.

Progress is material, moral, intellectual, social,

* P. 22.

political, artistic, religious, scientific, literary, and indefinitely manifold. Now, it is assumed that the diffusion of enlightenment is not merely promotive, but that it is an essential condition of progress in its widest and fullest meaning. This is the new faith—the goddess of culture, holding the torch of science and leading mankind into the palace of pleasure, the only true heaven.

By conduct, we have already said, both individuals and nations are saved or perish ; and we spoke of the civilized. Barbarous states are destroyed by catastrophes—they die a violent death ; but the civilized are wasted by internal maladies—*suis et ipsa Roma viribus ruit.* They grow and they decay, they progress and they decline. At first poverty, virtue, industry, faith, hopefulness, strong characters and heroic natures ; at last wealth, corruption, indolence, unbelief, despair, children too weak even to admire the strength of their fathers, too base to believe that they were noble. Public spirit dies out ; patriotism is in the mouths of politicians, but, like the augurs of Rome, they cannot speak the word and look one another in the face. The country is to each one what he can make out of it, and the bond of union is the desire of each citizen to secure his own interests. The bondholders love their country, and the *sansculottes* are disloyal ; class rises against class, civil discord unsettles everything, revolution succeeds revolution, and when the barbarian comes he holds an inquest over the corpse. It generally happens, too, that those civilizations which spring up quickest and promise most fair are fated to die earliest; as precocious children disappoint fond mothers. If the teaching of history is a trustworthy guide, we are certainly safe in affirming that civilized states and empires perish, not from lack of knowledge, but of virtue; not because the people are ignorant, but because they are corrupt.

The assumption, however, is that men become immoral because they are ignorant; that if they were enlightened, they would be virtuous.

"The superstition," says Mr. Herbert Spencer,* "that good behavior is to be forthwith produced by lessons learned out of books, which was long ago statistically disproved, would, but for preconceptions, be utterly dissipated by observing to what a slight extent knowledge affects conduct; by observing that the dishonesty implied in the adulterations of tradesmen and manufacturers, in fraudulent bankruptcies, in bubble companies, in 'cooking' of railway accounts and financial prospectuses, differs only in form, and not in amount, from the dishonesty of the uneducated; by observing how amazingly little the teachings given to medical students affect their lives, and how even the most experienced medical men have their prudence scarcely at all increased by their information."

It is not knowledge, but character, that is important; and character is formed more by faith, by hope, by love, admiration, enthusiasm, reverence, than by any patchwork of alphabetical and arithmetical symbols. The young know but little; but they believe firmly, they hope nobly, and love gen-

* *Study of Sociology,* p. 121.

erously; and it is while knowledge is feeble and
these spontaneous acts of the soul are strong that
character is moulded. The curse of our age is
that men will believe that, in education, to spell,
to read, to write, is what signifies, and they cast
aside the eternal faith, the infinite hope, the divine
love, that more than all else makes us men.

" The true test of civilization," says Emerson,
" is not the census, nor the size of cities, nor the
crops—no, but the kind of man the country turns
out." Is there some mystic virtue in printed words
that to be able to read them should make us men ?
And even in the most enlightened countries what
do the masses of men know ? Next to nothing ;
and their reading, for the most part, stupefies
them. The newspaper, with its murders, suicides,
hangings, startling disclosures, defalcations, embez-
zlements, burglaries, forgeries, adulteries, advertisements of nostrums, quack medicines, and secrets of
working death in the very source of life, with all
manner of hasty generalizations, crude theories, and
half-truths jumbled into intellectual *pot-pourris ;*
the circulating library, with its stories, tales, roman-
ces of love, despair, death, of harrowing accidents,
of hair-breadth escapes, of successful crime, and all
the commonplaces of wild, reckless, and unnatural
life—these are the sources of their knowledge. Or,
if they are ambitious, they read " How to get on in
the world," " The art of making money," " The secret of growing rich," " The road to wealth," " Successful men," " The millionaires of America," and
the Mammon-worship, and the superstition of mat-

ter, and the idolatry of success become their religion ; their souls die within them, and what wretched slaves they grow to be !

In the newspaper and circulating library God and man, heaven and earth—all things—are discussed, flippantly, in snatches, generally ; all possible conflicting and contradictory views are taken ; and these ignorant masses, who, in the common schools, have been through the Fourth Reader, and who know nothing, not even their own ignorance, are confused. They doubt, they lose faith, and are enlightened by the discovery that God, the soul, truth, justice, honor, are only nominal—they do not concern positivists. Can anything be more pitiful than the state of these poor wretches ?—neither knowing nor believing ; without knowledge, yet having nor faith nor love. God pity them that they are communists, internationalists, *solidaires ;* for what else could they be ? No enthusiasm is possible for them but that of destruction.

Religion is the chief element in civilization, and consequently in progress. For the masses, even though the whole energy of mankind should spend itself upon some or any possible common-school system, the eternal principles which mould character, support manhood, and consecrate humanity will always remain of faith, and can never be held scientifically. If it were possible that science should prove religion false, it would none the less remain true, or there would be no truth.

What children know when they leave school is mechanical, external to their minds, fitted on them

like clothes on the body; and it is soon worn
threadbare, and hangs in shreds and patches.
Take the first boy whom you meet, fourteen or fifteen years old, fresh from the common school, and
his ignorance of all real knowledge will surprise
you.   What he knows is little and of small value:
what is of moment is whether he believes firmly,
hopes strongly, and loves truly.   Not the diffusion
of enlightenment do we want so much, but the diffusion of character, of honest faith, and manly courage.

Man is more than his knowledge.   Simple faith
is better than reading and writing.   And yet the
educational quacks treat the child as though he
were mere mind, and his sole business to use it,
and chiefly for low ends, shrewdly and sharply,
with a view to profit; as though life were a thing
of barter, and wisdom the art of making the most
of it.

Poor child! who wouldst live by admiration,
hope, and love, how they dwarf thy being, stunt thy
growth, and flatten all thy soaring thoughts with
their dull commonplaces—thrift, honesty is the best
policy, time is money, knowledge is wealth, and
all the vocabulary of a shop-keeping and trading
philosophy.   Poor child! who wouldst look out into the universe as God's great temple, and behold
in all its glories the effulgence of heaven; to whom
morning, noon, and night, and change of season,
golden flood of day and star-lit gloom, all speak of
some diviner life, how they stun thy poetic soul,
full of high dreams and noble purposes, with their

cold teaching that man lives on bread alone—put money in thy purse! And when thou wouldst look back with awe and reverence to the sacred ages past, to the heroes, sages, saints of the olden times, they come with their gabble and tell thee there were no railroads and common schools in those days.

Is it strange that this education should hurt the nation's highest interests by driving in crowds, like cattle to the shambles, our youths from God and nature and tilling of the soil to town and city, or, worse, into professions to which only their conceit or distaste for hard labor calls them? What place for morality is there in this Poor Richard's Catechism—education of thrift and best policy? We grow in likeness to what we love, not to what we know. With low aims and selfish loves only narrow and imperfect characters are compatible.

Science, when cherished for itself—which it seldom is and in very exceptional cases—refines and purifies its lovers, and chastens the force of passion: though even here we must admit that the wisest of mankind may be the meanest, morally the most unworthy. But for the great mass of men, even of those who are called educated, the possession of such knowledge as they have or can have has no necessary relation with higher moral life. Their learning may refine, smooth over, or conceal their sin; it will not destroy it. The furred gown and intertissued robe hide the faults that peep through beggars' rags, but they are there all the same. There may be a substitution of pride for sensuality,

or a skilful blending or alternation of the finer with
the coarser. Vice may lose its grossness, but not
its evil. And herein we detect the wretched sophistry of criminal statistics, which deal, imperfectly and roughly enough, with what is open, shock-
ing, and repulsive. The hidden sins that, "like pit-
ted speck in garnered fruit," slowly eating to the core
of a people's life, moulder all ; the sapping of faith,
the weakening of character, the disbelief in goodness ; the luxury, the indulgence, the heartlessness
and narrowness of the rich ; the cunning devices
through which " the spirit of murder" works in the
very means of life,

> " While rank corruption, mining all within,
>   Infects unseen"

—cannot be appreciated by the gross tests of
numbers and averages. The poor, by statistics as
by the world, are handled without gloves. In the
large cities of civilized countries, both in ancient
and in modern times, we have unmistakable proof
of what knowledge can do to form character and
produce even the social virtues. These populations
have had the advantage of the best schools in the
most favorable circumstances, and yet in character
and morality they are far beneath the less educated
peasantry. Sensual indulgence, contempt of authority, hatred and jealousy of those above them,
make these the dangerous classes, eager for socialistic reforms, radical upheavals of the whole existing order ; and were it not for the more religious
tillers of the soil, chaos and misrule would already

prevail. In Greece and Rome it was in the cities that civilization first perished, as it was there it began—began with men who had great faith and strong character, but little knowledge ; perished among men who were learned and refined, but who in indulgence and debauch had lost all strength and honesty of purpose.

In the last report of the Commissioner of Education some interesting facts, bearing on the relation of ignorance to crime, are taken from the Forty-fifth Annual Report of the inspector of the State penitentiary for the Eastern District of Pennsylvania.

" It is doubted if in any State, or indeed in any country," says the commissioner, " forty-four volumes containing the annual statistical tables relating to the populations of a penal institution, covering nearly half a century, can, on examination, be regarded as more complete."

The number of prisoners received into the institution from 1850 to 1860 was 1,605, of whom 15 per cent. were illiterate, 15 per cent. were able to read, and 70 per cent., or more than two-thirds, knew how to read and write ; from 1860 to 1870, 2,383 prisoners were received into the penitentiary, and of these 17 per cent. were illiterate, 12 per cent. could read, and about 71 per cent. could read and write.

Of the 627 convicts who were in the penitentiary during the year 1867, 62 per cent., or five-eighths of the whole number, had attended the public schools of the State, 25 per cent., or two-eighths, had gone to private institutions, and 12 per cent., or one-eighth, had never gone to school.

But, as we have said, statistics deal with crime, and chiefly with the more open and discoverable sort, not with morality; whereas nations are destroyed not so much by crime as by immorality.

The thief is caught and sent to the penitentiary; but the trader who adulterates or gives short measure, the banker who puts forth a false or exaggerated statement, the merchant who fails with full hands, the stock-gambler who robs thousands, Crédit-Mobilier men and "ring" men generally who plunder scientifically, Congressmen who take money for helping to swindle the government, getters-up of "bubble companies"—salted diamond-fields and Emma Mines—compared with whom pickpockets and burglars are respectable gentlemen—these know not of penitentiaries; prisons were not built for such as they. The poor man abandons his wife, without divorce marries another, and is very properly sent to State prison. His rich and educated fellow-citizen gets a divorce, or is a free-lover, or keeps a harem, and for him laws were not made. Even that respectable old dame Society only gently shakes her head. We must not expect too much of gentlemen, you know. The ignorant girl falls, commits infanticide, and is incarcerated or hanged—heaven forbid that we should attempt to tell what she would have done had she been educated!—at any rate, she would not have gone to prison, though her guilt would not have been less.

Has the very great diffusion of enlightenment among our people during the hundred years that we have been an independent nation made them more moral and more worthy?

" The true test of civilization is not the census, nor the size of cities, nor the crops—no, but the kind of man the country turns out."

The Yankee is smarter than the Puritan—is he as true a man? Is the inventor of a sewing-machine or a patent bedstead as worthy as he who believes in God and in liberty against the whole earth with all his heart and soul, even though the heart be hard and the soul narrow? What compensation is there in all our philanthropies, transcendentalisms, sentimentalities, patent remedies for social evils, for the loss of the strong convictions, reverent belief, and simple dignity of character that made our fathers men? Do we believe in the goodness and honesty of men as they did, or is it possible that we should? What can come of beliefs in over-souls, whims, tendencies, abstractions, develop-ments? If we were shadows in a shadow-land, this might do.

Look at a famous trial where the very aroma and fine essence of our civilization was gathered : What bright minds, keen intellects! Poetry, eloquence, romance ; the culture, the knowledge, the scientific theories of the age—all are there. And yet, when the veil is lifted, we simply turn away heart-sick and nauseated. Not a hundred statistical prison reports would reveal the festering corruption and deep depravity, the coarse vulgarity and utter

11

heartlessness that is there, whatever the truth may be, if in such surroundings it can be found at all.

In Laing's *Notes of a Traveller* * we find a most striking example of almost incredible corruption united with great intellectual culture. " In this way," he says, " we must account for the singular fact that the only positively immoral religious sect of the present times in the Christian world arose and has spread itself in the most educated part of the most educated country in Europe—in and about Königsberg, the capital of the province of Old Prussia. The Muckers are a sect who combine lewdness with religion. The conventicles of this sect are frequented by men and women in a state of nudity ; and to excite the animal passion, but to restrain its indulgence, is said to constitute their religious exercise. Many of the highest nobility of the province, and two of the established clergy of the city, besides citizens, artificers, and ladies, old and young, belong to this sect ; and two young ladies are stated to have died from the consequences of excessive libidinous excitement. It is no secret association of profligacy shunning the light. It is a sect—according to the declarations of Von Tippelskirch and of several persons of consideration in Königsberg who had been followers of it themselves—existing very extensively under the leadership of the established ministers of the Gospel, Ebel and Diestel, of a Count von Kaniz, of a Lady von S——, and of other noble persons. . . .

* P. 221.

The system and theory of this dreadful combination of vice with religion are, of course, very properly suppressed. . . . The sect itself appears, by Dr. Bretscheider's account of it, to have been so generally diffused that he says ‘ it cannot be believed that the public functionaries were in ignorance of its existence ; but they were afraid to do their duty from the influence of the many principal people who were involved in it.’ ”

But we are not the advocates of ignorance. We will praise with any man the true worth and inestimable value of education. Even mere mental training is, to our thinking, of rare price. Water is good, but without bread it will not sustain life. Wine warms and gladdens the heart of man ; but if used without care, it maddens and drives to destruction. We are crying out against the folly of the age which would make the school-room its church, education its sacrament, and culture its religion. It is the road to ruin. Culture is for the few ; and what a trumpery patchwork of frippery and finery and paste diamonds it must ever remain for the most of these! For the millions it means the pagan debauch, the bacchanal orgy, and mere animalism.

“ The characters,” wrote Goethe—who was pagan of the pagans and “ decidirter Nicht-Christ ”— “ which we can truly respect have become rarer. We can sincerely esteem only that which is not self-seeking. . . . I must confess to have found through my whole life unselfish characters of the kind of which I speak only there where I found a

firmly-grounded religious life ; a creed, which had
an unchangeable basis, resting upon itself—not de-
pendent upon the time, its spirit, or its science."

This foundation of a positive religious faith is as
indispensable to national as to individual character,
and without it the diffusion of enlightenment cannot create a great or lasting civilization. Religion
ought to constitute the very essence of all primary
education. It alone can touch the heart, raise the
mind, and evoke from their brutish apathy the elements of humanity, especially the reason ; and it is
therefore the one indispensable element in any
right system of national education. A population
unable to read or write, but with a religious faith
and discipline, have before now constituted, and may
again constitute, a great nation ; but a people without religious earnestness have no solid political character. Religion is the widest and deepest of all
the elements of civilization ; it reaches those whom
nothing else can touch ; but for the masses of men.
there can be no religion without the authoritative
teaching of a church.

And now let us return to M. de Laveleye
" The general spread of education," he says,* " is
indispensable to the exercise of constitutional
liberty. . . . Education is the basis of national
liberty and prosperity."

In view of the facts that constitutional liberty has
existed, and for centuries, in states in which there
was no " general spread of education," and that

* P. 23.

" the diffusion of enlightenment " is found in our own day to co-exist with the most hateful despotisms, we might pass on, without stopping to examine more closely these loose and popular phrases ; but since the fallacies which they contain form a part of the culture-creed of modern paganism, and are accepted as indisputable truths by the multitude, they have a claim upon our attention which their assertion by Mr. Gladstone's friend could not give them.

There is no necessary connection between popular education and civil liberty, as there is none between the enlightenment and the morality of a people. This is a subject full of import—one which, in this age and country, ought to be discussed with perfect freedom and courage. Courage indeed is needed precisely here ; for to deny that there is a God, to treat Christ as a myth or a common man, to declaim against religion as superstition, to make the Bible a butt for witticisms and fine points, to deny future life and the soul's immortality, to denounce marriage, to preach communism, and to ridicule whatever things mankind have hitherto held sacred— this is not only tolerable, it is praiseworthy and runs with the free thought of an enlightened and inquiring age. But to raise a doubt as to the supreme and paramount value of intellectual training ; of its sovereign efficacy in the cure of human ills ; of its inseparable alliance with freedom, with progress, with man's best interests, is pernicious heresy, and ought not to be borne with patiently. In our civilization, through the action of majorities, there is special difficulty in such discussions, since with us nothing is true except what is popular. Majorities rule, and are therefore right. With rare eloquence we denounce tyrant kings and turn to lick the hands of the tyrant people. Whoever questions the wisdom of the American people is not to be argued with—he is to be pitied ; and therefore both press and pulpit, though they flaunt the banner of freedom, are the servants of the tyrant. To have no principles, but to write and speak what will please the most and offend the fewest—this is the philosophy of free speech. We therefore have no independent, and consequently no great, thinkers. It is dangerous not to think with majorities and parties ; for those who attempt to break their bonds generally succeed, like Emerson, only in becoming whimsical, weak, and inconclusive. It is not surprising, then, that the Catholics, because they do not accept as true or ultimate what is supposed to be the final thought and definite will of American majorities on the subject of education, should be denounced, threatened, and made a Trojan horse of to carry political adventurers into the White House.

Nevertheless, the observant are losing confidence in the theory, so full of inspiration to demagogues and declaimers, that superstition and despotism must be founded on ignorance. In Prussia at this moment universal education co-exists with despotism. Where tyrannical governments take control of education they easily make it their ally.

Let us hear what Laing says of the practical results of the Prussian system of education, which it is so much the fashion to praise.

" If the ultimate object," he says, " of all education and knowledge be to raise man to the feeling of his own moral worth, to a sense of his responsibility to his Creator and to his conscience for every act, to the dignity of a reflecting, self-guiding, virtuous, religious member of society, then the Prussian educational system is a failure. It is only a training from childhood in the conventional discipline and submission of mind which the state exacts from its subjects. It is not a training or education which has raised, but which has lowered, the human character. . . . The social value or importance of the Prussian arrangements for diffusing national scholastic education has been evidently overrated ; for now that the whole system has been in the fullest operation in society upon a whole generation, we see morals and religion in a more unsatisfactory state in this very country than in almost any other in the north of Europe; we see nowhere a people in a more abject political and civil condition, or with less free agency in their social economy. A national education which gives a nation neither religion, nor morality, nor civil liberty, nor political liberty is an education not worth· having. . . . If to read, write, cipher, and sing be education, the Prussian subject is an educated man. If to reason, judge, and act as an independent free agent, in the religious, moral, and social relations of man to his Creator and to his fellow-men, be the exercise of the mental powers which alone deserves the name

of education, then is the Prussian subject a mere
drum-boy in education, in the cultivation and use
of all that regards the moral and intellectual endowments of man, compared to one of the unlet-
tered population of a free country.   The dormant
state of the public mind on all affairs of public interest, the acquiescence in a total want of political
influence or existence, the intellectual dependence
upon the government or its functionary in all the
affairs of the community, the abject submission to
the want of freedom or free agency in thoughts,
words, or acts, the religious thraldom of the people
to forms which they despise, the want of influence of religious and social principle in society,
justify the conclusion that the moral, religious, and
social condition of the people was never looked at
or estimated by those writers who were so enthu-
siastic in their praises of the national education of
Prussia.''

In spite of the continued progress of education,
there is even less liberty, religious, civil, and political, in Prussia to-day than when these words were
written, thirty years ago.

Nothing more dazzles the eyes of men than great
military success ; and this, together with the habit
which belongs to our race of applauding whoever
wins, has produced, especially in England and the
United States, where Bismarck is looked upon, ig-
norantly enough, as the champion of Protestantism,
a kind of blind admiration and awe for whatever
is Prussian.   " Protestant Prussia," boasts M. de
Laveleye, " has defeated two empires, each con-

taining twice her own population, the one in seven weeks, the other in seven months"; and in the new edition of Appleton's *Cyclopædia* we are informed that these victories are attributed to the superior education of her people. As well might the tyranny of the government and the notorious unchastity and dishonesty of the Prussians be ascribed to their superior education. Not to the general intelligence of the people, but to the fact that the whole country has been turned into a military camp, and that to the one purpose of war all interests have been made subservient, must we seek for an explanation of the victories of Sadowa and Sedan.

Who would pretend that the Spartans were in war superior to the Athenians because they had a more perfect system of education and were more intelligent or had a truer religion? Or who would think of accounting in this way for the marvellous exploits of Attila with his Huns, of Zingis Khan with his Moguls, of Tamerlane with his Tartars, of Mahmood, Togrul-Bey, and Malek-Shah with their Turkish hordes?

In fact, it may be said, speaking largely and in general, that the history of war is that of the triumph of strong and ignorant races over those which have become cultivated, refined, and corrupt. The Romans learned from their conquered slaves letters and the vices of a more polished paganism. Barbarism is ever impending over the civilized world. The wild and rugged north is ever rushing down upon the soft and cultured south; the Scythian upon the Mede, the Persian, and the Egyptian ; the Macedonian upon Greece, and then upon Asia and Africa ; the Roman upon Carthage, and in turn falling before the men of the north—Goth, Vandal, Hun, Frank, and Gaul ; the Mogul and the Tartar upon China and India ; the Turk upon southern Europe, Asia, and Africa ; and to-day, like black clouds of destiny, the Russian hordes hang over the troubled governments of more educated Europe. Look at Italy during the middle ages—the focus of learning and the arts for all Christendom, and yet an easy prey for every barbarous adventurer ; and in England the Briton yields to the Saxon, who in turn falls before the Norman.   It would be truer to say that Prussia owes her military successes to the ignorance of her people, though they nearly all can read and write.   Had she had to deal with intelligent and enlightened populations, she could not have made the country a camp of soldiers.

The Prussian policy of "blood and iron" has been carried out, in defiance of the wishes of the people as expressed through their representatives, who were snubbed and scolded and sent back home as though they were a pack of school-boys; yet the people looked on in stolid indifference, and allowed the tax to be levied after they had refused to grant it.

We will now follow M. de Laveleye a step farther.

"With regard to elementary instruction," he says, " the Protestant states are incomparably more advanced than the Catholic.   England alone is no

more than on a level with the latter, probably because the Anglican Church, of all the reformed
forms of worship, has most in common with the
Church of Rome."

If any one has good reason to praise education,
and above all the education of the people, certainly we Catholics have. The Catholic Church created the people ; she first preached the divine doctrine of the brotherhood and equality of all men before God, which has wrought and must continue to
work upon society until all men shall be recognized
as equals by the law. She drew around woman her
magic circle; from the slave struck his fetters and
bade him be a man ; lifted to her bosom the child ;
baptized all humanity into the inviolable sacredness
of Christ's divinity ; she appealed, and still appeals,
from the tyranny of brute force and success, in the
name of the eternal liberties of the soul, to God.
Her martyrs were and are the martyrs of liberty ;
and if she were not to-day, all men would accept
accomplished facts and bow before whatever succeeds.

The barbarians, who have developed into the civilized peoples of Europe, despised learning as they
contemned labor. War was their business. The
knight signed his name with his sword, in blood ;
the pen, like the spade, was made for servile hands.
To destroy this ignorant, idle life of pillage and
feud, the church organized an army, unlike any the
world had ever seen, unlike any it will ever see outside her pale—an army of monks, who, with faith
in Christ and the higher life, believed in knowledge

and in work.   They became the cultivators of the mind and soil of Europe.

"The praise," says Hallam, speaking of the middle ages, " of having originally established schools belongs to some bishops and abbots of the sixth century."

Ireland is converted and at once becomes a kind of university for all Europe.   In England the episcopal sees became centres of learning.   Wherever a cathedral was built a school with a library grew up under its shadow.   Pope Eugenius II., in a council held in Rome in 826, ordered that schools should be established throughout Christendom at cathedral and parochial churches and other suitable places. The Council of Mayence, in 813, admonishes parents that they are in duty bound to send their children to school.   The Synod of Orleans, in 800, enjoins the erection in towns and villages of schools for elementary instruction, and adds that no remuneration shall be received except such as the parents voluntarily offer.   The Third General Council of Lateran, in 1179, commanded that in all cathedral churches a fund should be set aside for the foundation and support of schools for the poor. Free schools were thus first established by the Catholic Church, and her monasteries were the libraries where the arts and letters of a civilization that had perished were carefully treasured up for the rekindling of a brighter and better day.

As early as the twelfth century many of the universities of Europe were fully organized.   Italy took the lead, with universities at Rome, Bologna, Padua, Naples, Pavia, and Perugia—the sources

> "Whence many rivulets have since been turned,
> O'er the garden Catholic to lead
> Their living waters, and have fed its plants."

The schools founded at Oxford and Cambridge in the ninth and tenth centuries had in the twelfth grown to be universities. At Oxford there were thirty thousand, at Paris twenty-five thousand, and at Padua twenty thousand students. Scattered over Europe at the time Luther raised his voice against the church there were sixty-six universities.

"Time went on," says Dr. Newman, speaking of the mediæval universities; "a new state of things, intellectual and social, came in; the church was girt with temporal power; the preachers of St. Dominic were in the ascendant: now, at length, we may ask with curious interest, did the church alter her ancient rule of action, and proscribe intellectual activity? Just the contrary; this is the very age of universities; it is the classical period of the schoolmen; it is the splendid and palmary instance of the wise policy and large liberality of the church, as regards philosophical inquiry. If there ever was a time when the intellect went wild and had a licentious revel, it was at the date I speak of. When was there ever a more curious, more meddling, bolder, keener, more penetrating, more rationalistic exercise of the reason than at that time? What class of questions did that subtle metaphysical spirit not scrutinize? What premise was allowed without examination? What principle was not traced to its first origin, and exhibited in its most naked shape? . . . Well, I repeat, here was something which came somewhat nearer to theology than physical research comes; Aristotle was a somewhat more serious foe then, beyond all mistake, than Bacon has been since. Did the church take a high hand with philosophy then? No, not though that philosophy was metaphysical. It was a time when she had temporal power, and could have exterminated the spirit of inquiry with fire and sword; but she determined to put it down by *argument;* she said: ' Two can play at that, and my argument is the better.' She sent her controversialists into the philosophical arena. It was the Dominican and Franciscan doctors, the greatest of them being St. Thomas, who in those mediæval universities fought the battle of revelation with the weapons of heathenism." *

To find fault with the church because popular education in the middle ages was not so well organized nor so general as in our own day would be as wise as to pick a quarrel with the ancient Greeks for not having railroads, or with the Romans because they had no steamships. Reading and writing were not taught then universally as they are now, because the mechanism which renders this possible did not exist. Without steam and the printing-press, common-school systems would not now be practicable, nor would the want of them be felt. We have great reason to be thankful that the art of printing was invented and America discovered

* *The Idea of a University,* p. 469.

before Luther burned the Pope's bull, else we should be continually bothered with refuting the cause-and-effect historians who would have infallibly traced both these events to the Wittenberg conflagration.

All Europe was still Catholic when gunpowder drove old Father Schwarz's pestle through the ceiling, when Gutenberg made his printing-press, when Columbus landed in the New World; and these are the forces which have battered down the castles of feudalism, have brought knowledge within the reach of all, and some measure of redress to the masses of the Old World, by affording them the possibility and opportunity of liberty in the New. These forces would have wrought to even better purpose had Protestantism not broken the continuity and homogeneity of Christian civilization. The Turk would not rest like a blight from heaven upon the fairest lands of Europe and Asia, nor the darkness of heathenism upon India and China, had the civilized nations remained of one faith; and thus, though our own train might have rushed less rapidly down the ringing grooves of change, the whole human race would have advanced to a level which there now seems but little reason to hope it will ever reach.

We are slowly but inevitably rising to a position from which it will be possible to understand the injury done to Christian civilization by the disturbing influence of Protestantism. For a long time religious prejudice prevented men from seeing the plainest and most unmistakable facts of history, and we are therefore not surprised that the sixteenth century should have been glorified by an almost universal hymn of praise. In order to justify itself, Protestantism was under the sad necessity of misinterpreting or perverting the history of Christendom. The fifteenth century was robbed of its Catholic glories to crown the sixteenth with honors which were not its own.

"The fifteenth century," says Guizot, "is a century of voyages, enterprises, discoveries, and inventions of all kinds."*

The revival of letters, the invention of printing, the discovery of America, the mariner's compass, gunpowder, the establishment of universities, of banks; of postal service, the Gothic architecture, the mathematics, mining, smelting, weaving, engineering, paper, fire-arms, clocks, musical instruments, the modern languages, the greatest of modern poems, were all before Luther. Marsilius Ficin, who was born in 1433, understood his age when he called the fifteenth century the golden ; for it was beyond question the glorious dawn of a brighter era. "Aureum esse hoc sæculum," he says, "minime dubitabit, qui præclara sæculi hujus inventa considerare voluerit." And its greatest splendor was in Italy, where the influence of the popes was most powerful. Leonardo da Vinci, who was born in 1445, the painter of the "Last Supper" and the rival of Michael Angelo, rendered greater services even to science than to art. He it was who first proclaimed the principle that experiment and observation are the only

* *History of Civilisation in Europe,* Lesson xi.

right methods in scientific investigation. He excelled in painting, sculpture, architecture, engineering, and was thoroughly instructed in the astronomy, anatomy, and chemistry of his times. " To him," says Dr. Draper, " and not to Lord Bacon, must be attributed the renaissance of science. Bacon was not only ignorant of mathematics, but deprecated its application to physical inquiries. He contemptuously rejected the Copernican system, al·leging absurd objections to it. While Galileo was on the brink of his great telescopic discoveries, Bacon was publishing doubts as to the utility of instruments in scientific investigations. To ascribe the inductive method to him is to ignore history. His fanciful philosophical suggestions have never been of the slightest use. No one has ever thought of employing them. Except among English readers, his name is almost unknown." *

To Italy belongs the honor of the invention of the barometer, and also of the thermometer. Harvey owed his discovery of the circulation of the blood to the experiments of his teacher, Fabricius of Padua. The school of Salerno, the great medical authority in Europe from the eighth to the fourteenth century, was founded by the disciples of St. Benedict, who also called the attention of the afflicted to the value of mineral waters in the cure of disease. Baden, Kissingen, Marienbad, Pyrmont, Rippoldsau, and many other similar places were from the ear-

---

* *Conflict between Religion and Science*, p. 233. Dr. Draper but repeats what Liebig has satisfactorily proved in his work on Bacon. Both he and Goethe, who is no mean authority in such matters, hold that Bacon's influence retarded the progress of science.

liest times in the hands of the monks, who invited the suffering from every land to try the virtues of these waters.

Geographical discovery was carried on under the patronage and with the aid of the church. "In our day," says Ritter, "commercial and scientific interests are the motives which impel to a wider knowledge of the earth; in the middle ages these motives were drawn from religion and the church." * Even as late as the beginning of the present century our knowledge of the great Chinese Empire was derived principally from the writings of the Jesuit missionaries.

The most celebrated geographer of the middle ages was Father Mauro, a Camaldulese monk, who died in 1459. His chief labors were undertaken in the interests of the Republic of Venice and of Alfonso V. of Portugal. His geographical charts inspired Vasco da Gama and Christopher Columbus with the thoughts which led to such immortal results. Another priest, Hermann Martinez, was the first to suggest the idea which led to the discovery of the New World—that the best way to reach the east was to sail westward; and when Columbus was about to lose all hope, a Spanish monk won to his enterprise the heart of the great Catholic queen.

But we lose sight of M. de Laveleye's assertion that in popular education the Protestant nations are far in advance of the Catholic, with the exception of England, which is at least up to the standard of Catholic countries. In the report of the Commis-

* *Histoire des Découvertes Géographiques,* p. 141.

sioner of Education for 1874 there is a statistical
account of the state of education in foreign countries which throws some light upon this subject.

The school attendance, compared with the population, is in Austria as 1 to 10; in Belgium, as 1
to 10½ ; in Ireland, as 1 to 16; in Catholic Switzerland, as 1 to 16; in England, as 1 to 17. In
Bavaria it is as 1 to 7, upon the authority of Kay, in
his *Social Condition of the People in England and
Europe.* Catholic Austria, Bavaria, Belgium, and
Ireland have proportionately a larger school attendance than Protestant England. England and
Wales (report of 1874), with a population of 22,712,-
266, had a school population of 5,374,700, of whom
only about half were registered, and not half of
these attended with sufficient regularity to bring
grants to their schools. Ireland, with a population
of 5,411,416, had on register 1,006,511, or nearly
half as many as England and Wales, though her
population is not a fourth of that of these two
countries. "The statistical fact," says Laing, speaking of Rome as it was under the popes, "that
Rome has above a hundred schools more than Berlin, for a population little more than half that of
Berlin, puts to flight a world of humbug about systems of national education carried on by governments and their moral effects on society. . . . In
Catholic Germany, in France, Italy, and even Spain,
the education of the common people in reading,
writing, arithmetic, music, manners, and morals, is
at least as generally diffused and as faithfully promoted by the clerical body as in Scotland. It is

by their own advance, and not by keeping back the advance of the people, that the popish priesthood of the present day seek to keep ahead of the intellectual progress of the community in Catholic lands ; and they might, perhaps, retort on our Presbyterian clergy, and ask if they, too, are in their countries at the head of the intellectual movement of the age.   Education is in reality not only not repressed, but is encouraged, by the popish church, and is a mighty instrument in its hands, and ably used." *

Professor Huxley's testimony is confirmatory of this admission of Laing.   " It was my fortune," he says, " some time ago to pay a visit to one of the most important of the institutions in which the clergy of the Roman Catholic Church in these islands are trained ; and it seemed to me that the difference between these men and the comfortable champions of Anglicanism and Dissent was comparable to the difference between our gallant Volunteers and the trained veterans of Napoleon's Old Guard.   The Catholic priest is trained to know his business and do it effectually.   The professors of the college in question, learned, zealous, and determined men, permitted me to speak frankly with them.   We talked like outposts of opposed armies during a truce—as friendly enemies ; and when I ventured to point out the difficulties their students would have to encounter from scientific thought, they replied : ' Our church has lasted many ages, and has passed safely through many storms.   The

* *Notes of a Traveller*, pp. 402, 403.

present is but a new gust of the old tempest, and
we do not turn out our young men less fitted to
weather it than they have been in former times to
cope with the difficulties of those times.' " *

"It is a common remark," says Kay, "of the
operatives of Lancashire, and one which is only too
true : ' Your church is a church for the rich, but not
for the poor. It was not intended for such people
as we are.' The Roman church is much wiser than
the English in this respect. . . . It is singular to
observe how the priests of Romanist countries.
abroad associate with the poor. I have often seen
them riding with the peasants in their carts along
the roads, eating with them in their houses, sitting
with them in the village inns, mingling with them
in their village festivals, and yet always preserving
their authority. " †

With us, too, the masses of the people are fast
abandoning Protestantism. There is no Catholic
country in Europe in which the social condition of
the lower classes is so wretched as in England, the
representative Protestant country. For three hundred years, it may be said, the Catholic Church had
no existence there. The nation was exclusively
under Protestant influence; and yet the lower
classes were suffered to remain in stolid ignorance,
until they became the most degraded population in
Christendom.

"It has been calculated," says Kay, writing in
1850, "that there are at the present day, in Eng-

---

* *Lay Sermons,* p. 61.
† *The Social Condition,* etc., vol. i. p. 420.

land and Wales, nearly 8,000,000 persons who cannot read and write." That was more than half of
the whole population at that time. But this is not
the worst. A population unable to read or write
may nevertheless, to a certain extent, be educated
through religious teaching and influence; but these
unhappy creatures were left, helpless and hopeless,
to sink deeper and deeper beneath the weight of
their degradation, without being brought into contact with any power that could refine or elevate
them; and if their condition has somewhat improved in the last quarter of a century, this is no
more to be attributed to Protestantism than the
Catholic Emancipation Act or the Atlantic cable.

COMPARATIVE INFLUENCE OF CATHO-LICISM AND PROTESTANTISM ON NA-TIONAL PROSPERITY.

III. MORALITY.

THE keen relish which we all have for other people's sins is proverbial. As those who think with us are right, so are they virtuous who have only our own vices. Prodigality, which, to the miser's thinking, is the worst of sins, is, in the eyes of the spendthrift, merely an evidence of a generous nature. Men who wish to be thought gentlemen have a weakness for what are called gentlemanly vices; but from the coarser though less depraved wickedness of the vulgar they turn with loathing. This bias of our common nature is not confined in its action to individuals ; it affects classes, nations, races. The rich are shocked by the vices of the poor, and the poor, in turn, no less by those of the rich ; masters hate the sins of servants, and are repaid in their own coin.

When the free-born Briton sings, " England, with all thy faults, I love thee still," he means that faults, if only they be English, are after all not so bad. Wrapt up in the precious bundle of our self-love are all our pet sins and weaknesses. The universal hatred which existed between the nations of antiquity must be attributed in great part to the fact that their vices were unlike, and therefore repellant. The national contempt for foreigners is, in Christian times, strong in proportion to the barbarism of the people by whom it is felt; but in Greece and Rome such civilization as was then possible seemed to have no power over this prejudice. Not to be a Greek was to have been created for vile uses, and not to be a Roman was to be nobody. The French, as seen by the English, are giddy and lack dignity; the English appear to French eyes sulky and wanting in good nature; the Turk thinks both struck with madness, because they walk about and stretch their legs when they might sit still; and though he is at their mercy, yet he cannot persuade himself that they are anything but Christian dogs. The negro is quite sure the first man must have been black, and in this he is in accord with Mr. Darwin. The North American Indian will vanish from the earth through the golden portals of the western world still believing that he is the superior of the " pale face." The power of national prejudice is almost incredible. " Our country, right or wrong " is, we believe, an American phrase; but it expresses a sentiment which is almost universally held to be right and proper. In international disputes men nearly always take sides with their own country, without stopping to inquire into the merits of the quarrel, which, indeed, the strong feeling that at once masters them would pre-

vent them from being able to do. They act instinc-
tively like children who always think that in difficulties with neighbors their own parents are in the
right. We Americans are certainly not paragons
of virtue, and in this centennial year it is probably
wise to discuss almost anything rather than our
morals; yet we cannot but think that M. Louis
Veuillot was somewhat under the influence of national prejudice when he wrote that, if we were
sunk in the bottom of the ocean, civilization would
have lost nothing. Our form of government, it is
true, does not lead us to look for salvation, either
in church or state, from a king by divine right ;
still, he might just as well have let us alone, especially as he is at no loss for quarrels at home. Nor
can we think that the Germans who have raised
such a storm of indignation over the crime in Bre-
merhaven, committed, as it is supposed, by an
American, would have held the whole German people and their civilization responsible for the offence
had they known its author to be native there and
to the manner born.

As no passion takes hold of the human heart
with such sovereign power as that of religion, it follows that no bias of judgment is more fatal to truth
than religious prejudice; and now let us gently descend again to M. Emile de Laveleye and his pamphlet :

"It is agreed on all sides," he says,* " that the
power of nations depends on their morality. Everywhere is found the maxim, which is almost become

* P. 25.

13

an axiom of political science, that where morals are corrupted the state is lost. Now, it appears to be an established fact that the moral level is higher among Protestant than among Catholic populations. Religious writers confess this themselves, and explain it by the fact that the former remain more faithful to their religion than the latter, which explanation I believe to be the true one."

Here is fairness surely. The soft impeachment could not have been made in a more moderate or subdued tone. Catholics are notoriously more immoral than Protestants; but the subject is a painful one, and M. de Laveleye does not wish to emphasize the unpleasant truth by giving proof—which, indeed, would be superfluous, since Catholics themselves, we are assured, admit the fact and are concerned only about its explanation; and, strange to say, they have found the key to the mystery in the greater fidelity of Protestants to their religion: so M. de Laveleye and the Catholics shake hands and the dispute is at an end.

The position of Protestants with regard to this question is peculiar. The very life of their religion is intimately associated with a fixed belief in the preternatural wickedness of popes, priests, nuns, and Catholics generally. The sole justification of Protestantism was found in the abominable corruptions of Rome, and its only defence is that it is a purer worship, capable of creating a higher morality. The history of the Reformation, as written by Protestants, traces its origin to an awful and heaven-inspired indignation at the sight of papal iniquity, which resulted in a divine Protest against sin. It is this feeling, indeed, which is the living human magnetism in the words of Luther, Calvin, Zwingli, and Knox. They all felt that in so far as they protested against open and patent evil they were right, and therefore strong. Leo X., with God's eternal truth, but encircled by all the Graces and Muses, was at a disadvantage with those strong and plain-spoken men. In fact, the eternal ally of human error is human truth. It is because men who are right do wrong that men who are wrong seem right ; and if men in general were fit to be priests of God, there would be on earth no power to oppose the Catholic Church. St. Paul had protested, St. John Chrysostom had protested, St. Peter Damian had protested, St. Bernard had protested, St. Catherine of Sienna had protested, and yet there was no Protestantism. To protest was well and is well, but to seek to found a religion upon a protest is madness ; and this is Protestantism.⁣·

With Protestants purity of dogma is out of the question ; and nothing, therefore, remains to them but purity of morals. To this they must cling like drowning men to straws. Protestantism, if considered from a doctrinal point of view, is nihilism. Gather up the hundred sects which, taken collectively, are called Protestantism, and we will find every positive religious dogma excluded ; not even the personal existence of God remains. Mr. Matthew Arnold is a true Bible-Protestant, who has a little sect of his own, and all that he holds is that there is "a Power in us, not ourselves, which makes for righteousness"; and this he has discovered to be the sum and substance of all Scripture teaching. Doctrinal Protestantism is like the wrong side of a piece of tapestry with its fag-ends hanging in patches, twisted and jumbled; and yet they are the very substance out of which has been wrought a work of divine beauty. The dogmatic weakness of Protestantism throws its whole energy upon the moral side of religion. Its utter falseness, when we accept the fact that Christ has established a divine system of faith, is so manifest that no impartial thinker would hesitate to give his full assent to the sentiment of Rousseau: "Show me that in religious matters I must accept authority, and I shall become a Catholic at once." Supposing the Christian religion to be what it is commonly held to be by both Catholics and Protestants, it necessarily follows that the Catholic Church is the only logical as it is the only historical Christianity. This, we believe, is the almost universally-received opinion of non-Christian writers in our own day, in which, for the first time since the Reformation, a considerable number of learned men who are neither Catholic nor Protestant have been able to view this subject dispassionately. We do not mean to say that these writers prefer the church to the sects; on the contrary, they are partial to these because in their workings they perceive, as they think, the breaking-up and dissolution of the whole Christian system. Protestantism is valuable in their eyes as a stage in what Herbert Spencer calls "the universal religious thaw" which is going on around us.

If there has been no divine revelation, then whatever tends to weaken the claim of the church to be the depository of such revelation is good, especially as her claim is the only one which rests upon a valid historical basis. And it is because a very large number of men more than half suspect there never has been a revelation that Protestantism meets with so much favor from the unbelieving and pagan world, as serving the purpose of an easy stepping-stone from the strong and pronounced supernaturalism of the church to the nature-worship of Darwin and Spencer or the German *Culturists.*

Macaulay was struck and puzzled by what his keen eye could not fail to perceive to be so universal a phenomenon as to have the force of a law of history.

" It is surely remarkable," says this brilliant writer, "that neither the moral revolution of the eighteenth century nor the moral counter-revolution of the nineteenth should have in any perceptible degree added to the domain of Protestantism. During the former period whatever was lost to Catholicism was lost also to Christianity; during the latter whatever was regained by Christianity in Catholic countries was regained also by Catholicism. We should actually have expected that many minds, on the way from superstition to infidelity, or on the way back from infidelity to superstition, would have stopped at an intermediate point. Between the doctrines taught in the schools of the Jesuits, and those which were maintained at the little supper-parties of the Baron Holbach, there is

a vast interval in which the human mind, it should
seem, might find for itself some resting-place more
satisfactory than either of the two extremes; and
at the time of the Reformation millions found such
a resting-place.   Whole nations then renounced
popery without ceasing to believe in a First Cause,
in a future life, or in the divine authority of Christianity.   In the last century, on the contrary, when
a Catholic renounced his belief in the Real Presence, it was a thousand to one that he renounced
his belief in the Gospel too; and when the reaction
took place, with belief in the Gospel came back
belief in the Real Presence.   We by no means ven-
ture to deduce from these phenomena any general
law; but we think it a most remarkable fact that
no Christian nation which did not adopt the principles of the Reformation before the end of the sixteenth century should ever have adopted them.
Catholic communities have since that time become
infidel and become Catholic again, but none has become Protestant."

There could not be a more satisfactory proof of
the transitional and accidental nature of Protestantism.   Like all human revolutions, it grew out of
antecedent circumstances; and these were primarily political and social and only incidentally religious.   The faith in the divine authority of the
Christian religion was at that time absolute, and not
at all affected by the tendency to scepticism ob-
servable among a few of the Humanists.   The political power of the pope, however, together with his
peculiar temporal relations to the German Empire,

had gradually created throughout Germany a very strong national prejudice against his authority, which, upon the slightest provocation, was ready to break out into downright hatred of the Papacy. The worldly lives and ways of some of the popes had been as fuel for the conflagration which was to burst forth. Men, unconsciously it may be, grew accustomed to look upon the Christian religion and the Papacy as distinct and separable; and the temper of the public mind, while remaining reverential toward Christ and his religion, was embittered against his vicar. When, from amidst the social abuses and political antagonisms of Germany, Luther, in the name of Christ, denounced the pope, his voice struck precisely the note for which the public ear was listening, and, as Macaulay says, whole nations renounced allegiance to the pope without giving up faith in God and his Christ. This was done in the excitement of revolutionary enthusiasm, when passion and madness made deliberation impossible, and when a thoughtful and analytical study of the constitution of the church was out of the question. The Reformers imagined that they could abolish the pope and yet save Christianity, just as in France, two centuries and a half later, it was thought possible to abolish God and yet save the principle of authority, without which society cannot exist. And, indeed, it is as reasonable to suppose that this world, with its universal evidence of design and adaptation of means to ends, could have come into existence without the action of a supreme and intelligent Being, as to think that the system of religious truths taught by Christ can have either unity or authority amongst men without a living centre and visible representative of both. Protestants, in rejecting the primacy of the pope, were forced to accept as fundamental to their faith a principle of so purgative and drastic a nature that, in the general process of sloughing of religious thought which it brings on, it is itself finally carried away into the vacuum of nihilism.

This became evident as soon as the attempt was made to agree upon articles of belief. New heresies sprang up day after day, and complete chaos would have ensued from the beginning had not the different states taken hold of one or other of the sects and " established " it, thus, by the aid of the temporal power, giving to it a kind of consistency, but at the same time depriving it of vitality. Thus what Macaulay regarded as so remarkable—that no Christian nation which did not adopt the principles of the Reformation before the end of the sixteenth century should ever have adopted them—and he might as well have made the proposition universal, since there was no reason why he should limit it to Christian nations, as it is well known that in nothing has Protestantism given more striking proof of its impotence than in its utter failure to convert the heathen—this, we say, far from surprising us, seems so natural that we cannot understand how an observant mind should think it strange.

Protestantism was, in the main, the product of the peculiar political and social condition of Europe during the last period of the middle ages, and to

expect Catholic nations, or indeed individual Catholics of any intellectual or moral character, to become
Protestant in our day argues a total want of power
to grasp this subject. As well might one hope to
see the pterodactyls and ichthyosauri of a past
geologic era swimming in our rivers. Catholics
there are, indeed, now, as in the eighteenth century,
who become sceptics, who abandon all belief in
Christianity, but none who become Protestants ;
for we cannot consider such persons as Achilli or
Edith O'Gorman as instances of conversion of any
kind. A very limited acquaintance with Catholics
and Catholic thought will suffice to convince any
reflecting mind that for us there is no alternative
but to accept the doctrine of the church or to
renounce faith in Christ. Was there ever fairer
field for heresy to flourish in than that which
opened up before Old Catholicism at its birth?
But it was still-born. To this day its sponsors
have not dared define its relation to the pope; and
until this is done it remains without character. At
any rate, it does not claim to be Protestant.

Turning to view the present condition of Protestantism, we are struck by the contrast. The very
word " Protestant " is without meaning when
applied to two-thirds of the non-Catholics of Germany, England, and the United States. Their
mental state is one of disbelief in, or indifference
to, all forms of positive religion ; and if occasionally
they are roused to some feeling against the church,
it is through an association of ideas, traditional
with them, which places her in antagonism with

their political theories and national prejudices.
Among earnest and reflecting Protestants who are
united with one or other of the sects, there are two
opposite currents of religious thought of a strongly-
marked and well-defined character. Those who
are borne on the one are being carried farther and
farther away from the historic teachings of Christ,
and are busied in trying to dress out in Biblical
phraseology some of the various cosmic or pantheistic philosophies of the day. They very generally
assume that religion has nothing to do with theology, nor, consequently, with doctrines and dogmas.
As its home is the heart, its realm is the world of
sentiment ; and so it matters not what we believe,
provided only we feel good. Opposed to this current, which is bearing with it all the distinctive
landmarks of the Christian religion, is another which
is carrying men back to the church. In fact, all
great minds among Protestants who have been
strongly impressed by the objective character of
Christian truth have been drawn towards the Catholic Church. Who can have failed to perceive, for
instance—to mention only the three greatest who
have occupied themselves with religious questions—
how Leibnitz, Bacon, and Bishop Butler, in their
intellectual apprehension of the Christian system,
were, in spite of themselves, attracted to the
church ? Or who that is acquainted with the English Catholic literature of our own day is ignorant
of the divine illumination which many of the most
intellectual and reverent natures from the sects of
Protestantism have found in the teachings of the

one Catholic Church? In this way, by a process of supernatural or natural selection, the fragments of Protestantism are being assimilated to the church or are disappearing in the sea of unbelief in which even now they are seen only as barren islands in the wild waste of waters.

These considerations must be borne in mind by whoever would take a comprehensive view of the question which we propose now to discuss. In the first place, by reflecting upon them we shall find no difficulty in accounting for the marked difference in tone and character between Catholic and Protestant controversy, by which no attentive observer can have failed to be struck. Taking for granted the existence of God and the divinity of Christ, as admitted by the earlier Protestant sects, the logical position of the church is unassailable, which, as we have already stated, is generally conceded by impartial non-Christian thinkers.

As a consequence, Catholic controversialists, assured of the absolute coherence of their whole system with the fundamental dogma of the divine mission of Christ, have been chiefly concerned with showing the logical viciousness of the essential principles of Protestantism. They have, indeed, not omitted to remark upon the moral unfitness of such men as Henry VIII., Luther, Knox, and Zwingli to be the divinely-chosen agents of a reformation in the religion of Christ; but such observations have been incidental to the main course of the argument, and this is alike true of our more

learned discussions and of our popular controversies.

Catholic writers—allowing for individual exceptions—have not felt that, to show the falsity of
Protestantism, it was necessary to denounce Protestants or to stamp upon them any mark of infamy.
They have treated them as men who were wrong,
not as men who were wicked. Protestant controversy, on the other hand, presents for our consideration characteristics of a very different nature.
In the consciousness of their inability to settle upon
a fixed creed, which has been shown by history,
and from the necessarily feeble manner in which
articles of faith could be held by them, on account
of the disagreement and conflict of opinion among
themselves, Protestant writers were forced to treat
their religion, not as a doctrine, but as a tendency ;
and for this reason, together with the natural hatred
which men entertain for a church or government
against which they have rebelled, they were led to
draw contrasts between the results of Protestantism
and Catholicity ; so that it became customary to
attribute all the enlightenment, morality, progress,
and liberty of the world to Protestantism, and to
represent Catholics as cruel, ignorant, corrupt, and
in every way depraved. Luther, as we should
naturally expect, led the way in this style of controversy.

" The Papists," he said, " are for the most part
mere gross blockheads. . . . The pope and his
crew are mere worshippers of idols and servants of
the devil. . . . Pope, cardinals, bishops, not a soul

of them has read the Bible ; 'tis a book unknown to them. They are a pack of guzzling, stuffing wretches, rich, wallowing in wealth and laziness. . . . Seeing the pope is Antichrist, I believe him to be a devil incarnate. . . . The pope is the last blaze in the lamp which will go out and ere long be extinguished—the last instrument of the devil, that thunders and lightens with sword and bull ; . . . but the Spirit of God's mouth has seized upon that shameless strumpet. . . . Antichrist is the Pope and the Turk together. . . . The pope is not God's image, but his ape. . . . Popedom is founded on mere lies and fables. . . . A friar is evil every way ; the preaching friars are proud buzzards ; all who serve the pope are damned ; the Papists are devoid of shame and Christianity." *

This is the style of Protestant controversy which, except in form, still lingers in this nineteenth century. Protestant devotion, it may be said without sarcasm or exaggeration, consists essentially in a holy horror of popery. Were it possible to eliminate the Catholic Church from human society, Protestantism would at once fatally assume an attitude towards the world wholly different from that in which it now stands. At present, when attacked by evolutionistic pantheism—which means all the sophistries of the day—it takes refuge behind the historic fortress of Christianity, the Catholic Church, and, when encountered by the church, it makes an alliance with cosmism or anything else. Were the Catholic Church not in existence, it would be forced

* *The Table-Talk of Martin Luther,* pp. 200, 206, 213, *et passim.*

at once to build a fortress of its own ; for the Bible
is only a breastwork, which must be in charge of a
commander in-chief if we hope to hold it for the
sovereign Lord.   From the beginning, then, Protestants branded Catholics with a mark of infamy ;
they were idolaters, worse than pagans, for the
most part gross blockheads, who fall an easy prey
to the designing arts of priests and monks, who are
only knaves and rogues, whose chief aim is to carry
out the fiendish purposes of the pope, the arch-
enemy, Antichrist, the devil in the flesh ; and thus
the church becomes the Woman of Babylon, flam-
ing in scarlet, and alluring the nations to debauch.

No evidence, therefore, is needed to show that
Catholics are immoral, depraved, thoroughly corrupt.   To doubt it would be to question the truth
of Protestantism and to believe that something
good might come out of Nazareth.   In good sooth,
do not the Catholics, as M. de Laveleye says, admit
the fact themselves?

We often hear persons express surprise that intelligent and honest Protestants should still, after
such sad experience, be so eager to believe the
" awful disclosures " of " escaped nuns," and to
patronize that kind of lecture—of which, thank
God ! Protestants have the monopoly—delivered to
men or women only, in which the abominations of
the confessional are revealed and the general preternatural wickedness of priests, monks, and nuns
is made fully manifest.   This, to us, we must say,
has never seemed strange.   The doctrine of total
depravity is an article of Protestant faith, and, when

applied to Catholics, to none other have Protestants ever clung with such unwavering firmness and
perfect unanimity. When disagreeing about everything else, they have never failed to find a point of
union in this. Even after having lived and dealt
with Catholics who are kind-hearted, pure, and
fair-minded, in the true Protestant there still lurks
a vague kind of suspicion that there must be some
mysterious and secret diabolism in them which
eludes his observation ; that after all they may be
only " as mild-mannered men as ever scuttled ship
or cut a throat " ; and after his reason has been
fully convinced that the Catholic Church is the
only historical Christianity, he is still able to remain a strong Protestant by falling back upon the
undoubted total depravity of Papists. Dr. Newman, in his *Apologia,* the most careful and instructive self-analysis which has been written in this
century, or probably in any other, declares that
after he had become thoroughly persuaded of the
truth of the Catholic Church his former belief that
the pope was Antichrist still remained like a stain
upon his imagination ; and yet he had never been
an ultra-Protestant. Many a Protestant has ceased
to believe in Christ, without giving up his faith in
the pope as Antichrist.

It is not surprising, in view of all this, that Protestants should have habitually held the church responsible for the evil deeds of Catholics.

When quite recently the excited Germans charged
the dynamite plot of Thomassen upon our American civilization, we replied, with perfect justice, that

such crimes are anomalies, the guilt of which ought
not to be laid upon any nation, and all reasonable
men admitted the evident good sense of our answer;
but Protestants the world over have been unanimous
in seeking to hold up the church to the execration
of mankind as responsible for the St. Bartholomew
massacre. Is Protestantism answerable for Cromwell's massacres at Drogheda and Wexford? Religious fanaticism, no doubt, had much to do in
urging him to butcher idolaters and slaves of Satan;
but we should blush for shame were we capable of
thinking for a moment that such inhumanities are
either produced or approved by the real spirit of
the Protestant religion.

We know of nothing in the Catholic Church
which in any way corresponds to Protestant anti-
popery literature; indeed, we doubt whether in the
whole history of literature anything so disgraceful
and disreputable as this can be found, unless, possibly, it be that which is professedly obscene, but
which has nowhere ever had a recognized existence;
and we question whether even this is as discredita-
ble to human nature as the " awful disclosures " and
" lectures to men or women only " of Protestants.

In discussing the comparative morality of Catholic and Protestant nations it would be more satisfactory, even though it should not be more conclu-
sive, to consider their respective virtues rather than
their vices. There would seem to be neither good
sense nor logic in taking the individuals and classes
that are least brought under religious influences of
any kind, in order to use their depravity as an

argument for or against the church or Protestantism.
In the apostolic body one out of twelve was a thief
and traitor, yet neither Catholics nor Protestants are
in the habit of concluding from this that they must
all have been rogues and hypocrites. The amount
of crime, one would think, is but a poor test of the
amount of virtue. As the greatest sinners have
made the greatest saints, so in the church depravity
may co-exist with the most heroic virtue, though,
of course, not in the same individual. Our divine
Saviour plainly declares that in his church the good
shall be mingled with the bad ; that the cockle shall
grow with the wheat till the harvest time ; that
some shall call him Lord and Master, and yet do
not the will of his Father ; that even, with regard to
those who sit in the chair of Moses—and, let us add,
of Peter—though their authority must ever be acknowledged, yet are not their lives always to be
imitated, nor approved of even. It is manifestly
contrary to the teaching of Christ to make the note
of sanctity in his church consist in the individual
holiness of each and every member. He is no
Puritan, though he is the all-holy God. A puristic
religion is essentially narrow, self-conscious, and
unsympathetic ; it draws a line here on earth between the elect and the reprobate ; its disciples eat
not with sinners, nor enter into their abodes, nor
hold out to them the pleading hands of large-heart-
ed charity. Such a faith does not grow upon
men ; it does not win and convert them to God.

If, instead of comparing the crimes, we should
consider the respective virtues, of Catholic and Pro-

14

testant nations, we should at once be struck by the difference in their standards of morality. The most practical way of determining the real standard of morality of any religion is to study the character of its saints. There we find religious ideals made tangible and fully discernible. Here at once we perceive that there is an essential difference between the Catholic and the Protestant standard of morality. The lives of our saints, even when understood by Protestants, generally repel them. They are, in their eyes, useless lives, idle lives, superstitious lives, unnatural and inhuman. We take the words of Christ, " If thou wouldst be perfect, go sell what thou hast, give it to the poor, and come and follow me," in their full and complete literal meaning. The highest life is to leave father and mother, to have nor wife nor children, nor temporal goods except what barely suffices, and to cleave to Christ only with all one's soul in poverty, chastity, and obedience. Now, this life of prayer in poverty, chastity, and obedience is an offence to Protestants. They do not believe in perfect chastity, they hold religious obedience to be a slavery, and poverty, in their eyes, is ridiculous. Inasmuch as the monks tilled the earth, transcribed books, and taught school, they receive a partial recognition from the Protestant world ; but inasmuch as they were bound by religious vows they excite disgust. We should say, then, that the distinctive trait of Catholic morality is ascetic, while the Protestant is utilitarian. The one primarily regards the world that is to be, the other that which already is. The one inclines us to look upon this as a worthless world to lose or win; the other is shrewd and calculating—this is the best we have any practical experience of; it is the part of wisdom to make the most of it. The one seems to be more certain of the future life, the other of the present. It is needless to prolong the contrast, and we shall simply confess that we have always been inclined to the opinion of those who hold that Protestantism, in its aims and direct tendencies, is more favorable to what is called material progress than Catholicism. In fact, one cannot realize the personal survival of the soul through eternity, and at the same time be supremely interested in stocks or the price of cotton.

Not that the church discourages efforts which have as their object the material interests of mankind; but, in her view, our duties to God are of the first importance, and to these all others are subordinate. What doth it profit? she is always asking, whereas Protestantism is busy trying to show us how very profitable and pleasant the Reformation has made this world—and virtuous, too, since honesty is the best policy and enlightened self-interest the standard of morals. It is the old story—God and the world, the supernatural and the natural, progress from above and progress from below.

But we feel that it is time we should give our readers proof that we have no desire to avoid direct issue with M. de Laveleye. We flatly deny, then, his assertion that the Catholic nations are more immoral than the Protestant; and when he further affirms that Catholic writers themselves

—for his words can have no other meaning—admit
this, he lies under a mistake for which there can be
no possible excuse.   In the statement of facts,
however, which we propose now to give, we make
no use whatever of the testimony of Catholics, but
rely exclusively upon the authority of Protestants
and of statistics ; and that our readers may have the
benefit of observations extending over considerable
time as well as space, we will not confine ourselves
to the most recent writers or statistics on the subject under discussion.   Laing, a Scotch Presbyterian
and a most conscientious and observant traveller, who
wrote some thirty-five years ago, says of the French :
" They are, I believe, a more honest people than
the British. . . . It is a fine distinction of the
French national character and social economy that
practical morality is more generally taught through
manners among and by the people themselves than
in any country in Europe."*   Alison, the historian,
writing about the same time, but referring to the
early part of this century, says that the proportion
of crime to the inhabitants was *twelve times* greater
in Prussia than in France.†   To this may be added
the testimony of John Stuart Mill, in his *Autobiography*, published since his death, who passed a
considerable portion of his life in France.   Referring
to his sojourn there when quite a young man, he
says :
   " Having so little experience of English life, and
the few people I knew being mostly such as had

* *Notes of a Traveller*, pp. 79, 80.
† *History of Europe*, vol. iii. chap. xxvii. 10, 11.

public objects of a large and personally disinterested kind at heart, I was ignorant óf the low moral
tone of what in England is called society : the habit
of, not indeed professing, but taking for granted in
every mode of implication that conduct is of course
always directed towards low and petty objects ; the
absence of high feelings, which manifests itself by
sneering depreciation of all demonstrations of them,
and by general abstinence (except among a few of
the stricter religionists) from professing any high
principles of action at all, except in those preor-
dained cases in which such profession is put on as
part of the costume and formalities of the occasion.
I could not then know or estimate the difference
between this manner of existence and that of a people like the French, whose faults, if equally real, are
at all events different ; among whom sentiments
which, by comparison at least, may be called elevat-
ed are the current coin of human intercourse, both
in books and in private life, and, though often eva-
porating in profession, are yet kept alive in the nation at large by constant exercise and stimulated
by sympathy, so as to form a living and active part
of the existence of a great number of persons, and
to be recognized and understood by all.   Neither
could I then appreciate the general culture of the
understanding, which results from the habitual exercise of the feelings, and is thus carried down into
the most uneducated classes of several countries on
the Continent, in a degree not equalled in England
among the so-called educated, except where an
unusual tenderness of conscience leads to a habitual

exercise of the intellect on questions of right and wrong." *

This is strong testimony when we consider that it comes from an Englishman. In speaking of the elder Austin the same writer says: " He had a strong distaste for the general meanness of English life, the absence of enlarged thoughts and unselfish desires, the low objects on which the faculties of all classes of the English are intent."†   Mill's opinion of the French is confirmed by Lecky, who writes : " No other nation has so habitual and vivid a · sympathy for great struggles for freedom beyond its border.   No other literature exhibits so expansive and œcumenical a genius, or expounds so skilfully or appreciates so generously foreign ideas.   In no other land would a disinterested war for the support of a suffering nationality find so large an amount of support." ‡

Much has been said and written of the licentiousness of the French, which may, in part at least, be due to the fact that they, more than any other people, have known how to make vice attractive by taking from it something of the repulsive coarseness which naturally belongs to it, but must also be ascribed to the feeling that they are Catholic, and therefore sensual.   But let us examine the facts on this subject. We again bring Laing forward as a witness.

" Of all the virtues," he says, " that which the domestic family education of both the sexes most

* *Autobiography*, pp. 58, 59.   † *Ibid.* p. 177.
‡ *History of European Morals*, p. 160.

obviously influences—that which marks more clearly than any other the moral condition of a society, the home state of moral and religious principles, the efficiency of those principles in it, and the amount of that moral restraint upon passions and impulses which it is the object of education and knowledge to attain—is undoubtedly female chastity. Will any traveller, will any Prussian, say that this index-virtue of the moral condition of a people is not lower in Prussia than in almost any other part of Europe?" *

Acts which in other countries would affect the respectability and happiness of a whole family for generations are in Prussia looked upon as mere youthful indiscretions. What Laing affirms of Prussia, Madame de Staël, herself a Protestant, applies indiscriminately to the Protestant States of Germany.

" Love," she writes, " is a religion in Germany, but a poetic religion which tolerates too easily all that sensibility can excuse. It cannot be denied that the facility of divorce in the Protestant States is prejudicial to the sacredness of marriage. They change husbands with as much composure as if they were arranging the incidents of a drama; the good-nature common to both men and women accounts for the absence of bitterness in these ruptures; and as the Germans have more imagination than passion, the most extravagant events take place with astonishing tranquillity. In this way, nevertheless, manners and character lose all con-

* *Notes of a Traveller.* p. 172.

sistency; the spirit of paradox shakes the most sacred institutions, and all fixed rules of conduct are destroyed." *

But let us take the statistics of illegitimacy, which is a method of discussing the question made popular among Protestants by the Rev. Hobart Seymour in his *Evenings with the Romanists.*

The number of illegitimate births in France for every hundred was, in 1858, 7.8; in the same year in Protestant Saxony it was 16; in Protestant Prussia, 9.3; in Würtemberg (Prot.), 16.1; in Iceland (Prot.; 1838-47), 14; in Denmark (1855), 11.5; Scotland (1871), 10.1; Hanover (1855), 9.9; Sweden (1855), 9.5; Norway (1855), 9.3.

Catholic France, then, judged by this test, stands higher than any Protestant country of which we have statistical reports, except England and Wales, where the percentage was, in 1859, 6.5; but England and Wales are below other Catholic countries, and notably far below Ireland.   The rate of illegitimacy in the kingdom of Sardinia (1828-37) was 2.1; in Ireland (1865-66), 3.8; in Spain (1859), 5.6; in Tuscany, 6; in Catholic Prussia, 6.1.

In Scotland there are, in proportion to population, more than three times as many illegitimate births as in Ireland; and in England and Wales there are more than twice as many, and in Protestant Prussia the percentage is a third greater than in Catholic Prussia.†

---

* *L'Allemagne*, t. 1, ch. 3.
† For the full discussion of the statistics of this subject see THE CATHOLIC WORLD, vol. ix. pp. 52 and 845.

If chastity, to use Laing's expression, is the in-dex-virtue, the question as to the comparative mo-rality of Protestant and Catholic nations may be considered at an end. Lecky's words on the Irish people have often been quoted, to his own regret, we believe.

"Had the Irish peasants been less chaste," he says, "they would have been more prosperous. Had that fearful famine which in the present cen-tury desolated the land fallen upon a people who thought more of accumulating subsistence than of avoiding sin, multitudes might now be living who perished by literal starvation on the dreary hills of Limerick or Skibbereen." *

There is not in all Europe a more thoroughly Protestant country than Sweden. For three hun-dred years its people have been wholly withdrawn from Catholic influences. During all this time Pro-testantism, upheld by the state, undisturbed by dis-sent, with the education of the people in the hands of the clergy, and a population almost entirely ru-ral, has had the fairest possible opportunity to show what it is capable of doing to elevate the moral character of a nation. What is the result? In 1838 Laing visited Sweden and made a careful study of the moral and social condition of the peo-ple ; and he declares that they are at the very bot-tom of the scale of European morality. In 1836 one person out of every 112—women, infants, sick, all included—had been accused of crime, and one out of every 134 convicted and punished. In 1838

* *European Morals,* p. 153.

15

there were born in Stockholm 2,714 children, of whom 1,577 were legitimate and 1,137 illegitimate, leaving a balance of only 440 chaste mothers out of 2,714.

Drunkenness, too, was more common there than in any other country of Europe or of the world. Nearly 40,000,000 gallons of liquor were consumed in 1850 by a population of only 3,000,000, which gives thirteen gallons of intoxicating drink to every man, woman, and child in the kingdom.

If these things could be-said of any Catholic nation, the whole Protestant world would stand aghast, nor need other proof of the absolutely diabolical nature of popery. Compare this agricultural and pastoral population with the Catholic Swiss mountaineers—who to this day claim to have descended from a Swedish stock, and whose climate is not greatly different from that of Sweden— and we find that the Catholic Swiss are as moral and sober as the Protestant Swedes are corrupt and besotted. Or compare them with the Tyrolese, than whom there is no more Catholic and liberty-loving people on earth.

"Honesty may be regarded as a leading feature in the character of the Tyrolese," says Alison. . . . "In no part of the world are the domestic or conjugal duties more strictly or faithfully observed, and in none do the parish priests exercise a stricter or more conscientious control over their flocks. . . . Perhaps the most remarkable feature in the character of the Tyrolese is their uniform piety—a feeling which is nowhere so universally diffused as among their sequestered valleys. . . . On Sunday the *whole people* flock to church in their neatest and gayest attire; and so great is the number who thus frequent these places of worship that it is not unfrequent to see the peasants kneeling on the turf in the church-yard where Mass is performed, from being unable to find a place within its walls. Regularly in the evening prayers are read in every family; and the traveller who passes through the villages at the hour of twilight often sees through their latticed windows the young and the old kneeling together round their humble fire, or is warned of his approach to human habitation by hearing their evening hymns stealing through the silence and solitude of the forest. . . . In one great virtue the peasants in this country(in common, it must be owned, with most Catholic states) are particularly worthy of imitation. The virtue of *charity*, which is too much overlooked in many Protestant kingdoms, is there practised to the greatest degree and by all classes of people." *

With true Protestant condescension Alison adds : " Debased as their religion is by the absurdities and errors of the Catholic form of worship, and mixed up as it is with innumerable legends and visionary tales, it yet preserves enough of the pure spirit of its divine origin to influence in a great measure the conduct of their private lives."

Among rural populations more than elsewhere the divine power of the Christian religion is made manifest. To the poor, the frugal, and the single-hearted those heavenly truths which have changed

* Alison's *Miscellaneous Essays,* p. 119.

the world, but which were first listened to and received by fishermen and shepherds, appeal with a force and directness which the mere worldling and comfort-lover cannot even realize. In the presence of nature so silent and awful, yet so vocal, everything inclines the heart of man to hearken to the voice of God. Mountains and rivers; long-withdrawing vales and deep-sounding cataracts; winter's snows, and spring, over whose heaving bosom the unseen hand weaves the tapestry that mortal fingers never made; summer's warm breath, and autumn, when the strong year first feels the chill of death, and "tears from the depth of some divine despair rise in the heart and gather to the eyes"—all speak of the higher world which they foreshadow and symbolize. But in the hurry and noise of the city, with its extremes of wealth and poverty, of indulgence and want, of pride and degradation, the pleading voice of religion is not heard at all, or is heard only as a call from the shore is heard by men who are madly hurrying down some rapid stream. It is evident, therefore, that the easiest and surest way of getting at the relative moral influence of the Catholic and Protestant religions is to study their action upon rural populations. We have already established on the best authority the incalculable moral elevation of the Catholic rural populations of Switzerland and the Tyrol over the Protestants of the same class in Sweden. Let us now turn to Great Britain.

Kay, after having given a table of criminal statistics for England and Wales for the years 1841 and

1847, makes the following remarks upon the facts there presented :

" This table well deserves study. It shows that the proportional amount of crime to population calculated in two years, 1841 and 1847, was greater in both years in almost all the *agricultural* counties of England than it was in the *manufacturing* and mining districts. . . . With what terrible significance do these statistics plead the cause of the poor of our rural districts! Notwithstanding that a town-life necessarily presents so many more opportunities for, and temptations to, vice than a rural life; notwithstanding that the associations of the latter are naturally so much purer and so much more moral than those of the former; notwithstanding the wonderfully crowded state of the great manufacturing cities of Lancashire; notwithstanding the constant influx of Irish, sailors, vagrants, beggars, and starving natives of agricultural districts of England and Wales; and notwithstanding the miserable state of most of the primary schools of those districts and the great ignorance of the majority of the inhabitants, still, in the face of all these and other equally significant facts, the criminality of the *manufacturing* districts of Lancashire is LESS in proportion to the population than that of most of the rural districts of England and Wales !" *

In Scotland illegitimacy is more common in the country than in the towns and cities. In 1870 the rate of illegitimacy for the whole country was 9.4

* Kay's *Social Condition of the People*, vol ii. p. 392.

per cent., or 1 in every 10.6; whereas in the rural districts alone it was 10.5, or 1 in every 9.5. In 1871 it was for the whole country 10.1, or 1 in every 9.8, and in the rural districts 11.2, or 1 in every 8.9.* In England also the rate of illegitimacy is much larger in the rural districts than in the cities, whereas in Catholic France it is just the reverse. In the country districts of England we have the following rate :

Nottingham,	8.9
York, North Riding,	8.9
Salop,	9.8
Westmoreland,	9.7
Norfolk,	10.7
Cumberland,	11.4

In France :

Rural districts,	4 2
La Vendée,	2.2
Brittany—Côte d'Or,	1.2

Thus in the most Catholic rural districts of France there are only one or two illegitimate births in every hundred.

This is also true of Prussia, whose most strongly Catholic provinces are Westphalia and the Rhineland. In Westphalia there are only three and a half illegitimate births in every hundred, and in the Rhineland only three and a third; but in thoroughly Protestant Pomerania and Brandenburg there are ten and twelve illegitimate births in the hundred.† In Ireland, again, we find the same

* See *London Statistical Journal*, 1870, 1871.
† *Historische Politische Blätter*, 1867.

state of things. The rate of illegitimate births for all Ireland is 3.8 per cent. ; but the lowest proportion is in Connaught, nineteen-twentieths of whose people are Catholics, and the greatest is in Ulster, half of whose population is Protestant. " The sum of the whole matter," says the *Scotsman* (June, 1869), a leading organ of Presbyterian Scotland, " is that semi-Presbyterian and semi-Scotch Ulster is fully three times more immoral than wholly popish and wholly Irish Connaught—which corresponds with wonderful accuracy to the more general fact that Scotland as a whole is three times more immoral than Ireland as a whole." There is no reason why further proof should be given of what is a manifest truth : that rural populations—let us say, rather, the people—in proportion as they are Catholic, are also chaste ; and consequently that the Catholic Church, as every man who is competent to judge must know, is the mother of purity, which is the soul of Christian life, and without which we cannot draw near to the heart of the Saviour and supreme Lover of men. Protestants, however, will be at no loss for arguments. Should the worst come to the worst, illegitimacy, like the gallows, may be declared an evidence of civilization, and then it needs must follow, as the night the day, that it is more common in Protestant than in Catholic countries.

Let us now turn to the vice of intemperance. " I am sure," says Hill, " that I am within the truth when I state, as the result of minute and extensive inquiry, that, in four cases out of five,

when an offence is committed intoxicating drink
has been one of the causes." *

In an attempt, then, to form an estimate of the
relative morality of nations, we should not omit to
consider the vice of drunkenness, which is the
cause of half the crime and misery in the world.
Were it in our power to obtain accurate statistics
on this subject, as on that of illegitimacy, the superior sobriety of the Catholic nations would be
shown even more strikingly than their superior
chastity. The Spaniards, it is universally acknowledged, are the soberest people in Europe, as the
·Swedes are the most intemperate. Their respective geographical positions suggest at once what is
often assigned as a sufficient explanation of this
fact—the great difference of climate. It was long
supposed that the southern nations were more sensual than the northern, because it was thought a
warm climate must necessarily develop a greater
violence of passion. We know now, however, that
this is not the case. Though climate has an undoubted influence on morality, its action is yet so
modified or controlled among Christian and civilized nations that generalizations founded upon its
supposed effects are unreliable. The Swedes and
the Scotch are intemperate, the Spaniards and the
Italians are sober. The former are Protestant, the
latter Catholic ; it is therefore at once evident that
religion has nothing to do with this matter, which
can only be accounted for by the difference of

---

* *Crime : its Amount, Causes, and Remedies.* By Frederick Hill, Barrister-
at-law, late Inspector of Prisons. London, p. 65.

climate. These are the tactics of our opponents: those virtues in which the Catholic nations excel must be attributed to natural causes; but when some of them are found to lack the enterprise and industrial spirit of the English or the Americans, it would be altogether unreasonable to ascribe this to anything else than their religion.

Scotch statistics show a greater amount of intemperance in summer than in winter, which would seem to indicate that a high temperature does not tend to destroy the passion for intoxicating drink. But we do not propose to enter into a discussion of causes, which, however, we are perfectly willing to take up at the proper time. Our controversy with M. de Laveleye turns upon facts.

We have already cited the testimony of Laing to show that the Swedes, after they had been under the exclusive influence of Protestantism for three hundred years, were the most drunken people in Europe. Laing was in Venice on the occasion of a festival, when the whole population had turned out for pleasure, and he did not see a single case of intoxication; not a single instance, even among the boys, of rudeness; and yet all were singing, talking, and enjoying themselves. He gives the following account of a popular merry-making which he saw at Florence:

" It happened that the 9th of May was kept here as a great holiday by the lower class, as May-day with us, and they assembled in a kind of park about a mile from the city, where booths, tents, and carts, with wine and eatables for sale, were in crowds and clusters, as at our village wakes and race-courses. The multitude from town and country round could not be less than twenty thousand people, grouped in small parties, dancing, singing, talking, dining on the grass, and enjoying themselves. *I did not see a single instance of inebriety, ill-temper, or unruly, boisterous conduct;* yet the people were gay and joyous." *

Robert Dale Owen, writing from Naples, said: " I have not seen a man even partially intoxicated since I have been in the city, of 420,000 inhabitants, and they say one may live here for four years without seeing one."

Let us now turn to Protestant lands. St. Cuthbert's parish, Edinburgh, had in 1861 a population somewhat exceeding 90,000 souls. Of these, 1,953 were " drunk and incapable," 3,935 were " drunk and discharged"; making in all 5,888, or nearly 1 in 15.

In Salford jail (England), in 1870, the proportion of commitments for drunkenness was, as compared with commitments for all offences, 37 per cent.†

We have it upon the authority of the English government that in 1874 no fewer than 285,730 Britons were proceeded against for being drunk and disorderly, or drunk and not disorderly ; and, of course, to this must be added the probably greater number who escaped arrest. Mr. Granville, one of the secretaries of the Church of England Society in the diocese of Durham, estimates that there is an aggregate of 700,000 habitual drunkards in Eng-

* *Notes of a Traveller*, pp. 418-19.
† See *London Statistical Journal*, 1871.

land. " It is a melancholy but undeniable fact,"
says the *Alliance News*, " that, notwithstanding
vast agencies of improvement, intemperance, crime,
pauperism, insanity, and brutality are more ram-
pant than ever; and, if we except pauperism, these
evils have more than doubled in the last forty
years." We have not been able to get the statistics of drunkenness for Ireland, and can therefore
institute no comparison between England and that
country with regard to intemperance; * but we
have before us the criminal statistics of both countries for 1854, the population of England and Wales
in that year being about three times as great as
that of Ireland. The following table of convictions
will enable us to form an estimate of the comparative honesty of the two nations:

Robbery by persons armed, England and Wales, . . 210
Robbery by persons armed, Ireland, ... 2
Larceny from the person, England and Wales, . . . 1,570
Larceny from the person, Ireland, ... 389
Larceny by servants,† England and Wales, . . . 2,140
Larceny by servants, Ireland, ... 44
Larceny, simple, England and Wales, ... 12,562
Larceny, simple, Ireland, ... 3.329
Frauds and attempts to defraud, England and Wales, . 676
Frauds and attempts to defraud, Ireland, ... 62
Forgery, England and Wales, ... 149

* In 1871, 14,501,983 gallons of spirits were distilled in Scotland. What proportion of this was consumed at home we do not know. For the same year the number of gallons entered for home consumption in Ireland was 5,212,746. The population of Scotland is nearly three millions and a half, and that of Ireland about
five millions and a half.

† England and Wales, with not quite three times the population of Ireland, had
fifty times as many cases of dishonesty among servants, which clearly accounts for
those newspaper advertisements in which English housekeepers are careful to
state that "no Irish need apply."

Forgery, Ireland, ... 4
Uttering and having in possession counterfcit coin, England and Wales, ... 674
Uttering and having in possession counterfeit coin, Ireland, ... 4

On the other hand, the following crimes are proportionately more numerous in Ireland:

Convictions for manslaughter in 1854:
England and Wales, ... 96
Ireland, ... 50
Burglary, England and Wales, ... 384
"   Ireland, ... 240

We cannot think, however, that these returns are trustworthy, for the *Statistical Journal* of 1867 gives the following criminal tables for England in 1865:

Wilful murder cases tried, ... 60
Manslaughter, ... 316
Concealment of birth, ... 143
                                                    ———
Total, ... 519

And in Ireland from 1865 to 1871, a period of six years, only 21 persons were sentenced to death, of whom 13 were executed, Irish crime, in its worst phase, grows out of the injustice and wrongs inflicted upon the people by their Protestant rulers; and though no condemnation of agrarian outrages can be too severe, it must nevertheless be admitted that the landlords and their agents are more guilty than the victims whom their cruelties have driven to deeds of desperation.

It is greatly to be regretted that criminal statistics give us no information upon the religious

character of the persons accused or convicted of
offences against the law. Many have been baptized in infancy, and are called Catholics, who have
never been brought under the influence of the
church. In the absence of official statistics, Dr.
Descuret, who, in his capacity of legal physician in
Paris, had abundant opportunity to obtain data relative to this subject, made, about thirty years ago,
a careful study of the religious views and sentiments
of French criminals. The conclusion which he
reached was that, in every hundred persons accused
of crime, fifty are indifferentists in religion, forty
are infidels, and the remaining ten sincere believers.
In a hundred suicides he found only four persons
of known piety, three of whom were women subject to melancholia, and the other had been for
some time mentally deranged.*

* *La Médecine des Passions*, p. 116.

PRUSSIA AND THE CHURCH.

I.

THE first attempts to introduce the Christian religion into Prussia were unsuccessful. St. Adalbert in 997, and St. Bruno in 1009, suffered martyrdom whilst preaching the Gospel there, and the efforts of Poland to force the conquered Prussians to receive the faith only increased the bitterness of their anti-Christian prejudices. Early in the twelfth century Bishop Otto, of Bamberg, made many conversions in Pomerania; and finally, in the beginning of the thirteenth, the Cistercian monk Christian, with the approval and encouragement of Pope Innocent III., set to work to bring the Prussians into the church, and met with such success that in 1215 he was made bishop of the country. The greater part of the people, however, still remained heathens, and the progress of Christianity aroused in them such indignation that they determined to oppose its farther advance with the sword. To protect his flock Bishop Christian called to his aid the knights of the Teutonic Order; in furtherance of his designs, the Emperor Frederick II. turned the whole country over to them, and Pope Gregory IX. took measures

to increase their number, so that they might be
able to hold possession of this field, now first opened to the Gospel. Pope Innocent IV. also manifested special interest in the welfare of the church
in Prussia ; he urged priests and monks to devote
themselves to this mission, supported and encouraged the bishops in their trials and difficulties, and
exhorted the convents throughout Germany to
contribute books for the education. of the people.
But circumstances were not wanting which made
the position of the church in Prussia very unsatisfactory. The people had for the most part
been brought under her influence by the power
of arms, and consequently to a great extent remained strangers to her true spirit. The Teutonic
Order, moreover, gave ecclesiastical positions only
to German priests, so as to hold out inducements to
the people to learn German ; though, as a consequence, the priests were unable to communicate
with their flocks, except by the aid of interpre-
ters.

The grand master, too, had almost unlimited
control over the election of bishops, which was the
cause of many evils, especially as the order gradually grew lax in the observance of the rule, and
lost much of its Christian character. Unworthy
men were thrust into ecclesiastical offices, the
standard of morality among the clergy was lowered,
and the people lost respect for the priesthood. It
is not surprising, in view of all this, that the religious sectaries of the thirteenth and fourteenth
centuries should have found favor in Prussia, and

made converts among her still half-pagan populations.

In 1466 the Teutonic Order became a dependency of the crown of Poland. There was no hope of its freeing itself from this humiliating subjection without foreign aid; and with a view to obtain this, the knights resolved to choose their grand master from one or other of the most powerful German families. First, in 1498, they elected Frederick, Duke of Saxony; and upon his death, in 1510, Albrecht, Margrave of Brandenburg, was chosen to succeed him.

Albrecht refused the oath of supremacy to Sigismund, King of Poland, who thereupon, in 1519, declared war upon him.

To meet the expenses of the war, Albrecht had the sacred vessels of the church melted down and minted; but he was unable to stand against the arms of Poland, and therefore sought the mediation of the Emperor of Germany, through whose good offices he was able to conclude, in 1521, a four years' truce. He now went into Germany, where Luther was already preaching the Protestant rebellion, and asked aid from the imperial Parliament, which was holding its sessions at Nuremberg; and as this was denied him, he turned with favor to the teachers of the new doctrines. The Teutonic Order had become thoroughly corrupt, and Leo X. urged Albrecht to begin a reformation *in capite et membris;* but the grand master sought the advice of Luther, from whom he received the not unwelcome counsel to throw away the "stupid, unnatural rule of his order, take a wife, and turn Prussia into a temporal hereditary principality." Albrecht accordingly asked for preachers of the new doctrines, and in 1526 announced his abandonment of the order and the Catholic Church by his marriage with the daughter of the King of Denmark. Acting upon the Protestant principle, *cujus regio ejus religio*—the ruler of the land makes its religion—he forced the Prussians to quit the church from which they had received whatever culture and civilization they had.

At his death, in 1568, Lutheranism had gained complete possession of the country.

A few Catholics, however, remained, for whom, early in the seventeenth century, King Sigismund of Poland succeeded in obtaining liberty of conscience, which was still denied to those of Brandenburg. Frederick William, the second king of Prussia, and the first to form the design of placing her among the great powers of Europe by the aid of a strong military organization, in giving directions in 1718 for the education of his son, afterwards Frederick the Great, insisted that the boy should be inspired with a horror of the Catholic Church, " the groundlessness and absurdity of whose teachings should be placed before his eyes and well impressed upon his mind."

Frederick William was a rigid Calvinist ; and if he tolerated a few Catholics in his dominions, it was only that he might vent his ill-humor or exercise his proselytizing zeal upon them. He indeed granted Father Raymundus Bruns permission to

16

say Mass in the garrisons at Berlin and Potsdam, but only after he had been assured that it would tend to prevent desertions among his Catholic soldiers, and that, as Raymundus was a monk, bound by a vow of poverty, he would ask no pay from his majesty.

In 1746 permission was granted the Catholics to hold public worship in Berlin, and the St. Hedwig's Church was built ; in Pomerania, however, this privilege was denied them, except in the Polish districts.

During the eighteenth century congregations were formed at Stettin and Stralsund. In the principality of Halberstadt the Catholics were allowed to retain possession of a church and several monasteries, in which public worship was permitted ; and in what had been the archbishopric of Magdeburg there were left to them one Benedictine monastery and four convents of Cistercian nuns. These latter, however, were placed under the supervision of Protestant ministers.

Frederick the Great early in life fell under the influence of Voltaire and his disciples, from whom he learned to despise all religion, and especially the rigid Calvinism of his father. He became a religious sceptic, and, satisfied with his contempt for all forms of faith, did not take the trouble to persecute any. He asked of his subjects, whether Protestant or Catholic, nothing but money and recruits ; for the rest, he allowed every one in his dominions " to save his soul after his own fashion." He provided chaplains for his Catholic soldiers,

and forbade the Calvinist and Lutheran ministers
to interfere with their religious freedom, for reasons
similar to those which had induced his father to
permit Raymundus Bruns to say Mass in the garri-
son at Berlin. He had certainly no thought of
showing any favor to the church, except so far as
it might promote his own ambitious projects. His
great need of soldiers made him throw every ob-
stacle in the way of those who wished to enter the
priesthood, and his fear of foreign influence caused
him to forbid priests to leave the country. His
mistrust of priests was so great that he gave instructions to Count Hoym, his Minister of State, to
place them under a system of espionage. Catholics were carefully excluded from all influential and
lucrative positions. They were taxed more heavily
than Protestants, and professors in the universities
were required to take an oath to uphold the Reformation.

Notwithstanding, it was in the reign of Frederick
the Great that the Catholic Church in Prussia may
be said to have entered upon a new life. For more
than two hundred years it had had no recognized
status there ; but through the conquest of Silesia
and the division of Poland, a large Catholic population was incorporated into the kingdom of Prussia, and thus a new element, which was formally
recognized in the constitution promulgated by
Frederick's immediate successor, was introduced into
the Prussian state. Together with the toleration
of all who believed in God and were loyal to the
king, the law of the land placed the Catholic and

Protestant churches on an equal footing. To understand how far this was favorable to the church we must go back and consider the relations of Prussia to Protestantism.

What is known as the Territorial System, by which the faith of the people is delivered into the hands of the temporal ruler, has existed in Prussia from the time Albrecht of Brandenburg went over to the Reformers. Protestantism and absolutism triumphed simultaneously throughout Europe, and this must undoubtedly be in a great measure attributed to the fact that the Protestants, whether willingly or not, yielded up their faith into the keeping of kings and princes, and thus practically abandoned the distinction of the spiritual and temporal powers which lies at the foundation of Christian civilization, and is also the strongest bulwark against the encroachments of governments upon the rights of citizens. Duke Albrecht had hardly become a Protestant when he felt that it was his duty (" *coacti sumus* " are his words) to take upon himself the episcopal office. This was in 1530; in 1550 he treated the urgent request of the Assembly to have the bishopric of Samland restored as an attack upon his princely prerogative.

His successor diverted to other uses the fund destined for the maintenance of the bishops, and instituted two consistories, to which he entrusted the ecclesiastical affairs of the duchy.

During the seventeenth century Calvinism gained a firm foothold in Prussia. It became the religion of the ruling family, and Frederick William, called

the Great Elector, to whose policy his successors
have agreed to ascribe their power, sought in every
way to promote its interests, though he strenu-
ously exercised his *jus episcopale*, his spiritual supremacy over both the Lutherans and the Cal-
vinists.

His son, Frederick, who first took the title of
King of Prussia (1700), continued the policy of his
father with regard to ecclesiastical affairs. " To us,
alone," he declared to the Landstand, " belongs the
jus supremum episcopale, the highest and sovereign
right in ecclesiastical matters."

The Lutherans wished to retain the exorcism as
a part of the ceremony of baptism ; but Frederick
published an edict by which he forbade the appointment of any minister who would refuse to confer the sacrament without making use of this ceremony. In the same way he meddled with the
Lutheran practice of auricular confession ; and by
an order issued in 1703 prohibited the publication
of theological writings which had not received his
imprimatur.

His successor, Frederick William, the father of
Frederick the Great, looked upon himself as the
absolute and irresponsible master of the subjects
whom God had given him. " I am king and master," he was wont to say, " and can do what I
please." He was a rigid Calvinist, and made his
absolutism felt more especially in religious matters.
It seems that preachers then, as since, were sometimes in the habit of delivering long sermons ; so
King Frederick William put a fine of two thalers

upon any one who should preach longer than one
hour. He required his preachers to insist in *all*
their sermons upon the duty of obedience and loyalty to the king, and the government officials were
charged to report any failure to make special mention of this obligation. Both Lutherans and Cal-
vinists were forbidden to touch in their sermons
upon any points controverted between the two confessions. No detail of religious worship was insig-
nificant enough to escape his meddlesome tyranny.
The length of the service, the altar, the vestments
of the minister, the sign of the cross, the giving or
singing the blessing, all fell under his " high episcopal supervision."

This unlovely old king was followed by Frederick
the Great, who, though an infidel and a scoffer,
held as firmly as his father to his sovereign episcopal prerogatives, and who, if less meddlesome, was
not less arbitrary. And now we have got back to
the constitution which, after Silesia and a part of
Poland had been united to the crown of Prussia,
was partially drawn up under Frederick the Great,
and completed and promulgated during the reign
of his successor ; and which, as we have already
said, placed the three principal confessions of the
Christian faith in the Prussian states—the Lutheran, the Reformed, and the Catholic—on a footing
of equality before the law. Now, it must be noticed, this constitution left intact the absolute authority of the king over the Reformed and Lutheran churches, and therefore what might seem to be
a great gain for the Catholic Church was really none

at all, since it was simply placed under the supreme jurisdiction of the king. There was no express recognition of the organic union of the church in Prussia with the pope, nor of the right of the bishops to govern their dioceses according to the ecclesiastical canons, but rather the tacit assumption that the king was head of the Catholic as of the Protestant churches in Prussia. The constitution was drawn up by Suarez, a bitter enemy of the church, and in many of its details was characterized by an anti-Catholic spirit. It annulled, for instance, the contract made by parents of different faith concerning the religious education of their children, and manifested in many other ways that petty and tyrannical spirit which has led Prussia to interfere habitually with the internal discipline and working of the church.

As the Catholic population of Prussia increased through the annexation of different German states, this constitution, which gave the king supreme control of spiritual matters, was extended to the newly-acquired territories. Thus all through the eighteenth century the church in Prussia, though not openly persecuted, was fettered. No progress was made, abuses could not be reformed, the appointment of bishops was not free, the training of the priesthood was very imperfect ; and it is not surprising that this slavery should have been productive of many and serious evils.

The French Revolution and the wars of Napoleon, which caused social and political upheavals throughout Europe, toppled down thrones, overthrew empires, and broke up and reformed the boundaries of nations, mark a new epoch in the history of Prussia, and indeed of all Germany, whose people had been taught by these disastrous wars that they had common interests which could not be protected without national unity, the want of which had never before been made so painfully manifest.

After the downfall of Napoleon, the ambassadors of the Allied Powers met in Vienna to settle the affairs of all Europe. Nations, provinces, and cities were given away in the most reckless manner, without any thought of the interests or wishes of the people, to the kings and rulers who could command the greatest influence in the congress or whose displeasure was most feared. Germany demanded the restoration of Alsace and Lorraine, but was thwarted in her designs by Great Britain and Russia, who feared the restoration of her ancient power.

Prussia received from the congress, as some compensation for its sufferings and sacrifices during the Napoleonic wars, the duchies of Jülich and Berg, the former possessions of the episcopal sees of Cologne and Trèves, and several other territories, which were formed into the Rhine province. On the other hand, it lost a portion of the Sclavonic population which it had held on the east; so that, though it gained nothing in territory, it became more strictly a German state, and was consequently better fitted gradually to take the lead in the irrepressible movement toward the unification of Germany.

In the Congress of Vienna it was stipulated that Catholics and Protestants should have equal rights before the law. The constitutional law of Prussia was extended to the newly-acquired provinces, and " all ecclesiastical matters, whether of Roman Catholics or Protestants, together with the supervision and administration of all charitable funds, the confirming of all persons appointed to spiritual offices, and the supervision over the administration of ecclesiastics as far as it may have any relation to civil affairs, were reserved to the government."

In 1817, upon the occasion of the reorganization of the government, we perceive to what practical purposes these principles were to be applied. The church was debased to a function of the state, her interests were placed in the hands of the ministry for spiritual affairs, and the education of even clerical students was put under the control of government.

It was in this same year, 1817, that the tercentennial anniversary of the birth of Protestantism was celebrated. For two centuries Protestant faith in Germany had been dying out. Eager and bitter controversies, the religious wars and the plunder of church property during the sixteenth and early part of the seventeenth centuries, had given it an unnatural and artificial vigor. It was a mighty and radical revolution, social, political, and religious, and therefore gave birth to fanaticism and intense partisan zeal, and was in turn helped on by them.

There is a natural strength in a new faith, and when it is tried by war and persecution it seems to

17

rise to a divine power. Protestantism burst upon
Europe with irresistible force. Fifty years had not
passed since Luther had burned the bull of Pope
Leo, and the Catholic Church, beaten almost everywhere in the North of Europe, seemed hardly able
to hold her own on the shores of the Mediterra-
nean ; fifty years later, and Protestantism was saved
in Germany itself only by the arms of Catholic
France. The peace of Westphalia, in 1648, put an
end to the religious wars of Germany, and from
that date the decay of the Protestant faith was
rapid. Many causes helped on the work of ruin ;
the inherent weakness of the Protestant system
from its purely negative character, the growing and
bitter dissensions among Protestants, the hopeless
slavery to which the sects had been reduced by the
civil power, all tended to undermine faith. In the
Palatinate, within a period of sixty years, the rulers
had forced the people to change their religion four
times. In Prussia, whose king, as we have seen,
was supreme head of the church, the ruling house
till 1539 was Catholic ; then, till 1613, Lutheran ;
from that date to 1740, Calvinistic ; from 1740 to
1786, infidel, the avowed ally of Voltaire and
D'Alembert ; then, till 1817, Calvinistic ; and finally again evangelical.

During the long reign of Frederick the Great
unbelief made steady progress. Men no longer
attacked this or that article of faith, but Christianity itself. The quickest way, it was openly said
by many, to get rid of superstition and priestcraft,
would be to abolish preaching altogether, and thus

remove the ghost of religion from the eyes of the people. It seems strange that such license of thought and expression should have been tolerated, and even encouraged, in a country where religion itself has never been free ; but it is a peculiarity of the Prussian system of government that while it hampers and fetters the church and all religious organizations, it leaves the widest liberty of conscience to the individual. Its policy appears to be to foster indifference and infidelity, in order to use them against what it considers religious fanaticism. Another circumstance which favored infidelity may be found in the political thraldom in which Prussia held her people. As men were forbidden to speak or write on subjects relating to the government or the public welfare, they took refuge in theological and philosophical discussions, which in Protestant lands have never failed to lead to unbelief. This same state of things tended to promote the introduction and increase of secret societies, which, in the latter half of the eighteenth century, sprang up in great numbers throughout Germany, bearing a hundred different names, but always having anti-Christian tendencies.

To stop the spread of infidelity, Frederick William II., the successor of Frederick the Great, issued, in 1788, an "edict, embracing the constitution of religion in the Prussian states." The king declared that he could no longer suffer in his dominions that men should openly seek to undermine religion, to make the Bible ridiculous in the eyes of the people, and to raise in public the banner of unbelief,

deism, and naturalism. He would in future permit
no farther change 'in the creed, whether of the
Lutheran or the Reformed Church. This was the
more necessary as he had himself noticed with sorrow, years before he ascended the throne, that the
Protestant ministers allowed themselves boundless
license with regard to the articles of faith, and indeed altogether rejected several essential parts and
fundamental verities of the Protestant Church and
the Christian religion. They blushed not to revive
the long-since-refuted errors of the Socinians, the
deists, and the naturalists, and to scatter them
among the people under the false name of enlightenment (*Aufklärung*), whilst they treated God's Word
with disdain, and strove to throw suspicion upon the
mysteries of revelation. Since this was intolerable, he therefore, as ruler of the land and only law-
giver in his states, commanded and ordered that in
future no clergyman, preacher, or school-teacher of
the Protestant religion should presume, under pain
of perpetual loss of office and of even severer punishment, to disseminate the errors already named;
for, as it was his duty to preserve intact the law of
the land, so was it incumbent upon him to see that
religion should be kept free from taint; and he
could not, consequently, allow its ministers to substitute their whims and fancies for the truths of
Christianity. They must teach what had been
agreed upon in the symbols of faith of the de-
nomination to which they belonged; to this they
were bound by their office and the contract under
which they had received their positions. Never-

theless, out of his great love for freedom of conscience, the king was willing that those who were
known to disbelieve in the articles of faith might
retain their offices, provided they consented to
teach their flocks what they were themselves unable to believe.

In this royal edict we have at once the fullest
confession of the general unbelief that was destroying Protestantism in Prussia, and of the hope-
lessness of any attempt to arrest its progress. What
could be more pitiable than the condition of a church
powerless to control its ministers, and publicly recognizing their right to be hypocrites? How could
men who had no faith teach others to believe?
Moreover, what could be more absurd, from a
Protestant point of view, than to seek to force
the acceptance of symbols of faith when the whole
Reformation rested upon the assumed right of the
individual to decide for himself what should or
should not be believed? Or was it to be supposed
that men could invest the conflicting creeds of the
sects with a sacredness which they had denied to
that of the universal church? It is not surprising,
therefore, that the only effect of the edict should
have been to increase the energy and activity of
the infidels and free-thinkers.

Frederick William III., who ascended the throne
in 1797, recognizing the futility of his father's attempt to keep alive faith in Protestantism, stopped
the enforcement of the edict, with the express declaration that its effect had been to lessen religion
and increase hypocrisy. Abandoning all hope of

controlling the faith of the preachers, he turned his attention to their morals. A decree of the Ober-consistorium of Berlin, in 1798, ordered that the conduct of the ministers should be closely watched and every means employed to stop the daily-increasing immorality of the servants of the church, which was having the most injurious effects upon their congregations. Parents had almost ceased having their children baptized, or had them christened in the " name of Frederick the Great," or in the " name of the good and the fair," sometimes with rose-water.

But the calamities which befell Germany during the wars of the French Revolution and the empire seemed to have turned the thoughts of many to religion. The frightful humiliations of the Father-land were looked upon as a visitation from heaven upon the people for their sins and unbelief; and therefore, when the tercentennial anniversary of Protestantism came around (in 1817), they were prepared to enter upon its celebration with earnest enthusiasm. The celebration took the form of an anti-Catholic demonstration. For many years controversy between Protestants and Catholics had ceased; but now a wholly unprovoked but bitter and grossly insulting attack was made upon the church from all the Protestant pulpits of Germany and in numberless writings. The result of this wanton aggression was a reawakening of Catholic faith and life; whilst the attempt to take advantage of the Protestant enthusiasm to bring about a union between the Lutheran and Reformed churches in Prussia ended in causing fresh dissensions and divisions. The sect of the Old Lutherans was formed, which, in spite of persecution, finally succeeded in obtaining toleration, though not till many of its adherents had been driven across the ocean into exile.

As the Congress of Vienna had decided that Catholics and Protestants should be placed upon a footing of equality, and as Prussia had received a large portion of the *secularized* lands of the church, with the stipulation that she should provide for the maintenance of Catholic worship, the government, in 1816, sent Niebuhr, the historian, to Rome, to treat with the pope concerning the reorganization of the Catholic religion in the Prussian states. Finally, in 1821, an agreement was signed which received the sanction of the king, and was published as a fundamental law of the state.

In this Concordat with the Holy See there is at least a tacit recognition of the true nature of the church, of her organic unity—a beginning of respect for her freedom, and a seeming promise of a better future. In point of fact, however, in spite of Niebuhr's assurance to the Holy Father that he might rely upon the honest intentions of the government, Prussia began almost at once to meddle with the rights of Catholics. A silent and slow persecution was inaugurated, by which it was hoped their patience would be exhausted and their strength wasted. And now we shall examine more closely the artful and heartless policy by which, with but slight variations, for more than two centuries Prussia has sought to undermine the Catholic religion. In 1827 the Protestants of all communions in Prussia amounted to 6,370,380, and the Catholics to 4,023,513. These populations are, to only a very limited extent, intermingled; certain provinces being almost entirely Catholic, and others nearly wholly Protestant. By law the same rights are granted to both Catholics and Protestants; and both, therefore, should receive like treatment at the hands of the government.

This is the theory; what are the facts? We will take the religious policy of Prussia from the reorganization of the church after the Congress of Vienna down to the revolution of 1848, and we will begin with the subject of education. For the six millions of Protestants there were four exclusively Protestant universities, at Berlin, Halle, Königsberg, and Greifswalde; for the four millions of Catholics there were but two *half universities*, at Bonn and Breslau, in each of which there was a double faculty, the one Protestant, the other Catholic; though the professors in all the faculties, except that of theology, were for the most part Protestants. Thus, out of six universities, to the Catholics was left only a little corner in two, though they were forced to bear nearly one-half of the public burdens by which all six were supported. But this is not the worst. The bishops had no voice in the nomination of the professors, not even those of theology. They were simply asked whether they had any objections to make, *on proof*. The candidate might be a stranger, he might be wholly unfitted to teach theology, he might be free from open immorality or heresy ; and therefore, because the bishops could *prove* nothing against him, he was appointed to instruct the aspirants to the priesthood.

At Breslau a foreign professor was installed, who began to teach the most scandalous and heretical doctrines. Complaints were useless. During many years his pupils drank in the poison, and at length, after he had done his work of destruction, he was, as in mockery, removed. Nor is this an isolated instance of the ruin to Catholic faith wrought by this system. The bishops had hardly any influence over the education of their clergy, who, young and ignorant of the world, were thrown almost without restraint into the pagan corruptions of a German university, in order to acquire a knowledge of theology. At Cologne a Catholic college was made over to the Protestants; at Erfurt and Düsseldorf Catholic *gymnasia* were turned into mixed establishments with all the professors, save one, Protestants.

Elementary education was under the control of provincial boards consisting of a Protestant president and three councillors, *one* of whom might be a Catholic in Catholic districts. In the Catholic provinces of the Rhine and Westphalia the place of Catholic councillor was left vacant for several years till the schools were all reorganized. Indeed, the real superintendent of Catholic elementary education was generally a Protestant minister.

There was a government censorship of books of

religious instruction, the headquarters of which were in Berlin, but its agents were scattered throughout all the provinces. All who were employed in this department, to which even the pastorals of the bishops had to be submitted before being read to their flocks, were Protestants. The widest liberty was given to Protestants to attack the church; but when the Catholics sought to defend themselves, their writings were suppressed. Professor Freudenfeld was obliged to quit Bonn because he had spoken of Luther without becoming respect.

Permission to start religious journals was denied to Catholics, but granted to Protestants; and in the pulpit the priests were put under strict restraint, while the preachers were given full liberty of speech. Whenever a community of Protestants was found in a Catholic district, a church, a clergyman, and a school were immediately provided for them; indeed, richer provision for the Protestant worship was made in the Catholic provinces than elsewhere; but when a congregation of Catholics grew up amongst Protestants, the government almost invariably rejected their application for permission to have a place of worship. At various times and places churches and schools were taken from Catholics and turned over to Protestants; and though Prussia had received an enormous amount of the confiscated property of the church, she did not provide for the support of the priests as for that of the ministers.

At court there was not a single Catholic who held office; the heads of all the departments of government were Protestants; the Post-Office department, down to the local postmasters, was exclusively Protestant; all ambassadors and other representatives of the government, though sent to Catholic courts, were Protestants.

In Prussia the state is divided into provinces, and at the head of each province is a high-president (Ober-Präsident). This official, to whom the religious interests of the Catholics were committed, was always a Protestant. The provinces are divided into districts, and at the head of each district was a Protestant president, and almost all the inferior officers, even in Catholic provinces, were Protestants.

Again, in the courts of justice and in the army all the principal positions were given to Protestants. In the two *corps d'armées* of Prussia and Silesia, one-half was Catholic; in the army division of Posen, two-thirds; in that of Westphalia and Cleves, three-fifths; and, finally, in that of the Rhine, seven-eighths; yet there was not one Catholic field-officer, not a general or major. In 1832 a royal order was issued to provide for the religious wants of the army, and every care was taken for the spiritual needs of the Protestant soldiers; but not even one Catholic chaplain was appointed. All persons in active service, from superior officers down to private soldiers, were declared to be members of the military parish, and were placed under the authority of the Protestant chaplains. If a Catholic soldier wished to get married or to have his child baptized by a priest, he had first to obtain the permission of his Protestant curate. What was still more intolerable, the law regulating military worship was so contrived as to force the Catholic soldiers to be present at Protestant service.

Let us now turn to the relations of the church in Prussia with the Holy See. All direct communications between the Catholics and the pope were expressly forbidden. Whenever the bishops wished to consult the Holy Father concerning the administration of their dioceses, their inquiries had to pass through the hands of the Protestant ministry, to be forwarded or not at its discretion, and the answer of the pope had to be conveyed through the same channel. It was not safe to write; for the government had no respect for the mails, and letters were habitually opened by order of Von Nagler, the postmaster-general, who boasted that he had never had any idiotic scruples about such matters; that Prince Constantine was his model, who had once entertained him with narrating how he had managed to get the choicest selection of intercepted letters in existence; he had had them bound in morocco, and they formed thirty-three volumes of the most interesting reading in his private library. Thus the church was ruled by a system of espionage and bureaucracy which hesitated not to violate all the sanctities of life to accomplish its ends. · The bishops were reduced to a state of abject dependence; not being allowed to publish any new regulation or to make any appointment without the permission and approval of the Protestant high-president, from whom they constantly received the most annoying and vexatious despatches.

The election of bishops was reduced to a mere form. When a see became vacant, the royal commissary visited the chapter and announced the person whom the king had selected to fill the office, declaring at the same time that no other would receive his approval.

The minutest details of Catholic worship were placed under the supervision and control of Protestant laymen, who had to decide how much wine and how many hosts might be used during the year in the different churches.

We come now to a matter, vexed and often discussed, in which the trials of the church in Prussia, prior to the recent persecutions, finally culminated ; we allude to the subject of marriages between Catholics and Protestants.

When, in 1803, Prussia got possession of the greater part of her Catholic provinces, the following order was at once issued : " His majesty enacts that children born in wedlock shall all be educated in the religion of the father, and that, in opposition to this law, neither party shall bind the other." Apart from the odious meddling of the state with the rights of individuals and the agreements of parties so closely and sacredly related as man and wife, there was in this enactment a special injustice to Catholics, from the fact that nearly all the mixed marriages in Prussia were contracted by Protestant government officials and Catholic women of the provinces to which these agents had been sent.

As these men held lucrative offices, they found no difficulty in making matrimonial alliances; and as the children had to be brought up in the religion of the father, the government was by this means gradually establishing Protestant congregations throughout its Catholic provinces. In 1825 this law was extended to the Rhenish province, and in 1831 a document was brought to light which explained the object of the extension, which was that it might prove an effectual measure against the proselyting system of Catholics.

The condition of the church was indeed deplorable. With the name of being free, she was, in truth, enslaved; and while the state professed to respect her rights, it was using all the power of the most thoroughly organized and most heartless system of bureaucracy and espionage to weaken and fetter her action, and even to destroy her life. This was the state of affairs when, in the end of 1835, Von Droste Vischering, one of the greatest and noblest men of this century, worthy to be named with Athanasius and with Ambrose, was made archbishop of Cologne.

The Catholic people of Prussia had long since lost all faith in the good intentions of the government, of whose acts and aims they had full knowledge; and it was in order to restore confidence that a man so trusted and loved by them as Von Droste Vischering was promoted to the see of Cologne. The doctrines of Hermes, professor of theology in the University of Bonn, had just been condemned at Rome, but the government ignored the papal brief, and continued to give its support to the Hermesians; the archbishop, nevertheless, denounced their writings, and especially their organ, the *Bonner Theologische Zeitschrift*, forbade his students to attend their lectures at the university, and finally withdrew his approbation altogether from the Hermesian professors, refusing to ordain students unless they formally renounced the proscribed doctrines.

By a ministerial order issued in 1825, priests were forbidden, under pain of deposition from office, to exact in mixed marriages any promise concerning the education of the offspring. A like penalty was threatened for refusing to marry parties who were unwilling to make such promises, or for withholding absolution from those who were bringing up their children in the Protestant religion. To avert as far as possible any conflict between the church and the government, Pius VIII., in 1830, addressed a brief to the bishops of Cologne, Treves, Münster, and Paderborn, in which he made every allowable concession to the authority of the state in the matter of mixed marriages. The court of Berlin withheld the papal brief, and, taking advantage of the yielding disposition of Archbishop Spiegel of Cologne, entered, without the knowledge of the Holy See, into a secret agreement with him, in which still farther concessions were made, and in violation of Catholic principle. Von Droste Vischering took as his guide the papal brief, and paid no attention to such provisions of the secret agreement as conflicted with the instructions of the Holy Father.

The government took alarm, and offered to let

fall the Hermesians, if the archbishop would yield
in the affair of mixed marriages ; and as this expedient failed, measures of violence were threatened, which were soon carried into effect ; for on the
evening of the 20th of November, 1837, the archbishop was secretly arrested and carried off to the
fortress of Minden, where he was placed in close
confinement, all communication with him being cut
off. The next morning the government issued a
"Publicandum," in which it entered its accusations
against the archbishop, in order to justify its arbitrary act and to appease the anger of the people.
Notwithstanding, a cry of indignation and grief was
heard in all the Catholic provinces of Prussia, which
was re-echoed throughout Germany and extended
to all Europe. Lukewarm Catholics grew fervent,
and the very Hermesians gathered with their sympathies to uphold the cause of the Church.

The Archbishop of Posen and the Bishops of
Paderborn and Münster announced their withdrawal
from the secret convention, which the Bishop of
Treves had already done upon his death-bed ; and
henceforward the priests throughout the kingdom
held firm to the ecclesiastical law on mixed marriages, so that in 1838 Frederick William III. was
forced to make a declaration recognizing the rights
for which they contended. But the Archbishop of
Cologne was still a prisoner in the fortress of Minden. Early, however, in 1839, his health began to
fail ; and as the government feared lest his death
in prison might produce unfavorable comment, he
received permission to withdraw to Münster. The

next year the king died, and his successor, Frederick William 1V., showed himself ready to settle the dispute amicably, and in other ways to do justice to the Catholics. A great victory had been gained—the secret convention was destroyed—a certain liberty of communication with the pope was granted to the bishops. The election of bishops was made comparatively free, the control of the schools of theology was restored to them, the Hermesians either submitted or were removed, and the Catholics of Germany awoke from a deathlike sleep to a new and vigorous life.

An evidence of the revival of faith was given in the fall of 1844, when a million and a half of German Catholics went in pilgrimage, with song and prayer, to Treves.

Nevertheless, many grievances remained unredressed. The censorship of the press was still used against the church ; and when the Catholics asked permission to publish journals in which they could defend themselves and their religious interests, they were told that such publications were not needed ; but when Ronge, the suspended priest, sought to found his sect of "German Catholics," he received every encouragement from the government, and the earnest support of the officials and nearly the entire press of Prussia ; though, at this very time, every effort was being made to crush the " Old Lutherans."

The government continued to find pretexts for meddling with the affairs of the bishops, and the newspapers attacked the church in the most insult-

18

ing manner, going so far as to demand that religious exercises for priests should be placed under police supervision. We have now reached a memorable epoch in the history of the Catholic Church in Prussia—the revolution of 1848, which convulsed Germany to its centre, spread dismay among all classes, and filled its cities with riot and bloodshed. When order was re-established, the liberties of the church were recognized more fully than they had been for three centuries.

PRUSSIA AND THE CHURCH.

II.

IN February, 1848, Louis Philippe was driven from his throne by the people of Paris, and the Republic was proclaimed. This revolution spread rapidly over the whole of Europe. The shock was most violent in Germany, where everything was in readiness for a general outburst. Most of the governments were compelled to yield to the popular will and to make important concessions. New cabinets were formed in Würtemberg, Darmstadt, Nassau, and Hesse. Lewis of Bavaria was forced to abdicate. Hanover and Saxony held out until Berlin and Vienna were invaded by the revolutionary party, when they too succumbed. On the 13th of March the Vienna mob overthrew the Austrian ministry, and Metternich fled to England. Italy and Hungary revolted. Berlin was held all summer by an ignorant revolutionary faction. In September fierce and bloody riots broke out in Frankfort.

Popular meetings, secret societies, revolutionary clubs, violent declamations, and inflammatory appeals through the press kept all Germany in a state of agitation. Occasional outbreaks among the peasantry, followed by pillage and incendiarism, increased the general confusion.

It was during this time of wild excitement that the elections for the Imperial Parliament were held. To this assembly many avowed atheists, pantheists, communists, and Jacobins were chosen—men who fully agreed with Hecker when he declared that "there were six plagues in Germany: the princes, the nobles, the bureaucrats, the capitalists, the parsons, and the soldiers." The parties in the Parliament took their names from their positions in the assembly hall, and were called the extreme left, the left, the left centre, the right centre, the right, and the extreme right. The first three were composed of red republicans, Jacobins, and liberals. To the right centre belonged the constitutional liberals; and on the right and right centre sat the Catholic members, the predecessors of the party of the *Centrum* of the present day. The extreme right was occupied by functionaries and bureaucrats, chiefly from Prussia. The Parliament of Frankfort, in the *Grundrechte*, or *Fundamental Rights*, which it proclaimed, decreed universal suffrage, abolished all the political privileges of the aristocracy, the hereditary chambers in all the states of Germany, set aside the existing family entails, and, though it nominally retained the imperial power, degraded the emperor to a republican president by giving him merely a suspensive veto.

While this Parliament was sitting the Catholic bishops of Germany assembled in council at Würzburg, and, at the conclusion of their deliberations, drew up a Memorial as firm in tone as it was clear and precise in expression, in which they set forth the claims of the church.

" To bring about," they said, " a separation from the state—that is to say, from public order, which necessarily reposes on a moral and religious foundation—is not according to the will of the church. If the state will perforce separate from the church, so will the church, without approving, tolerate what she cannot avoid ; but, unless compelled by the duty of self-preservation, she will not break the bonds of union made fast by mutual understanding.

" The church, entrusted with the solemn and holy mission, ' As my Father hath sent me, so send I ye,' requires for the accomplishment of this mission, whatever the form of government of the state may be, the fullest freedom and independence. Her holy popes, prelates, and confessors have in all ages willingly and courageously given up their life and blood for the preservation of this inalienable freedom."

In virtue of these principles the bishops, in their Memorial, claimed the right of directing, without any interference on the part of the state, theological seminaries, and of founding schools, colleges, and all kinds of educational establishments ; of exerting canonical control, unfettered by state meddling, over the conduct of their clergy, as well as that of introducing into their dioceses religious orders, congregations, and pious confraternities, for which they demanded the same privileges which the new political constitution had granted to secu-

lar associations. Finally, they asserted their right
to free and untrammelled communication with the
Holy See ; and, as included in this, that of receiving and publishing all papal bulls, briefs, and other
documents without the Royal Placet, which they
declared to be repugnant to the honor and dignity
of the ministers of religion.

The Frankfort Parliament decreed the total separation of church and state, and was therefore compelled to guarantee the freedom of all religions.
This separation was sanctioned by the Catholic
members of the Assembly, who looked upon it as
less dangerous to the cause of religion and morality
than ecclesiastical Josephism.   In the present conflict between the church and the German Empire
the Catholic party has again demanded, and in vain,
the separation of church and state.   In rejecting
their urgent request Dr. Falk declared that the
leading minds in England and America are already
beginning to regret that their governments have so
little control over the ecclesiastical organizations
within their limits.

Whilst the representatives of the German people
at Frankfort were abolishing the privileges of the
nobles, decreeing the separation of church and
state, and forgetting the standing armies, the governments were quietly gathering their forces.   Mar-
shal Radetzky put down the Italian rebellion, Prince
Windischgrätz quelled the democracy of Vienna,
and General Wrangel took possession of Berlin,
without a battle.   Russia, at the request of Austria, sent an army into Hungary to destroy the

rebellion in that country, and the disturbances in
Bavaria and in the Palatinate were suppressed by
Prussian troops under the present Emperor of
Germany. The representatives of the larger states
withdrew from the Frankfort Parliament, which
dwindled, and finally, amidst universal contempt
and neglect, came to an end at Stuttgart, June 18,
1849.

But the liberties of the church were not lost. In
Prussia, as we have seen, a better state of things
had begun with the imprisonment of the heroic
Archbishop of Cologne in 1837. In the face of the
menacing attitude of the German democrats and
republicans, Frederick William IV. confirmed the
liberties of the Catholic Church by the letters-
patent of 1847.

The constitutions of December 5, 1848, and January 31, 1850, were drawn up in the lurid light of
the revolution, which had beaten fiercest upon the
house of Hohenzollern. The king had capitulated
to the insurgents, withdrawn his soldiers from the
capital, and abandoned Berlin, and with it the
whole state, for nine months to the tender mercies
of the mob. He was forced to witness the most
revolting spectacles. The dead bodies of the
rioters were borne in procession under the windows
of his palace, while the rabble shouted to him:
" Fritz, off with your hat."

It is not surprising, in view of this experience,
that we should find in the constitution of 1850
(articles 15 to 18 inclusive) a very satisfactory recognition of the rights of the church. Why these

paragraphs granting the church freedom to regulate
and administer its own affairs; to keep possession
of its own revenues, endowments, and establishments, whether devoted to worship, education, or
beneficence; and freely to communicate with the
Pope, were inserted in the constitution, we know
from Prince Bismarck himself. In his speech in
the Prussian Upper House, March 10, 1873, he
affirmed that "they were introduced at a time
when the state needed, or thought it needed, help,
and believed that it would find this help by leaning
on the Catholic Church. It was probably led to
this belief by the fact that in the National Assembly of 1848 all the electoral districts with a preponderant Catholic population returned—I will not
say royalist representatives, but certainly men who
were the friends of order, which was not the case
in the Protestant districts."

The provisions of the constitution of 1850 with
regard to the church were honorably and faithfully
carried out down to the beginning of the present
conflict. Never since the Reformation had the
church in Prussia been so free, never had she made
such rapid progress, whether in completing her internal organization or in extending her influence.
The Prussian liberals and atheists, who had fully
persuaded themselves that without the wealth and
aid of the state the Catholic religion would have no
force, were amazed. The influence of the priests
over the people grew in proportion as they were
educated more thoroughly in the spirit and discipline of the church under the immediate super-

vision of the bishops, unfettered by state interference ; the number of convents, both of men and women, rapidly increased ; associations of all kinds, scientific, benevolent, and religious, spread over the land; religious journals and reviews were founded in which Catholic interests were ably advocated and defended ; and all the forces of the church were unified and guided by the harmonious action of a most enlightened and zealous episcopate.

This was the more astonishing as the Evangelical Church, whose liberties had also been guaranteed by the constitution of 1850, had shown itself unable to profit by the greater freedom of action which it had received. In fact, the Evangelical Church was lifeless, and it needed only this test to prove its want of vitality. It was a state creation, and in an age when the world had ceased to recognize the divine right of kings to create religions. It was only in 1817 that the Lutheran and Calvinistic churches of Prussia, together with the very name of Protestant, were abolished by royal edict and a new Prussian establishment, under the title of "evangelical," was imposed by the civil power upon a Protestant population of nearly eight millions, whose religious and moral sense was so dead that they seemed to regard with stolid indifference this interference of government with all that freemen deem most sacred in life. Acts of parliament may make "establishments," but they cannot inspire religious faith and life ; and it was therefore not surprising that, when the mummy of evangeli-

19

calism was put out into the open air of freedom by the constitution of 1850, it should have been revealed to all that the thing was dead.

Nevertheless, the Prussian government continued to act toward the Catholic Church with great justice, and even friendliness, and the war against Catholic Austria in 1866 wrought no change in its ecclesiastical policy. Even the opening of the Vatican Council caused no alarm in Prussia; on the contrary, King William, as it was generally believed at least, was most civil to the Holy Father; and Prince Bismarck himself at that time saw no reason for apprehension, though he had been the head of the ministry already eight years. To what, then, are we to attribute Prussia's sudden change of attitude toward the church? Who began the present conflict, and what was its provocation?

This is a question which has been much discussed in the Prussian House of Deputies and elsewhere. Prince Bismarck has openly asserted in the House of Deputies within the past year that the provocation was the definition of papal infallibility by the Vatican Council on the 18th of June, 1870, and subsequently the hostile attitude of the party of the *Centrum* toward the German Empire.

Herr von Kirchmann, a member of the German Parliament and of the Prussian House of Deputies, a national liberal, and not a Catholic, but in the main a sympathizer with the spirit of the Falk legislation, has recently discussed this whole subject with great ability, and—as far as it is possible for one who believes in the Hegelian doc-

trine that "the state is the present god"—also
with fairness.*

.To Prince Bismarck's first assertion, that the
definition of papal infallibility was the unpardonable offence, which has been so strongly emphasized
by Mr. Gladstone and re-echoed with parrot-like
fidelity by the anti-Catholic press of Europe and
America, Herr von Kirchmann makes the following
reply :

"It is difficult to understand how so experienced a statesman as Prince Bismarck can ascribe to
this decree of the council such great importance
for the states of Europe, and particularly for Prussia and Germany. To a theorizer sitting behind
his books such a decree, it may be allowed, might
appear to be something portentous, since, taken
from a purely theoretical stand-point and according
to the letter, the infallibility of the Pope in all
questions of religion and morals gives him unlimited control over all human action ; and many a Catholic, when called upon to receive this infallibility
as part of his faith, may have found that he was
unable to follow so far ; but a statesman ought to
know how to distinguish, especially where there is
question of the Catholic Church, between the literal import of dogmas and their use in practical
life. In the Catholic Church as a whole this infallibility, as is well known, has existed from the
earliest times ; its organ hitherto has been the
Œcumenical Council in union with the Pope ; but

* *Der Culturkampf in Preussen und seine Bedenken*—"Considerations on
the Culture-Struggle in Prussia"—von J. H. von Kirchmann. Leipzig, 1875.

already before 1870 it was disputed whether the
Pope might not alone act as the organ of infallibility. In 1870 the question was decided in favor of
the Pope; but we must consider that the œcumenical councils have, as history shows, nearly always
framed their decrees in accordance with the views
of the court of Rome; and this, of itself, proves
that the change made in 1870 is rather one of form
than of essence. Especially false is it to maintain
that by this decree a complete revolution in the
constitution of the church has been made. To the
theorizer we might grant the abstract possibility
that something of this kind might some day or
other happen; but such *possibilities* of the abuse
of a right are found in all the relations of public
life, in the state and its representatives as well as
in the church. Even in constitutions the most
carefully drawn up such possibilities are found in
all directions. What a statesman has to consider
is not mere possibilities, but the question whether
the possessor of such right is not compelled, from
the very nature of things, to make of it only the
most moderate and prudent use. So long, therefore, as the Pope does not alter the constitution
of the church, that constitution remains, precisely
in its ancient form, such as it has been recognized
and tolerated by the state for centuries; and
wherever the relations between particular states
and the court of Rome have been arranged by
concordats, these too remain unchanged, unless
the states themselves find it convenient to depart
from them. We see, in fact, that this infallibility

of the Pope has in no country of Europe or America altered one jot or tittle in the constitution of the Catholic Church; and where in particular countries such changes have taken place, they have not been made by the ecclesiastical government, but by the state and in its interest. In Germany even, and in Prussia itself, the Pope has, since 1870, made no change in the church constitution, as determined by the Canon Law; and when, in some of his encyclicals and other utterances, he has taken up a hostile attitude towards the German Empire and the Prussian state, he has done this only in defence against the aggressive legislation of the civil government. He has never hesitated to express his disapprobation of the new church laws, but he has in no instance touched the constitution of the Catholic Church or the rights of the bishops." *

It seems almost needless to remark that there is no necessary connection between the doctrine of Papal infallibility and that of the essential organization of the church; that the jurisdiction of the Pope was as great, and universally recognized as such by Catholics, before the Vatican Council as since; and consequently that it is not even possible that the definition of 1870 should make any change in his authoritative relation to, or power over, the church. His jurisdiction is wider than his infallibility, and independent of it; and the duty of obedience to his commands existed before the dogma was defined precisely as it exists now; and therefore it is clearly manifest that the Vatican

* *Culturkampf*, pp. 5-7.

decree cannot give even a plausible pretext for
such legislation as the Falk Laws.

" Not less singular," continues Herr von Kirchmann, " does it sound to hear the party of the
Centrum in the Reichstag and Prussian Landtag
denounced as the occasion of the new regulations
between church and state. The members of this
party notoriously represent the views and wishes
of the majority of their constituents, and just as
faithfully as the members of the parties who side
with the government. The reproach that they receive their instructions from Rome is not borne
out by the facts; and if there were an understanding with Rome of the kind which their adversaries
affirm, this could only be the result of a similar
understanding on the part of their constituents.
Nothing could more strikingly prove that the Catholic party faithfully represent the great majority
in their electoral districts than the repeated re-
election of the same representatives or of men of
similar views. To this we must add that the
Centrum, though strong in numbers, is yet in a
decided minority both in the Reichstag and the
Prussian Landtag, and has always been defeated in
its opposition to the recent ecclesiastical legislation.
If in other matters, by uniting with opposition
parties, it has caused the government inconve-
nience, we have no right to ascribe this to feelings
of hostility ; for on such occasions its orators have
given substantial political reasons for their opposition, and instances enough might be enumerated
in which, precisely through the aid of the *Centrum*,

many illiberal and dangerous projects of law have fallen through ; and for this the party deserves the thanks of the country.

"The present action of the state against the Catholic Church would be unjustifiable, if better grounds could not be adduced in its favor. For the attentive observer, however, valid reasons are not wanting. They are to be found, to put the whole matter in a single word, in the great power to which the Catholic Church in Prussia had attained by the aid of the constitution and the favor of the government—a power which, if its growth had been longer tolerated, would have become, not indeed dangerous to the existence of the state, but a hindrance to the right fulfilment of the ends of its existence." *

Neither the Vatican Council, then, nor the Catholics of Prussia have done anything to provoke the present persecution. To find fault with the German bishops for accepting the dogma of infallibility, after having strongly opposed its definition by the council, would be as unreasonable as to blame a member of Congress for admitting the binding force of a law the sanctioning of which he had done everything in his power to prevent. Their duty, beyond all question, was to act as they have acted. This was not the offence ; the unpardonable crime was that the church, as soon as she was unloosed from the fetters of bureaucracy, had grown too powerful. We doubt whether any more forcible argument in proof of the indestructible vitality

* Page 9.

of the church can be found than that which may
be deduced from the universal consent of her enemies, of whatever shade of belief or unbelief, that
the only way in which she can be successfully opposed is to array against her the strongest of
human powers—the state. A complete revolution
of thought upon this subject has taken place within the last half-century. Up to that time it was
confidently held by Protestants as well as infidels
that, to undermine and finally destroy the church,
it would be simply necessary to withdraw from her
the support of the state; that to her freedom would
certainly prove fatal. The experiment, as it was
thought, had not been satisfactorily tried. Ireland,
indeed, had held her faith for three hundred years,
in spite of all that fiendish cruelty could invent to
destroy it; but persecution has always been the life
of the faith. In the United States the church had
been free since the war of independence, but of us
little was known; and, besides, down to, say, 1830
even the most thoughtful and far-sighted among us
had serious doubts as to the future of the church
in this country.

But with the emancipation of the Catholics in
Great Britain, the new constitution of the kingdom
of Belgium, and the completer organization of the
church in the United States, the test as to the action of freedom upon the progress of Catholic faith
began to be applied over a wide and varied field
and under not unfavorable circumstances. What
the result has been we may learn from our enemies.
Mr. Gladstone expostulates for Great Britain, and

reaches a hand of sympathy to M. Emile de Laveleye in Belgium. Dr. Falk, Dr. Friedberg, and
even the moderate Herr von Kirchmann, defend
the tyrannical *May Laws* as necessary to stop the
growth of the church in Germany ; and at home
the most silent of Presidents and the most garrulous
of bishops, forgetting that the cause of temperance
has prior claims upon their attention, have raised
the cry of alarm to warn their fellow-citizens of the
dangerous progress of popery in this great and free
country.   Time was when "the Free Church in
the Free State" was thought to be the proper word
of command ; but now it is " the Fettered Church
in the Enslaved State," since no state that meddles
with the consciences of its subjects can be free.

If there is anything for which we feel more
especially thankful, it is that henceforth the cause
of the church and the cause of freedom are insepa-
rably united.   We have heard to satiety that the
Catholic Church is the greatest conservative force
in the world, the most powerful element of order in
society, the noblest school of respect in which mankind have ever been taught.   Praised be God that
now, as in the early days, he is making it impossible that Catholics should not be on the side of liberty, as the church has always been ; so that all men
may see that, if we love order the more, we love not
liberty the less !

" I will sing to my God as long as I shall be,"
wrote an inspired king; " put not your trust in
princes."   No, nor in governments, nor in states,
but in God who is the Lord, and in the poor whom

Jesus loved. From God out of the people came
the church; through God back to the people is
she going. We know there are still many Catholics who trust in kings and believe in salvation
through them; but God will make them wiser.
The Spirit that sits at the roaring Loom of Time
will weave for them other garments. The irresistible charm of the church, humanly speaking, lies
in the fact that she comes closer to the hearts of
the people than any other power that has ever
been brought to bear upon mankind.

Having shown that the oppressive ecclesiastical
legislation of Germany was not provoked by the
church, and that its only excuse is the increasing
power of the church, Herr von Kirchmann reduces
all farther discussion of this subject to the two following heads: 1st. How far ought the state to go
in setting bounds to this power of the Catholic
Church? and 2d. What means ought it to em-
ploy?

In view of the dangers with which every open
breach of the peace between church and state is
fraught for the people, it would have been advisable,
he thinks, from political motives, to have tried to
settle the difficulty by a mutual understanding between the two powers; nor would it, in his opinion,
be derogatory to the sovereignty of the state to
treat the church as an equal, since she embraces in
her fold all the Catholics of the world, who have
their directing head in the Pope, whose sovereign
ecclesiastical power cannot, therefore, as a matter
of fact, be called in question.

That Prussia did not make any effort to see what could be effected by this policy of conciliation may, in the opinion of Herr von Kirchmann, find some justification in the fact that the government did not expect, and could not in 1871 foresee, the determined opposition of the Catholics to the May Laws of 1873. At any rate, as he thinks, the high and majestatic right of the state is supreme, and it alone must determine, in the ultimate instance, how far and how long it will acknowledge any claim of the church. Thus even this statesman, who is of the more moderate school of Prussian politicians, holds that the church has no rights which the state is bound to respect; that political interests are paramount, and conscience, in the modern as in the ancient pagan state, has no claim upon the recognition of the government. English and American Protestants, where their own interests are concerned, would be as little inclined to accept this doctrine as Catholics; in fact, this country was born of a protest against the assumption of state supremacy over conscience; and yet so blinding and misleading is prejudice that the Falk Laws rêceive their heart-felt sympathy.

Though Herr von Kirchmann accepts without reservation the principles which underlie the recent Prussian anti-Catholic legislation, and thinks the May Laws have been drawn up with great wisdom and consummate knowledge of the precise points at which the state should oppose the growing power of the church, he yet freely admits that there are grave doubts whether the present policy of Prussia can be successfully carried out. That Prince Bismarck and Dr. Falk had but a very imperfect knowledge of the difficulties which lay in their path, the numerous supplementary bills which have been repeatedly introduced in order to give effect to the May Laws plainly show. Where there is question of principle and of conscience Prince Bismarck is not at home. He believes in force ; like the first Napoleon, holds that Providence is always on the side of the biggest cannons ; sneers about going to Canossa, as Napoleon mockingly asked the pope whether his excommunication would make the arms fall from the hands of his veterans. He knows the workings of courts, and is a master in the devious ways of diplomacy. He can estimate with great precision the resources of a country ; he has a keen eye for the weak points of an adversary. His tactics, like Napoleon's, are to bring to bear upon each given point of attack a force greater than the enemy's. He has, in his public life, never known what it is to respect right or principle. With the army at his back he has trampled upon the Prussian constitution with the same daring recklessness with which he now violates the most sacred rights of conscience. Nothing, in his eyes, is holy but success, and he has been consecrated by it, so that the Bismarck-cultus has spread far beyond the Fatherland to England and the United States. Carlyle has at last found a living hero, the very impersonation of the brute force which to him is ideal and admirable ; and at eighty he offers incense and homage to

the idol. We freely give Prince Bismarck credit
for his remarkable gifts—indomitable will, reckless
courage, practical knowledge of men, considered as
intelligent automata whose movements are directed
by a kind of bureaucratic and military mechanism;
and this is the kind of men with whom, for the
most part, he has had to deal. For your thorough
Prussian, though the wildest of speculators and the
boldest of theorizers, is the tamest of animals. No
poor Russian soldier ever crouched more submis-
sively beneath the knout than do the Prussian pantheists and culturists beneath the lash of a master.
Like Voltaire, they probably prefer the rule of one
fine Lion to that of a hundred rats of their own
sort. Prince Bismarck knew his men, and we give
him credit for his sagacity. Not every eye could
have pierced the mist, and froth, and sound, and
fury of German professordom, and beheld the cra-
ven heart that was beneath.

Only men who believe in God and the soul are
dangerous rebels. Why should he who has no faith
make a martyr of himself? Why, since there is
nothing but law, blind and merciless force, throw
yourself beneath the wheels of the state Juggernaut
to be crushed? The religion of culture is the religion of indulgence, and no godlike rebel against
tyranny and brute force ever sprang from such worship. So long as Prince Bismarck had to deal with
men who were nourished on "philosophy's sweet
milk," and who worshipped at the altar of culture,
who had science but not faith, opinions but not
convictions, amongst whom, consequently, organic

union was impossible, his policy of making Germany " by blood and iron " was successful enough. But, like all great conquerors, he longed for more kingdoms to subdue, and finding right around him a large and powerful body of German citizens who did not accept the " new faith " that the state— in other words, Prince Bismarck—is "the present god," just as a kind of diversion between victories, he turned to give a lesson to the *Pfaffen* and clerical *Dummköpfe*, who burnt no incense in honor of his divinity.   In taking this step it is almost needless to say that Prince Bismarck sought to pass over a chasm which science itself does not profess to have bridged—that, namely, which lies between the worlds of matter and of spirit. Of the new conflict upon which he was entering he could have only vague and inaccurate notions. Nothing is so misleading as contempt—a feeling in which the wise never indulge, but which easily becomes habitual with men spoiled by success. To the man who had organized the armies and guided the policy which had triumphed at Sadowa and Sedan what opposition could be made by a few poor priests and beggar-monks? Would the arms fall from the hands of the proudest soldiers of Europe because the *Pfaffen* were displeased? Or why should not the model culture-state of the world make war upon ignorance and superstition?

Of the real nature and strength of the forces which would be marshalled in this great battle of souls a man of blood and iron could form no just estimate.   " To those who believe," said Christ,

" all things are possible " ; but what meaning have
these words for Prince Bismarck? The soul, firm
in its faith, appealing from tyrant kings and states
to God, is invincible. Lifting itself to the Infinite,
it draws thence a divine power. Like liberty, it is
brightest in dungeons, in fetters freest, and conquers with its martyrdom. Needle-guns cannot
reach it, and above the deadly roar of cannon it
rises godlike and supreme.

> " For though the giant Ages heave the hill
> And break the shore, and evermore
> Make and break and work their will ;
> Though world on world in myriad myriads roll
> Round us, each with different powers
> And other forms of life than ours,
> What know we greater than the soul ?
> On God and godlike men we build our trust."

Men who have unwrapt themselves of the garb
and vesture of thought and sentiment with which
the world had dressed them out, who have been
born again into the higher life, who have been
clothed in the charity and meekness of Christ, who
for his dear sake have put all things beneath their
feet, who love not the world, who venerate more
the rags of the beggar than the purple of Cæsar,
who fear as they love God alone, for whom life is
no blessing and death infinite gain, form the invincible army of Christ foredoomed to conquer. " This
is the victory which overcometh the world—our
Faith."

Who has ever forgotten those lines of Tacitus,
inserted as an altogether trifling circumstance in
the reign of Nero?—" So for the quieting of this

rumor [of his having set fire to Rome] Nero judicially charged with the crime, and punished with most studied severities, that class, hated for their general wickedness, whom the vulgar call *Christians*. The originator of that name was one *Christ*, who in the reign of Tiberius suffered death by sentence of the procurator, Pontius Pilate. The baneful superstition, thereby repressed for the time, again broke out, not only over Judea, the native soil of the mischief, but in the City also, where from every side all atrocious and abominable things collect and flourish." *

"Tacitus," says Carlyle, referring to this passage, "was the wisest, most penetrating man of his generation ; and to such depth, and no deeper, has he seen into this transaction, the most important that has occurred or can occur in the annals of mankind."

We doubt whether Prince Bismarck to-day has any truer knowledge of the real worth and power of the living Catholic faith on which he is making war than had Tacitus eighteen hundred years ago, when writing of the rude German barbarians who were hovering on the confines of the Roman Empire, and who were to have a history in the world only through the action of that "baneful superstition" which he considered as one of the most abominable products of the frightful corruptions of his age.

That the Prussian government was altogether

* Tacit. *Annal.* xv. 44.

unprepared for the determined though passive opposition to the May Laws which the Catholics have
made, Herr von Kirchmann freely confesses. It
was not expected that there would be such perfect union between the clergy and the people; on
the contrary, it was generally supposed that, with
the aid of the Draconian penalties threatened for
the violation of the Falk Laws, the resistance of
the priests themselves would be easily overcome.
These men love their own comfort too much, said
the culturists, to be willing to go to prison and
live on beans and water for the sake of technicali-
ties; and so they chuckled over their pipes and
lager-beer at the thought of their easy victory
over the *Pfaffen*. They were mistaken, and Herr
von Kirchmann admits that the courage of the bishops and priests has not been broken but strengthened by their sufferings for the faith.

"So long as we were permitted to hope," he
says, "that we should have only the priests to deal
with, there was less reason for doubt as to the policy of executing the laws in all their rigor; but the
situation was wholly altered when it became manifest that the congregations held the same views as
the bishops and priests. . . . It is easy to see that
all violent, even though legal, proceedings of the
government against these convictions of the Catholic people can only weaken those proper, and in
the last instance alone effective, measures through
which the May Laws can successfully put bounds
to the growing power of the church. These measures— viz., a better education of the people and a

higher culture of the priests—can, from the nature
of things, exert their influence only by degrees.
Not till the next generation can we hope to gather
the fruit of this seed ; and not then, indeed, if the
reckless execution of the May Laws calls forth an
opposition in the Catholic populations which will
shake confidence in the just intentions of the government, and beget in the congregations feelings of
hatred for everything connected with this legislation.   Such feelings will unavoidably be communi-
cated to the children, and the teacher will in consequence be deprived of that authority without which
his instructions must lack the persuasive force that
is inherent in truth.   In such a state of warfare
even the higher culture of the clergy must be useless.   Those who stand on the side of the government will, precisely on that account, fail to win the
confidence of their people ; and the stronger the
aged pastors emphasize the Canon Law of the
church, the more energetically they extend the
realms of faith even to the hierarchical constitution
of the church, the more readily and faithfully will
their congregations follow them.

"It cannot be dissembled that the government,
through the rigorous execution of the May Laws,
is raging against its own flesh and blood, and is
thereby robbing itself of the only means by which
it can have any hope of finally coming forth victo-
rious from the present conflict.   It may be objected
that the resistance which is now so wide-spread cannot be much longer maintained, and that all that
is needed to crush it and bring about peace with

the church is to increase the pressure of the law.
Assertions of this kind are made with great confidence by the liberals of both Houses of the Landtag whenever the government presents a new bill;
and the liberal newspapers, which never grow tired
of this theme, declare that the result is certain and
even near at hand.

" Now, even though we should attach no importance to the contrary assertions of the Catholic party, it is yet evident, from the declarations of the
government itself, that it is not at all confident of
reaching this result with the aid of the means which
it has hitherto employed or of those in preparation,
but that it is making ready for a prolonged resistance of the clergy, who are upheld and supported by the great generosity of the Catholic people.
The ovations which the priests receive from their
congregations when they come forth from prison
are not falling off, but are increasing; and this is
equally true of the pecuniary aid given to them.
It is possible that much of this may have been gotten up by the priests themselves as demonstration ;
but the displeasure of the still powerful government
officials which the participants incur, and the greatness of the money-offerings, are evidence of earnest
convictions.

" Nothing, however, so strongly witnesses to the
existence of a perfect understanding between the
congregations and the priests as the fact that,
though the law of May, 1874, gave to those congregations whose pastors had been removed or had
not been legally appointed by the bishops the right

to elect others, yet not even one congregation has up to the present moment made any use of this privilege. When we consider that the number of parishes where there is no pastor must be at least a hundred ; that in itself such right of choice corresponds with the wishes of the congregations; farther, that the law requires for the validity of the election merely a majority of the members who put in an appearance ; that a proposition made to the *Landrath* by ten parishioners justifies him in ordering an election ; and that, on the part of the influential officials and their organs, nothing has been left undone to induce the congregations to demand elections, not easily could a more convincing proof of the perfect agreement of the people with their priests be found than the fact that to this day in only two or three congregations has it been possible to hunt up ten men who were willing to make such a proposal, and that not even in a single congregation has an election of this kind taken place." *

This is indeed admirable ; and it may, we think, be fairly doubted whether, in the whole history of the church, so large a Catholic population has ever, under similar trials, shown greater strength or constancy. Of the peculiar nature of these trials we shall speak hereafter; the present article we will bring to a close with a few remarks upon what we conceive to have been one of the most important agencies in bringing about the perfect unanimity

---

* *Culturkampf*, pp. 16–19.

and harmony of action between priests and people
to which the Catholics of Prussia must in great
measure ascribe their immovable firmness in the
presence of a most terrible foe. We refer to those
Catholic associations in which cardinals, bishops,
priests, and people have been brought into immediate contact, uniting their wisdom and strength for
the attainment of definite ends.

Such unions have nowhere been more numerous
or more thoroughly organized than in Germany,
though their formation is of recent date. It was
during the revolution of 1848, of which we have
already spoken, that the German Catholics were
roused to a more comprehensive knowledge of the
situation, and resolved to combine for the defence
of their rights and the protection of their religion.
Popular unions under the name and patronage of
Pius IX. (Pius-Vereine) were formed throughout
the fatherland, with the primary object of bringing
together once a week large numbers of Catholic
men of every condition in life. At these weekly
meetings the questions of the day, in so far as they
touched upon Catholic interests, were freely discussed, and thus an intelligent and enlightened
Catholic public opinion was created throughout
the length and breadth of the land. In refuting
calumnies against the church the speakers never
failed to demand the fullest liberty for all Catholic
institutions.

On the occasion of beginning the restoration and
completion of the Cathedral of Cologne, the most
religious of churches, the proposition that an annual

General Assembly of all the unions should be held was made and received with boundless enthusiasm. The first General Assembly took place at Mayence in October, 1848; and thither came delegates from Austria, Prussia, Bavaria, Saxony, Hanover, and all the other states of Germany, whose confidence and earnestness were increased by the presence of the Catholic members of the Parliament of Frankfort. For the first time since Luther's apostasy the Catholics of Germany breathed the air of liberty. The bishops assembled at Würzburg, gave their solemn approbation to the great work, and Pius IX. sent his apostolic benediction. Since that time General Assemblies have been held at Breslau, May, 1849; Ratisbon, October, 1849; Linz, 1850; Mayence, 1851; Münster, 1852; Vienna, 1853; Linz, 1856; Salzburg, 1857; Cologne, 1858; Freyburg, 1859; Prague, 1860; Munich, 1861; Aix-la-Chapelle, 1862; Frankfort, 1863, and in other cities, down to the recent persecutions.

These assemblies represented a complete system of organization, in which no Catholic interest was forgotten. Every village and hamlet in the land was there, if not immediately, through some central union. We have had the honor of being present at more than one of these assemblies, and the impressions which we then received are abiding. Side by side with cardinals, bishops, princes, noblemen, and the most learned of professors sat mechanics, carpenters, shoemakers, and blacksmiths—not as in the act of worship, in which the presence of the Most High God dwarfs our universal human littlenesses to the dead-level of an equal insignificance, but in active thought and co-operation for the furtherance of definite religious and social ends. The brotherhood of the race was there, an accomplished fact, and one felt the breathing as of a divine Spirit compared with whose irresistible force great statesmen and mighty armies are weak as the puppets of a child's show.

We have not the space to describe more minutely the ends, aims, and workings of the numberless Catholic associations of Germany ; but we must express our deep conviction that no study could be more replete with lessons of practical wisdom for the Catholics of the United States. Organization is precisely what we most lack. Our priests are laborious, our people are devoted, but we have not even an organized Catholic public opinion—nay, no organ to serve as its channel, and make itself heard of the whole country. Many seem to think that the very question of the necessity of Catholic education is still an open one for us; and this is not surprising, since we have no system of Catholic education. Catholic schools, indeed, in considerable number, there are, but the discipline, plan of studies, and even the religious instruction, are left to be determined by the fancy or whims of individuals. The great need of the church in this country is the organization of priests and people for the promotion of Catholic interests. Through this we will learn to know one another; our views will be enlarged, our sympathies deepened, and the truth will dawn upon us that, if we

wish to be true to the great mission which God
has given us, the time has come when American
Catholics must take up works which do not spe-
cially concern any one diocese more than another,
but whose significance will be as wide as the nation's life.

PRUSSIA AND THE CHURCH.

III.

E have already alluded to that feature in the recent ecclesiastical legislation of Prussia which gives to the people the right to choose their pastors, and we have also seen how nobly the Catholics of Germany have thwarted this unholy attempt to create dissension and discord in the church. When it could no longer be doubted that the German bishops were immovable in their allegiance to the pope, Prussia sought, by holding out every possible inducement to apostasy, to create disunion between the priests and the bishops; but in this, too, she met with signal defeat. Nothing, therefore, remained to be done but to devise measures whereby the administration of ecclesiastical affairs would be placed exclusively in the hands of the laity; since the breaking of the bonds which unite church and state would not have as a result that weakening of ecclesiastical power which is so ardently desired. This Professor Friedberg, in his *German Empire and the Catholic Church*, expressly states in the following words :

"If the government were to adhere to the plan of a total separation of church and state, what

21

would be the consequence? Would the bishops lose their authority because the state no longer recognized it? Would the parochial system be broken up if unsupported by the state? In a word, would the church lose any of her power? It would argue an absolute want of perception and a total ignorance of Catholic history to affirm that she would. The stream which for centuries has flowed in its own channel does not run dry because its course is obstructed. It only overflows and floods the country. To continue the metaphor, we must first seek with all care to draw off the waters, and to lead them into pools and reservoirs, where what remains will readily evaporate."

The Protestants of Prussia are opposed to the separation of church and state, because they are well aware that in the present condition of religious opinion in Germany the rationalists and socialists would at once get control of most of the parishes of the Evangelical church, if it were deprived of the support of the government; and, on the other hand, both they and the infidels are persuaded that the Catholic Church is quite able to maintain herself, and even to wax strong, without any help from the temporal power.

"One thing," says the *Edinburgh Review*, "the state is quite at liberty to do. The state is not bound to pay or maintain churches or sects which it does not approve. Indeed, if these conditions are annexed to the acceptance of state payment, the church herself would do well to reject the terms. But will Prince Bismarck withdraw the stipend and set the church free? Nothing of the kind. There is no freedom of religious orders or communities in Prussia. The whole spirit of these laws is to make every form of religious belief and organization as subservient to the state as a Prussian recruit is to the rattan of a corporal. That we abhor and denounce as an intolerable oppression ; and it is only by the strangest perversion of judgment that any Englishman can have imagined that the cause of true religious liberty was identical with the policy of Prince Bismarck." *

To consent to a separation of church and state would be a recognition of the independent existence of the church, which Prussia holds to be contrary to the true theory of the constitution of human society in relation to government and religion. This theory is that man exists for the state, to which he owes his supreme and undivided allegiance ; whose duty it is to train and govern him for its own service alike in peace and war. All the interests of society, therefore, material, political, educational, and religious, must be subjected to the state, independently of which no organization of any kind ought to be permitted to exist. And in fact the whole spirit of the recent ecclesiastical legislation of Prussia is in perfect consonance with this theory. The Falk Laws deny to the church the right to educate her priests, to decide as to their fitness for the care of souls, to appoint them to or remove them from office ; in a word, the right to administer her own affairs,

* April, 1874, p. 195.

and consequently to exist at all as an organization separate from the state.

It can hardly surprise us that the attempt should have been made to prove that this is in accordance with the teachings of the Bible.

" The New Testament," says the *British Quarterly*, " requires that the Christian shall be a loyal subject of the government under which he lives. ' Let every soul be subject unto the higher powers. For there is no power but of God; the powers that be are ordained of God : whosoever therefore resisteth the power, resisteth the ordinance of God.' " *

After quoting several texts from the Epistles of St. Paul, of the same general import, the writer in the *British Quarterly* continues :

" Now, it is impossible to find in the New Testament any injunctions of obedience to organized ecclesiastical power, like those here given of obedience to the civil government. It is not ecclesiastical authority, nor a corporate ecclesiastical institution, but the personal God, and the individual conscience in its direct personal relations with God, which is set over against an unrighteous demand of the civil authority in the crucial motto of Peter, ' We ought to obey God rather than men,' and in the teaching of Christ, ' Render unto Cæsar the things which are Cæsar's, and unto God the things which are God's.' Of conscience as an ecclesiastical corporation, or of conscience as an imputed or vicarious faculty, determined and exercised by one

* Romans xiii. 1, 2.

for another, the ethics of the New Testament have no knowledge." *

It is hard to realize the ignorance or the bad faith of a man who is capable of making such statements as these. Let us take the last words of the gospel of St. Matthew : "And Jesus coming, spoke to them, saying : All power is given to me in heaven and in earth. Going, therefore, teach ye all nations, . . . teaching them to observe all things whatsoever I have commanded you ; and, behold, I am with you all days, even to the consummation of the world." Here surely is an organized body of men, receiving from Christ himself the divine command to teach all the nations of the earth their religious faith and duties, which necessarily carries with it the right to exact obedience. But, lest there be any room for doubt, let us hear Christ himself: "He that heareth you, heareth me : and he that despiseth you, despiseth me. And he that despiseth me, despiseth him that sent me." †

Again : "And if he will not hear the church, let him be to thee as the heathen and the publican. Amen I say to you, whatsoever you shall bind upon earth, shall be bound also in heaven : and whatsoever you shall loose upon earth, shall be loosed also in heaven." ‡

When Peter and John were brought into court and "charged not to speak at all, nor teach in the name of Jesus," they should have submitted at

---

* The *British Quarterly*, January, 1875, p. 17.
† Luke x. 16.　　‡ Matthew xviii. 17, 18.

once, upon the theory that the state has the right
to exact supreme and undivided allegiance ; but
they appealed to their divine commission, just as
the bishops of Germany do to-day, and answered,
" We cannot but speak the things which we have
seen and heard." *

And in the council at Jerusalem, " an ecclesiastical corporation " surely, the apostles say : " For
it hath seemed good to the Holy Ghost, and to
us, to lay no further burden upon you than these
necessary things " ; † plainly indicating and using
their right to impose commands and exact obedience.
But enough of this. The persecutors of the church
to-day are not at all concerned about the teachings
of the New Testament. The attempt, however, to
make it appear that only Catholics protest against
the doctrine of absolute and undivided allegiance
to the state is wholly unjustifiable. There is no
Protestant sect in England or the United States
which would submit to the intervention of the
government in its spiritual life and internal discipline. Would the Methodists, or the Baptists, or
the Presbyterians permit the state to decide what
kind of education their ministers are to receive, or
to determine whether they are capable of properly
discharging their spiritual duties, or to keep in
office by force those whom the church had cast off?
They would go out to pray on the hillside and by
the river-banks rather than submit to such tyranny.

Is not the right of revolution, which in our day,
especially outside of the Catholic Church, is held

* Acts iv 20.   † Acts xv. 28.

to be divine, based upon the principle of divided allegiance? Practically it is impossible to distinguish between loyalty to the government and loyalty to the state ; and no man in this age thinks of questioning the right of rebellion against a tyrannical government. This divided allegiance marks the radical difference between Christian and pagan civilization. Before Christ there was no divided allegiance, because the individual was absorbed by the state, and nothing could have wrested mankind from this bondage but a great spiritual organization such as the Catholic Church ; and this, we believe, is generally admitted by our adversaries. They fail to perceive, however, that there is no other institution than the Catholic Church which has the power to prevent the state from again absorbing the individual and destroying all civil and political liberty. If the church could be broken up into national establishments, and the entire control of education handed over to the state, the bringing all men to the servile temper which characterizes the Russians and Protestant Prussians would be only a question of time. Many will be inclined to hold that the general freedom, and even license, of thought of our time would be a sufficient protection against any such danger.

A little reflection, however, will suffice to dispel this illusion. No number of individuals, unless they are organized, can successfully oppose tyranny ; and mere speculations or opinions as to the abstract right of resistance cannot stop the march of the state toward absolutism. The most despotic states have often encouraged the most unbounded freedom of thought, and we need not go beyond Prussia for an example. In no country in the world has there been more of what is called free-thinking, nor has any government been more tolerant of wild theories and extravagant speculations ; and yet the free-thinkers and *illuminati* have done nothing to promote the growth of free institutions or to encourage civil or religious liberty. They are without unity or organization or programme. Many of them to-day are the strongest supporters of Bismarckian despotism. Even in 1848 they succeeded only in getting up a mob and evaporated in wild talk.

The divine right of resistance to tyranny would have no sanction or efficacy if it were not kept living in the hearts of men by supernatural religion.

This is thoroughly understood by the advocates of absolutism, who do not trouble themselves about doctrines of any kind, except when they are upheld by organizations, and for this reason all their efforts are directed to the destruction of the organic unity of the church. Had Prince Bismarck succeeded in his attempt to get the Catholic congregations which have been deprived of their priests to elect pastors for themselves, there would have been but another step to open schism, which would have inevitably resulted in favor of Old Catholicism. But, as we have seen, out of more than a hundred parishes, not one has lent itself to the iniquitous designs of the enemies of the church.

Another striking example of the perfect unanimity of thought and action which in Prussia exists between priests and people was given last year when the so-called State-Catholics tried to get up a protest against the encyclical letter of the Pope, in which he declared that the May Laws were not binding upon the consciences of Catholics. All the liberal papers of Germany were loud in praise of this project, which presented the fairest opportunity to Catholic government officials to curry favor by showing their acceptance of the Falk laws; and yet, in spite of every effort that was made, only about a thousand signatures were obtained, most of which were found outside of the eight millions of Prussian Catholics.

Mr. Gladstone, in his article on the " Speeches of Pope Pius IX.,"* says of the Catholic clergy that they " are more and more an army, a police, a caste; further and further from the Christian Commons, but nearer to one another and in closer subservience to the pope." However near the Catholic clergy may be to one another, it certainly shows a great lack of power to see things as they are to maintain that they are losing the hold which more than any other class of men they have always had on the hearts of the people. The persecution in Germany has shown there that inseparable union of priest and people which is to-day as universal as the life of the church. Had there existed any seed of discord, it

* The *London Quarterly Review*, January, 1875, p. 160.

certainly would have sprung up and flourished in Prussia during the last four or five years.

What circumstances could have been more favorable to such development than those created by the Old Catholics in league with Bismarck? The unprecedented victories over Austria and France had set all Germany wild with enthusiasm. " Deutschland über alles, über alles in der Welt," was the refrain of every song. On the other hand, many Catholics, especially in Germany, had been prejudiced and somewhat soured by the false interpretations which were everywhere put on the dogma of papal infallibility. Just at this moment Dr. Döllinger, whose reputation was greater than that of any other German theologian, announced his separation from the church, and at once there gathered around him a party of dissatisfied or suspended priests and rationalistic laymen. Reinkens was made bishop, and the Emperor of Germany publicly prayed that the "certainly correct conviction of the *Hochwürdiger Herr Bischof* might win ground more and more." Fortune smiled upon the new religion and everything seemed to promise it the brightest future. What has been the result? In a population of eight millions of Catholics this sect, with the aid of the state, German enthusiasm, and the whole liberal press, has been able to gather only about six thousand adherents; and they are without zeal, without doctrinal or moral unity, having as yet not even dared to define their position towards the Pope. Dr. Döllinger himself has lost interest in the movement, and its most sanguine friends have yielded to despondency. Old Catholicism was, in fact, impossible from the beginning. But two roads open before those who to-day go forth from the fold of the church; the one leads to the Babel and decomposition of Protestant sectarianism, the other to the unbelief of scientific naturalism.

To declare that Christianity is lying disjointed, in shattered fragments, and yet to pretend that human hands, with paste and glue, out of these broken pieces can remake the heavenly vase once filled with God's spirit of faith, hope, and love, is an idle fancy. Into this patchwork no divine life will come; men will not believe in it, nor will it inspire enthusiasm or the heroic courage of martyrdom. Therefore they who leave the church, their native soil, have indeed all the world before them, and yet no place where they can find rest for their souls.

What the religious policy of the Prussian Liberals is, Herr von Kirchmann, to whom in a previous article we introduced our readers, informs us in the following words:

" The majority of the Liberal representatives are highly-educated men who have fallen out with the Christian churches, because they no longer accept their creed, and therefore hold as a principle that freedom of conscience for the individual is abundantly sufficient to satisfy the religious wants of the people. At best, they would consent to the existence of congregations; any organization beyond this they consider not only unnecessary but hurtful."

This, then, is the Liberal programme: the individual shall have perfect freedom to believe, as he pleases, in God or the devil; but there shall be no ecclesiastical organization, unless a kind of congregationalism, which, having neither unity nor strength, can be easily rendered harmless by being placed under police supervision. These men of culture, as Herr von Kirchmann says, have fallen out with all the churches; and they are liberal enough to be willing to do everything in their power to make it impossible that any of them shall exist at all, since without organic unity of some kind there can be no church, as there can be no state.

But let us hear what Herr von Kirchmann has to remark upon this subject.

" This view," he says, " may satisfy those who have reached the high degree of culture of the Liberals; but those who take it, utterly ignore the religious wants of the middle and lower classes, and fail to perceive the yearning, inseparable from all religious feeling, for association with persons of like sentiments, in order, through public wor-hip, to obtain the strength and contentment after 'hich this fundamental craving of the human heart ngs."

To the existence of this feeling, and its yearn-
· for the largest possible association, the history
ll Christian peoples, down even to the present
bears witness; for this reason nowhere have
been satisfied with the freedom of the indi-
but have ever demanded a church with

acknowledged rights and the privilege of free intercommunion.

" To the dangers which would threaten society if religious associations should be broken up, and faith left to the whim of individuals, these highly-cultivated men give no heed, because they do not themselves feel the need of such support; but they forget that their security, the very possibility, indeed, of reaching the point at which they stand, rests upon the power of the church over the masses ; and should they destroy this by allowing the congregations to break up into atoms, leaving the Christian creed to be fashioned by passion and ever-varying interests, according to the fancy of each and every one, nothing would remain but the brute force of the state, which, without the aid of the internal dispositions of the people, cannot save society from complete dissolution." *

Herr von Kirchmann, then, adds his testimony to that of many other observers who, though they do not believe in the divine origin and truth of the Christian religion, yet hold that its acceptance by the masses as a system of belief, received on the authority of a church, is essential to the preservation and permanence of our civilization. This is a subject to which we Americans might with great profit give our thoughts.

As Emerson, who is probably our most characteristic thinker, has declared that he would write over the portal of the Temple of Philosophy WHIM, American Protestantism seems more and

* *Der Culturkampf,* § 28, 29.

more inclined to accept this as the only satisfactory, or indeed possible, shibboleth in religion. The multiplication of sects holding conflicting creeds, while it has weakened faith in all religious doctrines, has helped on the natural tendency of Protestantism to throw men back upon their own feelings or fancies for their faith. This, of course, results in the breaking up even of congregations into atoms of individualism, and will, if not counteracted, necessarily destroy our character as a Christian people ; and for us it is needless to say Christianity is the only possible religion.

Our statesmen—politicians may be the more proper word—though not irreligious, lack grasp of mind and depth of view, else they could not fail to perceive, however little they may sympathize with the doctrines or what they conceive to be the social tendencies of the Catholic Church, that just such a strong and conservative Christian organism as she is, is for us an indispensable political requirement. That none of the leading minds of the country should have taken this view is a sad evidence of want of intellectual power or of moral courage. The most that any of them feel authorized in saying in our favor is that a country which tolerates free-love, Mormonism, and the joss-house of the Chinaman ought not, if consistency be a virtue, to persecute Catholics. In spite of appearances which mislead superficial observers, we are the most secular people in the world. No other people is so ready to sacrifice religious to material interests ; no other people has

ever to an equal extent banished all religious instruction from its national education ; no other
people has ever taken such a worldly view of its
religion. The supernatural in religion is lost sight
of by us, and we value it chiefly for its social and
æsthetic power. The popular creed is that religion is something which favors republicanism, pro-
motes the exploitation of the material resources
of the globe, softens manners, and makes life
comfortable.

The proposition to tax church property shows
that a large portion of the American people have
ceased to believe in religion as a moral and social
power. A church is like a bank or theatre or coal-
mine—something which concerns only those who
have stock in it, and has nothing whatever to do
with the public welfare. The school-house occupies quite other ground. The country is interested in having all its citizens intelligent ; this is for
the general good ; but whether they believe in God
or the soul is a matter of profound indifference,
unless, possibly, to themselves, since this can in
no way affect the progress or civilization of the
American people. This is evidently the only possible philosophy for those who would tax church
property. The popular contempt for theology encouraged by nearly all Protestant ministers is another evidence of the tendency to religious disintegration. There is but little danger that any
church will ever get a controlling influence in the
national life of this country ; our peril lies in the
opposite direction ; and that so few of those who

think should see this is to us the saddest sign of the times; but those who do recognize it cannot help knowing that the Catholic Church is the strongest bulwark against this flood-tide.

The social dangers of an open persecution of the Catholic Church are most clearly seen in Prussia to-day. Since the German chancellor entered upon his present course of violence five bishops and fifteen thousand priests have been imprisoned or fined, and about the same number of laymen have suffered for daring to speak unfavorably of these proceedings. Never before, probably, have the police been so generally or constantly employed in arresting men who are loved and venerated by the people, and whose only crime is fidelity to conscience. The inevitable consequence of this is that the officers of the government come to be looked upon, not as the ministers of justice, but as the agents of tyranny and oppression, which must, of course, weaken respect for authority. These coercive measures, from the nature of things, tend only to confirm the Catholics in their conscientious convictions, and the government is thereby instigated to harsher methods of dealing with this passive resistance. The number of confessors of the faith increases, the enthusiasm and devotion of the people are heightened, and it becomes an honor and a glory to be made a victim of tyranny. The feeling of disgrace which is attached to the penalties for violation of law is more efficacious in repressing crime than the suffering which is inflicted; but this feeling is destroyed, or

rather changed, into one of an opposite character
in the minds of the people when they behold their
venerated bishops and much-loved priests dragged
to prison for saying Mass or administering the sacraments. No amount of reasoning, no refinement
of logic, can ever convince them that there can be
anything criminal in the performance of these sacred functions. In this way the ignominy which
in the public mind follows conviction for crime is
wiped away, and the sacredness of the law itself
endangered.

This alone is sufficient to show how blind and
thoughtless Prince Bismarck has been in making
war upon the Catholic Church just at the moment
when wise counsels would have led him to seek to
add the strength of reverence and respect to the
enthusiasm with which the creation of the new
empire had been hailed. The spoilt child of success, wounded pride made him mad. How ser-
viceable he might have found the moral support
of the Catholic clergy Herr von Kirchmann has
informed him.

" I myself," he says, " from 1849 to 1866, with
the exception of some intervals, lived in Upper
Silesia, a wholly Catholic province, and, as the
president of the Criminal Senate of a Court of
Appeals, had the fullest opportunity to study the
moral and religious state of the people, which in
nothing is so truly seen as in those circumstances
out of which spring offences against the law. Now,
although this province of more than a million of
men was thoroughly Catholic and entirely in the

hands of the clergy; although the school system was still very imperfect, and the population, with the exception of the land-owners and the inhabitants of the large cities, not speaking the German language, was thereby deprived of culture and of intercourse with the German provinces, yet can I unhesitatingly affirm that the moral condition of the people was in no way worse than in Saxony or the Margravate where formerly I held similar official positions. The number of crimes was rather less, the security of person and of property greater, and the relations between the different classes of society far more peaceable and friendly than in the provinces to which I have just made allusion. The socage and heavy taxes pressed hard upon the peasantry; nevertheless in 1848 insurrections against the landlords were not more frequent here than elsewhere. It was unquestionably the powerful influence of the clergy which, in spite of so many obstacles, gave to the people their moral character, and produced the general contentment and obedience which reflected the greatest honor upon the whole population. The vice of drunkenness, through the agency of temperance societies established solely by the priests, had been in an almost marvellous manner rooted out from among the people, and the general welfare made manifest progress. By means of my official and political position I had the opportunity to make the acquaintance of a large number of the pastors and curates, and still to-day I recall with pleasure my intercourse with these men, for the most part cultivated, but above all distinguished by their thorough gentleness of character. They were firm in maintaining the rights of their church, they were filled with the excellence of their mission, but they never thought of thwarting the civil authorities; on the contrary, they found in the clergy a great and efficacious support, so that this province needed fewer protective and executive officials than others." *

No enlightened and fair government has anything to fear from the influence of men who are as firm in upholding the authority of the state as they are in asserting their own liberty of conscience; who will neither do wrong nor tamely submit to it. If, in the social, religious, and political crisis through which the nations of Christendom are passing, sound reason is ultimately to prevail and civilization is to be preserved, the necessity of an institution like the Catholic Church will come to be recognized by all who are capable of serious thought. The divided allegiance, the maintenance of the supremacy of conscience, is essential to the preservation of the principle of authority in society. If it were possible to nationalize religion by placing all churches under state control, the authority of the state would necessarily become that of brute force, and would in consequence be deprived of its sacredness. The respect of Christian nations for the civil power is a religious sentiment; and if the church could cease to be, there would be a radical revolution in the attitude of the people toward the

* *Culturkampf*, pp. 33, 34.

state. In Europe even now, in consequence of the progress of unbelief, respect for authority and the duty of obedience has been so far destroyed in the minds and hearts of the masses that government is possible only with the support of immense standing armies, which help on the social dissolution ; and with us things would be in a still worse condition, were it not that the vast undeveloped resources of the country draw off the energies which else would be fatal to public order. Our strength and security are rather in our physical surroundings than in our moral character. Our greatest moral force, during the century of our existence, has been the universal veneration of the people for the Constitution, which was regarded with a kind of religious reverence ; but this element of strength is fast wasting away and will not pass over as a vital power into the second century of our life. The criticisms, the amendments, the patchings, which the Constitution has been made to suffer, have, more than civil strife, debased it to the common level of profane parchments and robbed it of the consecration which it had received in the hearts of the people. The change which has taken place, though it have something of the nature of growth and development, is yet, unquestionably, more a breaking down and dissevering. The Catholic Church, by the reverence which she inspires for institutions, is, and in the future will be yet more, the powerful ally of those who will stand by the Constitution as our fathers made it.

Our statesmen, we know, are in the habit of

looking elsewhere for the means which are to give permanence to our free institutions. The theory now most in favor is that universal education is the surest safeguard of liberty, and it is upon this more than upon anything else that we, as a people, rely for the perpetuity of our form of government. This hope, we cannot but think, is based upon an erroneous opinion of the necessary tendency of intellectual culture ; which is to increase the spirit of criticism, and consequently, by dissatisfying the mind with what is, to direct it continually to new experiments, with the hope of finding something better. Now, though this may be well enough in the realms of speculation, and may be a great help to the progress of science, it most assuredly does not tend either to beget or to foster reverence for existing institutions of any kind ; and this same mental habit which has already made American Protestantism so fragmentary and contradictory will beyond doubt weaken and, unless counteracted, destroy the unity of our political life. This is a question which does not concern us alone ; with it is bound up the future of the human race. If the American experiment of government by the people fails, all hope of such government perishes. If we allow our personal prejudices to warp our judgment in a matter so catholic and all important, no further evidence of our unfitness for the great mission which God seems to have assigned us is needed. Unfortunately, we are at the mercy of politicians for whom all other questions than the present success of party have no interest, and who

therefore flatter the passions of the people instead
of seeking to enlighten them; and the insane hatred and fear of the church which the Protestant
masses have inherited from the Old World prevents
them from seeing what a source of strength and
bond of union is her strong and firmly-knit organism in a social state like ours, in which there are
so many elements of dissolution and disintegration.

Herr von Kirchmann, though, as we have seen,
not a Catholic nor a Christian, is yet too profound
a statesman not to recognize the supreme social
importance of the church to the modern world.

" Human society," he says, " cannot do without
the principle of authority, of obedience, of respect
for law, any more than it can do without the principle of individual freedom; and now that the
family has been shoved into the background, there
remains to uphold this principle of authority only
one great institution, and that is the Christian
churches, and, above all, the Catholic Church.

" The Reformation has so filled the Evangelical
Church with the principle of self-examination and
self-determination that she cannot at all take upon
herself the mission of protectress of authority, of
respect for law, as law; which is essential to modern society. She is also too far removed from
the laity, and lacks those special institutions which
would enable her energetically to uphold this
principle.

" The same is true of all reform parties within
the church, and must be applied to the Old
Catholics, should they succeed in acquiring any

importance. The Roman Catholic Church alone must be considered the true mother of respect for authority. She does not permit the individual to decide in matters of faith and discipline; and she most perfectly realizes the essence of religion, which cannot proceed from the individual, but must have its source in the commandments of God. In the bishops, in the councils, in the pope, the individual finds authorities who announce to him religious truth, and by the administration of the sacraments bring him nearer to God. Changes in faith and worship which, with the progress of science and of general culture, become necessary, are here withdrawn from the disputes of the learned and the criticism of individuals; in the councils and in their head, the pope, an institution is found by which modifications may be permitted without shaking faith in the teachings of the church.

" In the position of the priest toward the laity this relation of the individual to the church becomes most intimate, and numerous special ordinances cultivate the spirit of obedience and respect for the commands of ecclesiastical superiors, while they also serve the ends of Christian charity and benevolence. It ought not, indeed, to be denied that this repression of individual self-determination and this fostering of obedience may be carried too far, and to some extent has, in the Catholic Church, been exaggerated, as in civil society the cultivation of individual freedom and the repression of authority have produced an opposite excess; but precisely through the interaction of these extremes

will the true mean be obtained; and therefore
ought the state to seek in the Catholic Church
that powerful institution which alone, by virtue
of her whole organization, is able to ward off the
dangers which threaten society from the exaggeration of the principle of individual freedom. But
to do this the church must be left in the possession of her constitution as it has hitherto existed,
and the state, consequently, should not interfere
with her external power any further than its own
existence demands. In this respect the principle
of individual freedom which pervades all modern
life is so powerful an auxiliary of the state that no
fear of the influence of the church need be felt,
of which too much is far less dangerous to society
than too little.

"These are considerations, indeed, which are
not in harmony with the programme of modern
liberalism, and will therefore have but little weight
with those who swim with the current of the time;
nevertheless, if we look around us, we perceive
many evidences of the instinctive feeling of human
society that in the Catholic Church may be found
a protection for the harmony of social life which
now no longer exists elsewhere. Only in this way
can we explain the rapid growth of the Catholic
Church in her strictly hierarchical constitution in
America, and the increasing Catholic movement
in England, together with the efforts of the Established Church to draw nearer to the Catholic;
and this tendency would be far more pronounced
had it not to contend against historical reminis-

cences, which in England are more vivid than elsewhere. Similar reasons influence the government of France to seek rather to strengthen than to weaken the power of the church ; and in this matter the unbelieving Thiers has not acted otherwise than the religious MacMahon.

" After the principle of authority had been shaken by revolutions and an unhappy war in France more than in any other country, the people knew not where to seek help, except in the fostering of religion and the support of the Catholic Church. Like grounds prevent Italy and Austria from coming to an open rupture with the church ; they prefer to yield somewhat in the execution of the laws rather than suffer themselves to be deprived of her indispensable aid. Similar tendencies exist in the other German governments, and also among the rich and powerful families of Germany and Prussia. Everywhere, even where these families are not adherents of the Catholic faith, they feel that this church is a fortress against the anarchy of individual freedom, which should be defended and not destroyed. The members of these families are not blind to the defects of the church; but they know that in the present age these are the least to be feared, while her power against the self-exaltation of the individual is indispensable to modern society. It is altogether a mistake to attribute this bearing of the wealthy classes of all civilized nations toward the church to selfish motives or to the cunning of priests; these motives may, as in all great things, slip in in isolated cases ; but this whole

23

movement in Europe and America springs from deeper causes—from causes which lie at the very root of our common nature, which can neither suffer the loss of freedom nor yet do without order and authority.

"About every ten years we are assured that if only this or that point is reached, the Catholic Church will of herself fall to pieces. Never has the attempt to bring about this consummation been made with more spirit and energy than in the literature and political constitutions of the last century ; and yet this church lives still in our day, and what she has lost in temporal sovereignty is doubly and trebly made up to her in the growing number of her children and the gradually-increasing insight into the significance of her mission for human society.

"For this reason the present conflict with the church in Prussia ought not to be pushed so far as to bring her power as low as the state has brought that of the Evangelical Church. If the Catholic Church is to fulfil the great social mission which we have just described, and which consists essentially in her maintaining an equilibrium between freedom and obedience, which is indispensable to society and the state, her external power and internal organization must not be interfered with in a way to render the accomplishment of this exalted mission impossible." *

Herr Joerg, the editor of one of the first reviews of Germany, has said that Prince Bismarck

* *Culturkampf,* pp. 44-47.

has done more to strengthen and make popular the Catholic cause in the empire than the two hundred Jesuits whom he has exiled could have done in half a century. This, we believe, is coming to be generally recognized. The war on the church was begun with loud boastings. Men of high position declared that in two years not a Catholic would be left in Germany. The prince chancellor disdained to treat with the Pope or the bishops, and defiantly entered upon his course of draconic legislation to compel to his stubborn will the consciences of eight millions of Prussian subjects. He is not able to conceal his disappointment. With glory enough to satisfy the most ambitious he could not rest content, but must court defeat. All his hopes have fallen to the ground. The Old Catholics who were to have been his most powerful allies have sunk into the oblivion of contempt; the priests whom he expected to throw off the authority of their bishops have not been found; the uprising of the laity against their pastors has not taken place ; the bishop who was to have put himself at the head of a German Catholic Church has not appeared; the Falk laws have not served the purpose for which they were enacted, nor have the numerous supplementary bills met with better success. He has indeed made his victims personally most uncomfortable ; bishops and priests he has cast into dungeons, monks and nuns he has driven forth from their homes and their country to beg the bread of exile; laymen he has sent to jail for speaking and writing the truth; but with

all this he has not advanced one step towards
the end he aims at.   He has not made a breach in
the serried Catholic phalanx.   His legislation has
nearly doubled the number of Catholic representatives in the parliament ; it has given new life
and wider influence to the Catholic press ; it
has welded the union of bishops, priests, and people, and bound all closer to the Pope.   From their
dungeons the bishops and priests come forth and
are received in triumph like conquering heroes ;
imprisonments and fines of Catholic editors serve
only to increase the circulation of their journals.
In the meantime the radicals and revolutionists are
gaining strength, crime is becoming more common,
and the laws aimed at the church are beginning to
tell upon the feebler organizations of Protestantism.   Since the law on civil marriage has been
passed comparatively few contract matrimony in
the presence of Protestant ministers ; great numbers refuse to have their children baptized or to
have the preachers assist at the burial of the dead.
The government has become alarmed, and quite
recently circulars have been sent to the officials
charged with carrying out the law on civil marriage, in which they are instructed to inform the
contracting parties that the law does not abrogate
the hitherto existing regulation concerning ecclesiastical marriage, and that they are still bound to
present themselves before the clergyman and to
have their children baptized as formerly.   The
service of the police, we need scarcely say, is not
required to induce the Catholics to seek the bless-

ing of the church upon their marriage contracts or
to have their children baptized.

The result of all this is that many wise and large-
minded men, like Von Hoffmann, Von Gerlach,
and Von Kirchmann, have lost all sympathy with
the policy of Bismarck towards the Catholic
Church, as well as confidence in its success. They
now thoroughly understand that, were it possible
to destroy the church, this would be an irrepara-
ble misfortune for the Fatherland. The state needs
the church more than the church the state. She
can live with Hottentots and Esquimaux, but without her neither liberty nor culture can be permanent. It must also be humiliating to Prince
Bismarck to see with what little success those who
have sought to ape him have met. Mr. Gladstone,
from faith in the chancellor, thought to bolster up
a falling party by "expostulating" with the Pope,
and he has succeeded only in finding himself in
the company of Newdegate and Whalley. President Grant has been made to believe that the Pope
is such a monstrous man that by means of him
even a third term might become possible ; and he
will retire to the obscurity of private life with the
stigma of having sought to stir up religious strife
for the furtherance of his own private interest.

GERMAN JOURNALISM.*

HE universal hymn of journalistic praise, sung throughout the civilized world with hardly a discordant note, is of itself no mean evidence of the power of the press. " Great is journalism," says Carlyle. " Is not every able editor a ruler of the world, being a persuader of it?" From France M. Thiers declares that the liberty of the press is theoretically and practically the most necessary of all; and was it not our own Jefferson who solemnly affirmed that he would rather live in a country with newspapers and without a government than in a country with a government but without newspapers? And did not Napoleon himself stand in greater awe of a newspaper than of a hundred thousand bayonets? "Give me but the liberty of the press," cried Sheridan, " and I will give to the minister a venal House of Peers; I will give him a corrupt and servile House of Commons; I will give him the full sway of the patronage of office; I will give him the whole host of ministerial influence; I will give him all the power that place can confer upon him to

* Die deutsche Zeitschriften und die Entstehung der öffentlichen Meinung. Ein Beitrag zur Geschichte des Zeitungswesens. Von Heinrich Wuttke.—The German newspapers and the origin of public opinion : a contribution to the history of journalism. Leipzig; 1875.

purchase up submission and overcome resistance ; and yet, armed with the liberty of the press, I will go forth to meet him undismayed ; I will attack the mighty fabric he has reared with that mightier engine ; I will shake down from its height corruption and bury it amidst the ruins of the abuses it was meant to shelter."

But we do not propose to treat our readers to a dissertation written in the style of him who declared that, were the starry heavens deficient of one constellation, the vacuum could not be better supplied than by the introduction of a printing-press. We fully recognize, however, the very great power of the press which controls public opinion, and indeed often makes it. Nothing is unimportant which throws light upon the constitution and workings of this " Fourth Estate," into whose hands the destinies of modern nations and civilization seem to have been delivered ; and it is for this reason that we take pleasure in bringing to the notice of the American public the work of Professor Wuttke on *German Journalism and the Origin of Public Opinion.*

It would be difficult to find a more curious or instructive book. For years connected with the press, a leader of the " great German party," and the author of several valuable historical and philosophical works, Herr Wuttke has brought to his present task the thoroughgoing and painstaking conscientiousness of a German professor. He is wholly in earnest ; neither smiles nor laughs ; does not even stop to give smoothness and polish to his phrase,

but without remorse or fear invades the editorial
sanctum, and pours upon its most hidden mysteries
the profane light ; holds them up before vulgar
eyes, and leaves not the suspicion of a doubt but
that he is resolved to tell all he knows.   His courage no one can deny.   The enterprise to which he
has devoted himself was full of perils, none of which
were hidden from him.

German newspapers before the revolution of 1848
were chiefly of a literary character.   Their columns
were filled with criticisms of books, philosophical
and theological discussions, æsthetic treatises, accounts of travel, entertaining stories, and theatrical
notices.   Scarcely any attention was paid to events
of the day, and least of all to those of a political
character.   The explanation of this anomaly is
simple.   The governments of Germany exercised a
rigorous censorship over the press, and allowed nothing to be published which might set people to
thinking about what their rulers were doing.   But
the storm of 1848 blew the pen from the hand of
the official censor, and opened the columns of the
newspaper to all kinds of political theories and discussions.   The governments were at sea, borne
helpless by the popular wave which had broken
them loose from their ancient moorings and was
carrying them they knew not whither.   Their official organs, with unlimited financial support from
the state, were powerless, because people refused to
read them whilst independent journals were within
their reach.   But this revolutionary outburst was
soon followed by a reaction, partly brought on by

its own excesses; and with the aid of the military the former governments were restored. . Restrictions were again placed upon the liberty of the press; but so universal had the political agitation been that to think of carrying through a policy of rigorous repression was manifestly out of the question. It became necessary, therefore, to devise some expedient by which the press might be controlled without being muzzled.

With this view Von Manteuffel, the Prussian minister, established in Berlin a "Central Bureau of the Press," which stood in intimate relations with the government and received from the "Secret Fund" a yearly support of from forty to fifty thousand thalers. With this money the pens of a crowd of needy scribes were bought, who for twenty or thirty thalers a month agreed to write articles in support of the views which the director of the Bureau should inspire. The next step was to make an opening for these articles in the columns of journals in different parts of the kingdom. This was not difficult, as the contributions were well written, by persons evidently thoroughly informed, and were offered at a nominal price, or even without pay. On the 9th of March, 1851, the director of the Bureau sent a circular to "those editors and publishers of the conservative party with whom he has not at present the honor of holding personal relations," in which he promised, with special reference to his connection with the Ministry of State, to send them from time to time communications concerning the real condition of political affairs, in order to furnish them indispensable materials for the successful prosecution of their labors. This assistance was to be given free of cost, and many editors were eager to avail themselves of it without inquiring with much care into its special significance. In this way the "Central Press-Bureau" wove a net-work of lines of communication over the whole kingdom, which, however, was carefully hidden from public view. It also kept up constant intercourse with the representatives of Prussia at the various European courts, which enabled it to give tone to public opinion on foreign affairs as well as on matters at home. Through the influence of the government, and by spending money, the Bureau gradually succeeded in introducing its agents into the offices of many newspapers, and occasionally in getting entire control of this or that journal. By this cunning policy the Prussian government was able to lead the unsuspecting public by the nose.

Whilst confiding readers throughout the land were receiving the views of their favorite journals as the honest expression of public opinion, these newspapers were in fact only the whispering-galleries of the Berlin ministry. The editors themselves were often ignorant of the fact that the pens of their co-laborers had been bought and sold. Even foreign journals, in England and France, did not escape the meshes of the "Press-Bureau," but were entrapped and made to do service for Prussia.

Another contrivance for working up public opinion was the "Lithographic Correspondence-Bureau," which is a French invention. This is an agency for the manufacture of correspondence from all parts of the world, at home and abroad, which is lithographed and sent to journals that are willing to pay for it ; and nearly all of them find this the cheapest and easiest method of keeping abreast of the times.

As the men who found these Bureaus are chiefly intent upon making money, and live, moreover, in salutary awe of the government, they generally find it advisable to place themselves at its disposition. The correspondence-agency of Havas-Büllier in Paris was Orleanistic under Louis Philippe, and Napoleonic under the Empire. In return it obtained the monopoly of "lithographic correspondence"; so that, during the reign of Louis Napoleon, France received its knowledge of the foreign world through the single channel of this Bureau, which was carefully supervised by the government. This was too excellent a device not to find ready acceptance in Berlin, and in the most natural way in the world the "Lithographic Correspondence-Bureau" was placed alongside the "Press-Bureau"; the journals which had already fallen under the influence of the latter yielded without resistance to the seductions of the new ally, and thus became to a still greater extent the tools of the government. In this way the "eunuchs of the court and press" were in position deliberately and with malice to falsify and pervert public opinion, which soon came to mean the utterances of the herd of venal scribes in Berlin who had sold themselves, body and soul, to the " Press-Bureau." One of the five sins which, according to Confucius, is unpardonable, is from under the mantle of truth to scatter broadcast lies which are hurtful to the people; and this is the charge which Professor Wuttke brings against the crowd of German newspaper-writers.

Telegraphy, which was first introduced into Germany in 1849, led to further improvements in the art of manipulating the press. The " Correspondence-Bureau " of Havas-Büllier became a telegraphic agency and furnished despatches free of charge to the Parisian journals, in order to prevent the starting of a rival business ; and when, notwithstanding, the *Agence Continentale* was organized, it was suppressed by Persigny, the Minister of State, who by this means was enabled to control the publication of telegrams in all the leading journals of France. In Italy the Stefani Agency, at Turin, rendered similar services to the government of Victor Emanuel ; sending out the most shameless falsehoods to the four corners of the earth, and carefully suppressing whatever the authorities wished to conceal from the public. These despatches were printed in the leading journals of Europe and America as coming from unsuspected sources, when they were in fact the " cooked " telegrams of the secret agents of Cavour and the Revolution.

In 1850 Reuter established his telegraphic Agency in Aix-la-Chapelle, but removed it in the following year to Berlin ; and a few months later, when the cable between Calais and Dover was laid, he

made London the central point of his operations.
In Berlin a similar business was opened by. Dr.
Wolf, a Jew. In 1855 he sold out to a number
of capitalists, who organized the *Continentale Tele-
grafenkompagnie*, and then entered into a combination with Reuter and Havas, through which they
controlled the telegraphic despatches furnished to
the press of all Europe. To have the latest news
was a journalistic necessity ; and yet to maintain
special agents in the great centres, and to pay the
high rates for sending special telegrams, would
have been too heavy a burden. Nothing remained, therefore, but to take the despatches of the
Agencies, which were now in league with one another.

In Prussia nearly all the telegraphic lines, most
of which were put up during the reaction after the
revolution of 1848, were in the hands of the government ; and this, of itself, was sufficient to place
the Agencies at its disposal. And in point of fact,
it is no secret that in Prussia there exists a censorship of the telegraph, and that the government de-
cides as to the despatches which the newspapers
shall receive. Whoever will take the trouble to
weigh this matter will see what a terrible instrument for the perversion of public opinion is thus
placed in the hands of the state. A despatch has
always in its favor the force of first impressions.
When, after days or weeks, explanations follow,
they are passed over, new events having already
preoccupied public attention. All the world reads
the telegram ; comparatively few pay any attention

to the later-coming corrections of inaccurate or false statements.

Prussia, then, through her " Central Press-Bureau," her " Correspondence-Bureau," and her " Telegram-Bureau," succeeded in getting control of the leading German journals, which, while keeping up the appearance of independence and honesty, were either in her pay or under the influence of her agents. Public opinion in Germany was at her mercy; so that, after she had made the most thorough preparations for the war of 1866, she found no difficulty in having it proclaimed throughout the Fatherland that Austria had been arming and was ready to fall upon her in order to rob her of Silesia. The newspapers even lent themselves, when the war had begun, to the publication of a spurious address to the army by Benedek, the Austrian leader, in which there was not one word of truth, but in which he was made to speak in a way that could not fail to arouse the indignation of the Prussian soldiers. This forged document was circulated by the press and read by the captains to their men as soon as they had entered Bohemia.

The creation of the new empire has not improved German journalism. The " Press-Bureau " has enlarged the circle of its activity, while the government has invented other means not less effective for controlling the newspapers. " We care not for public opinion," said a high official in Berlin some months ago; " for the entire press belongs to us." Prussia has German public opinion, in so far as it is allowed to find expression, in her keeping. After the war with Austria the annual secret fund of the "Press-Bureau" was increased to 70,000 thalers; but this is in reality a very inconsiderable portion of the money at its disposition. The incorporation of Hanover and Hesse with Prussia threw into the hands of the government very large resources. From George of Hanover King William exacted 19,000,000 thalers, and from the Prince Elector of Hesse property with an annual rental of 400,000 thalers. Both these sums were placed at the disposal of Bismarck by the Landtag, that he might use them to defeat the "intrigues" of the enemies of Prussia. It was on the occasion of this grant that Bismarck used the words which have given to the "Press-Bureau" fund a name which it can never lose. "I follow," he said, "malignant reptiles into their very holes, in order to watch their doings." The money which he received to carry on this dark underground business was appropriately designated by the Berlin wits the "Reptile-fund" (*Reptilienfond*). A vocabulary of slang has been invented to designate the hired scribes of the Bureau and their operations. Bismarck calls them "my swine-herds" (*meine Sauhirten*). To write for the "Press-Bureau" is to take mud-baths (*Schlammbäder nehmen*); and the writers themselves, who are classified as "officious," "high-officious," "half-officious," and "over-officious," are called "mud-bathers" (*Schlammbäder*), and they devour the "Reptile-fund." The instructions issued by the directors for the preparation of articles for the·different journals are styled "wash-tickets" (*Waschzettel*). The directors who are not immediately connected with the Bureau are known by the name of "Piper" (*Pfeifer*), which, in the jargon of Berlin, has a peculiar and by no means flattering signification.

As the buzzards fly to the carcass, so gathered the hungry German scribes around the "Reptile-fund"; but their pens were cheap and the "Press-Bureau" was able to feed a whole army of them, and yet have abundant means to devote to other methods for influencing public opinion. · Its machinations are, of course, conducted with the greatest secrecy. All manner of blinds are used. Its agents assume in their articles a style˜ of great independence, deal largely in loud and· captious epithets, occasionally even criticise this or that measure of the government, and ape the ways of honest and patriotic men. The "Central Press-Bureau" itself is pushed as far out of sight as possible; stalking-horses and scarecrows are put forward; and the institution is made to appear as only a myth. But the Cave of Æolus is in Berlin, and the winds which are let loose there blow to and fro, hither and yon, through all Germany, starting currents in other parts of the world. In this cave the old snake-worship of so many ages and peoples still exists, and the god is the "Reptile-fund." Out of this cavern are blown the double-leaded leaders which fall thick all over the land, and always, as if by magic, just in the right place. False reports eddy through the air; stubborn facts are pulled and bent and beaten until they get into the proper shape. The light which is permitted to fall upon them is managed as skilfully as in an art-gallery or a lady's drawing-room. With the aid of the " Reptile-fund " the " Press-Bureau " found little difficulty in extending its business of buying up journals, paying sometimes as high as a hundred thousand thalers for a single newspaper; and where this could not be done money was freely spent to start an opposition sheet. Whenever a journal was found to be growing weak, aid was proffered on condition that it should open its columns to the " Press-Bureau "; sometimes with the understanding that one of its agents should be placed in the editorial chair. So thoroughly has this system of bribery taken possession of Prussian journalism that the court decided (October, 1873), in a suit against the *Germania* newspaper, that to accuse an editor of being in the pay of the " Press-Bureau " is not a criminal offence, since it does not in the public estimation tend to lower his character.

Occasionally, in spite of the greatest care, the secrets of the Bureau are betrayed. Thus in February, 1874, a circular was sent to various journals, and amongst others to the *Neue Wormser-Zeitung*, with the offer to furnish from the capital, first, a tri-weekly original article on the political situation; second, original political and diplomatic advice from all the departments of the government, also three times a week; third, a short but exhaustive parliamentary report; fourth,

24

special correspondence from other capitals (written in Berlin); fifth, original accounts of foreign affairs, drawn from the special sources of the Bureau; and, sixth, a short daily, as well as a more lengthy weekly, exhibit of the Berlin Bourse. For these services nothing was demanded; but, that the thing might not appear too bald, it was stated that the editor should fix his own price. Now, it so happened that when this circular was received by the *Neue Wormser-Zeitung* that paper was in the hands of Herr Westerburg, a Social Democrat, who straightway took the public into his confidence.

The newly-acquired provinces of Prussia were a favorite field for the operations of the Berlin Bureau. General Manteuffel, in 1866, suppressed the *Schleswig-Holsteinische Zeitung*, and handed the country over to the reptile-press. In Alsace and Lorraine also journals were suppressed, and others established, by the government. In these provinces the independent press has wholly disappeared, with the exception of two tame and unimportant sheets. In fact, if we except the Catholic and a few Social Democratic newspapers, there is hardly a journal of any weight in the German Empire in which the press-reptile is not found. "I know," wrote to Professor Wuttke an author well acquainted with the circumstances—"I know few German newspapers in which there is not a mud-bather." For even passing services the Bureau is ready to pay cash. Chaplain Miarka, the editor of the *Katholik*, has declared publicly that he was offered 7,500 thalers on condition of consenting to write in a milder manner during the elections.

The working up of public opinion through the press extends far beyond the boundaries of the German Empire. The proceedings of the court in the trial of Von Arnim in 1874 developed the fact that he, whilst representing Prussia at the Tuileries, had entered into relations with various journals in Paris, Vienna, and Brussels; and it is generally understood that 50,000 thalers were annually placed at the disposition of Herr Rudolf Lindau for the purpose of manipulating the Parisian press. Through these and similar means an opening for the articles of the " Press-Bureau " was made in English, French, and Belgian newspapers; and these articles, which had been first written in German, were translated back into German and published by the reptile-press as the expression of public opinion in foreign countries on Prussian affairs. " I could give the names," says Professor Wuttke, " of the press-reptiles who write for the *Indépendance Belge*, of those who take care of the *Hour*, and of others whose duty it is to furnish articles to the Italian and Scandinavian newspapers." * To hold the English in leading-strings, Berlin had, in 1869, a *North-Germany Correspondence*, and then, under the supervision of Aegidi, the director of the " Press-Bureau," a *Norddeutsche Correspondenz*, which is still the chief source from which both English and American journals draw their information on German affairs. The attempt made from Berlin to buy Katkoff's *Journal*

* *Die deutsche Zeitschriften*, p. 309.

of Moscow was defeated by the incorruptibility of the proprietor.

The reptile-press, of course, ignores and strives to hush whatever may throw light upon the dark workings and intrigues of the " Press-Bureau "; and no better instance of its power in this respect can be given than the history of Professor Wuttke's book on German journalism. Its existence was not recognized by the press-reptiles; its startling revelations were ignored or received in profound silence; and so successful was this policy that a year after the publication of the work only three hundred copies had been sold; and it is chiefly through the efforts of a Catholic newspaper—the *Germania*—and of Windthorst, a leader of the party of the *Centrum*, that it has finally been brought to public notice and has now reached a third edition. In the German Parliament, on the 18th of December, 1874, Windthorst took Professor Wuttke's book with him to the speaker's stand, and, in a powerful address against any further grant of the " Secret Fund " (*Reptilienfond*), made special reference to this work, which he characterized as "conscientious" and full of startling revelations which leave room to suspect even worse things. A year before (December 3, 1873) the same speaker declared in the Prussian Landtag that in Germany the government had nearly succeeded in getting entire control of the press; that the influence of the " Reptile-fund " was already noticeable in foreign countries, particularly in the newspapers of Vienna; and that the attempt had been made to establish a " Reptile-

Bureau " in connection with the London embassy; and when this was found not to work well, a " Press-Bureau " for England, France, and Italy was organized in Berlin. These charges, made in public parliamentary debate, were allowed to pass without contradiction, although Aegidi, the director of the Central Bureau, was a member of the Assembly and present during the discussion.

Eugen Richter, the member for Hagen, brought forward other accusations of like import on the 20th of January, 1874. We have already given an example of the uses to which the Prussian government puts the reptile-press, in the instance of the forged army address attributed to Benedek, and published throughout Germany at the outbreak of the war with Austria in 1866.* Similar services were rendered by the " mud-bathers " at the time of the crisis with France in 1870. A false telegram, purporting to come from Ems, dated July 13, 1870, in which the French minister, Count Benedetti, was said to have grossly insulted King William, was eagerly taken up by the venal press and commented upon in a way which excited the greatest indignation in the minds of the Germans against Napoleon, who, they firmly believed, was bent upon humiliating Prussia. In this way public feeling in both countries was fanned into a heat which could be cooled only by blood. The account of the interview at Ems was a fabrication, as Benedetti has since clearly shown; but Bis-

* This spurious document has got into many books; *e.g.*, into Hahn's *Geschichte des preussischen Vaterlandes.*

marck's "swine-herds" had faithfully done their unholy work.*

When, just at the beginning of the war, the French army made an attack on Saarbrücken, the reptile-press spread the report that they had reduced the city to ashes ; and this infamous falsehood made a deep impression throughout Germany.   A similar lie had been propagated at the commencement of the Austrian war.   On the 27th of June, 1866, the Prussians were driven from Trautenau by General Gablenz, and forthwith the reptile-press raised the cry that the citizens of Trautenau had poured from their houses hot water and boiling oil on the retreating soldiers; and the government lent itself to the spreading of this detestable calumny by dragging off the mayor of Trautenau, Dr. Roth, to prison, where he was detained in close confinement nearly three months.†

There is no subject on which the organs of the "Press-Bureau" are more united or more eloquent than the necessity of keeping up the full strength of the standing army ; nay, they have gone so far as to demand that the Reichstag shall consent to take from the representatives of the people the right to legislate on military affairs during the next seven years.   But before taking this step, hitherto unheard of in the history of constitutional government, it was necessary to manipulate public opinion, so that the members of parliament might seem to be compelled to this decision by the will of the

---

* See *Ma Mission en Prusse*, by Benedetti, Paris, 1871, p. 372 et seq.
† Roth, *Achtzig Tage in preussischen Gefangenschaft*, p. 13.

people themselves. With this view packed meetings were gotten up in various parts of the empire
which the telegraph lyingly announced to the
world as very numerously attended and unanimous
in demanding the seven-year enactment; but the
popular gatherings which were held to protest
against this violation of constitutional rights were
passed over in dead silence, and their action, consequently, did not become known outside of their
own immediate neighborhood. The reptile-press
acted in full harmony with the " Telegraph-Bu-
reau." The *Spener'sche Zeitung*, in Berlin, went so
far as to declare that no protests had been heard,
whereupon the *Provinzialkorrespondenz* exclaimed
that the movement, which had proceeded from
the depths of the nation's heart with unexpected
power, should force the Reichstag to yield to the
demand of the government.

As a part of the same programme, the " Press-
Bureau" just a year ago raised the cry that France
was buying horses, and that in less than three
months she would declare war on Germany. On
the same day and at the same hour this startling
announcement was made in Frankfort, in Leipzig,
in Stuttgart, and other cities. The following day
hundreds of newspapers throughout the Fatherland
took up the chorus and began to shout that the
empire was threatened. Now, all the world knows
that France at that time was as little thinking of
making war on Germany as of tunnelling the Atlantic Ocean ; but this piece of journalistic legerde-
main roused the Teutonic mind to the necessity of

strengthening the army and increasing the military
resources of a country which was already a camp
of soldiers.

No figure of rhetoric is more forcible than repetition, and we may calculate with mathematical
precision just how many leading articles, all saying
the same thing in fifty different localities, are required in order to fabricate a public opinion on a
given subject.

Another trick of the reptile-press is employed to
prevent the people from getting a knowledge of
the speeches of the opposition in parliament. The
arguments of these orators are either excluded
from its columns or caricatured so as to appear
childish or ridiculous. When, for instance, Sonne-
mann, the member for Frankfort, made an appeal
in behalf of the Alsacians, who had themselves
been reduced to dead silence, and showed from
authentic documents the pitiable condition to
which that province had been brought, the organs
of the " Press-Bureau " declared that " to answer
such utterances would be beneath the dignity of a
chancellor of the empire ; such want of political
honor had no claim to pass as the honest views of
an individual " ; and when Mallinckrodt placed his
hand on Lamarmora's book to prove his charges
against Bismarck, the *Spener'sche Zeitung* announced that " the national parties were filled with deepest disgust at the conduct of the *Centrum's* faction, and were not able to conceal their regret
that Prince Bismarck should deign to answer these
Ultramontane brawlers, since, by consenting to

notice the tricks of Windthorst, Mallinckrodt, and Schorlemer, he was giving prominence to what ought to be completely ignored " ; and then closed with the phrase of Frederick the Great, " Shall we play at fisticuffs with the rabble ?" The *Norddeutsche Allgemeine* and *National Zeitung* indulged in similar strains, and these articles were then republished by nearly the entire German press. When an opponent is especially troublesome the press-reptiles raise the cry that he has been bought up by foreign gold ; and in this they are probably sincere, since it must be difficult for them to understand how any man could refuse to sell himself for a proper consideration.

For five years now Bismarck's venal press has poured the full tide of its wrath upon the bishops and priests of Germany. Here was a subject upon which the reptiles could distil their venom to their hearts' content. What magnificent opportunities were here offered to the " mud-bathers " to hunt through the sewers of centuries and to wallow in the mire of ages; to revive Luther's vocabulary and refurbish the rusty weapons that for hundreds of years had lain idle and hurtless ! What an open field was here in which to ventilate historical calumnies, to produce startling effects by the dramatic grouping of striking figures ; to bring out the light of the golden present by causing it to fall upon the dark and bloody background of the past ! And what divine occasions for indignation, wrath, horror, word-painting to cause the hair to stand on end and the eyes to start ! Here was

25

place for withering scorn, patriotic thunder, lurid
lightning to sear the Jesuitic head bent upon the
ruin of the new empire.   And with what demoniac
delight the hired crew ring the changes on each
popular catch-word—progress, liberty, culture, free
thought; and how they foam and rage when a
bishop or a priest has the " boundless impudence"
·to speak in defence of the church !   " It has come
to this," says the *Dresdener Volksbote* (April 17,
1873): " Minorities must keep silence."

" Gone," exclaims a former German minister of
state—" gone is the reign of noble ideas; the power
of the love of country and of freedom ; the worth
and honor of the national character !   Money alone
is loved, and all means by which it is acquired seem
natural and praiseworthy."   The very foundations
of the moral order are attacked by this vile press.
The events of 1866 and 1870 are now spoken of
as "an historical phenomenon, which cannot be
judged by the current notions of morality, but
In accordance with which these moral principles
themselves must be widened and corrected."   This
is the low and degrading philosophy to which the
idolatry of success fatally leads.

But, for the honor of journalism, a portion of
the German press has remained closed against the
insidious power of the " Reptile-fund."   No Catholic newspaper has lent itself even covertly to
this conspiracy against truth and liberty ; and it
must be admitted, too, that the socialistic journals
have refused the government bribes; their circulation, however, which is not large, is confined

almost exclusively to the laboring classes, and
their influence is but little felt. The power of
the Catholic press in Germany is of recent growth.
In the early part of the present century the only
periodical of any weight devoted to the defence
of the interests of the church in Germany was the
Theologische Quartalschrift, founded in 1819 as the
organ of the Tübingen professors. Twenty years
later Joseph Görres established in Munich the
Historisch-politischen Blätter, which soon caused
the influence of his powerful mind to be felt
throughout the Fatherland, and which, under the
editorial management of the historian Jörg, is
still to-day one of the ablest reviews in Germany.
The censorship of the press which, prior to the
revolution of 1848, was maintained in all the German governments, was exercised in a way that
rendered Catholic journalism impossible. No
sooner, however, had the Parliament of Frankfort
proclaimed the liberty of the press than the Catholics hastened to take advantage of it by creating newspapers to advocate their religious interests. The bishops and priests, in obedience to
the earnest exhortations of Pius IX., threw themselves into the work with a will; the people followed their example; press-unions were formed
and a large number of Catholic newspapers sprang
into life. Bismarck's persecution of the church
has given yet greater force to this movement and
increased both the number and the circulation of
Catholic journals. In the new German Empire
there are to-day two hundred and thirty news-

papers devoted to the interests of the church. The *Augsburger Wochenblatt* has a subscription list of thirty-two thousand ; the *Mainzer Volksblatt,* one of thirty thousand. Twelve thousand copies of the *Germania* (in Berlin) are sold daily, and many other Catholic journals have a circulation of from five to ten thousand copies. As this powerful Catholic press could not be bought, nothing remained to be done but to silence it.

At the close of the year 1872 all Prussian journals were warned, under pain of confiscation, not to publish the Christmas Allocution of Pope Pius IX. Mallinckrodt, the vigilant Catholic leader, raised his voice in protest against this attempt upon the liberty of the press; but the Reichstag was silent, and the newspapers which had not heeded the warning were seized. The *Mainzer Journal* was brought into court for having presumed to print an open letter to the emperor, in which was found the following sentence : " The emperor is bound by the laws of the moral order just like the least of his subjects." The government procurator (Schön, in Mainz, on the 19th of December, 1873) declared that the emperor is a " sanctified " person, whose majesty is '' above the laws of the state,'' and the bare address " to the emperor " is a punishable offence. For republishing this open letter the editors of the *Kölner Volkszeitung* and the *Mühlheimer Anzeiger* were condemned to prison for two months. Siegbert, the managing editor of the *Deutscher Reichszeitung* (Catholic), was called upon to give the name of the writer of a certain article which he had published; and upon his declaration that this would be a breach of honor he was thrown into prison.

On the 1st of July, 1874, a new law came into force, by which still further restrictions were placed upon the liberty of the press; and on the 15th of the same month the Minister of Justice enjoined upon the government officials to keep sharp watch upon the newspapers. Within six months from this date the *Germania* newspaper in Berlin had been condemned thirty-nine times; and there were besides twenty-four untried charges against it in court. In January, February, March, and April, 1875—four months—one hundred and thirty-six editors were condemned either to prison or to pay a fine. The most of these were Catholics, though some of them belonged to the democratic and socialistic press. It is not necessary to say that the "press-reptiles" were not represented among them. These editors were thrust into the cells of common criminals, were refused books and writing material, and were forced to live upon "prison fare," which many found so unpalatable that they could eat nothing but rye-bread.

The reptile-press alone is tolerated. If a man wishes to be honest, and has, notwithstanding, no desire to go to jail, the most unwise thing which he could do would be to become a journalist in the new German Empire. To refuse to eat of the "Reptile-fund" is to condemn one's self to Bismarck's "prison fare" of beans and cold water.

To poison the wells is not held to be lawful, even in war; but to taint the fountain-sources of knowledge, and to corrupt the channels through which alone the public receives its general information, is not thought to be unworthy of a great hero, if we may judge from the Prussian chancellor's popularity with Englishmen and Americans, which is not diminished even by his determined efforts to crush all who refuse to sell their souls or renounce their manhood.

"The only man," said Carlyle of Bismarck— "the only man appointed by God to be his vice-gerent here on earth in these days, and knowing he was so appointed, and bent with his whole soul on doing and able to do God's work." And our great centennial celebration of the reign of popular government is to be desecrated by a colossal statue of the man who is its deadliest enemy.

We have not, in this country, wholly escaped the evil effects of the vast European conspiracy against truth and honor which is carried on through the agency of "Press-Bureaus," "Telegram-Bureaus," "Correspondence-Bureaus," and "Reptile-funds." One may, for instance, readily detect the "trail of the serpent" in many of the cable despatches to the Associated Press, and not less evidently in the European correspondence of some of our leading journals. Is it not worthy of remark that so few of our great newspapers should have taken up the defence of the persecuted and imprisoned German editors? The American press, which can upon such slight compulsion be blatant and loud-mouthed, has been most reserved in its treat-ment of Bismarck ; has, indeed, hardly attempted to veil its sympathy with his despotic and arbi-trary measures. If this approval of tyranny went merely the length of applauding his persecution of the Catholic Church, it might be explained by the desire to pander to popular Protestant preju-dice. But how shall we account for it when there is question of the degradation and enslavement of the press itself; of the violation of every prin-ciple of liberty ; and of the systematic consolida-tion of the most complete military despotism which the world has ever seen ? Might it not be possible, even, to trace to the *Reptilien-fond* the recent attempts to rekindle in the United States the flame of religious hate and fanaticism ? How-ever this may be, it is unfortunately true that mon-ey is the controlling power in American as in Ger-man journalism. Its influence is as discernible in the columns of our own " independent" press as in a genuine Berlin " mud-bather's" double-leaded leader.

 " How can we help it ? " said a well-known edi-tor of Vienna. " A newspaper office is a shop where publicity is bought and sold." " I will be frank," said another journalist. " I am like a wo-man of the town (*Ich bin die Hure von Berlin*): if you wish to have this and that written, pay your money." Praise and blame, approval and condemnation, are the articles of merchandise of the press, and they are offered to the highest bid-der.

"When the proprietor of a journal," says Sacher-Mosach, a widely-known writer, who was for
some time connected with the Vienna newspaper,
the *Presse*, and afterwards with the *Neue Freie
Presse*—"when the proprietor of a journal has
entered into lucrative relations with a bank, he
is not content with placing his sheet at its disposition in whatever relates to financial matters; but
if the director of the bank, as sometimes happens,
is a man of fancy who patronizes an actress who
has beauty but not talent, he will order his theatrical critic to praise this lady without stint; and
the critic will reserve all his squibs for some old
comédienne who is not protected by a bank director or by any one else. If a great publisher has
all the works which appear in his house advertised
in the journal, the proprietor will direct his book
critic to find them all admirably written, profound,
and full of the freshest and most delightful
thoughts; and the author is just as certain to be
praised in this sheet as he is to be torn to pieces
by the newspapers in which his book has not been
advertised. The first principle of journalistic industry and of the criticism at its command is to
recognize merit only when and so far as it is finan-
cially profitable to do so." *

It is far from our thought to wish to deny the
vast power for good exercised by the press; but
this is its own constant theme, and we have deemed it a more worthy, even though a less pleasant,
task to point out at least some of the ways in

* Sacher-Mosach, *Ueber den Werth der Kritik*, Leipzig, 1873, p. 55.

which its power may be turned against the highest interests of truth and the dearest liberties of the people. A thoughtful and fearless work on the influence of journalism on our American civilization would be a fitting contribution to the centennial literature, and at the same time a most instructive chapter in the history of the country. The only attempt of this kind which so far has been made does not rise above the dignity of a compilation, and is without value as a philosophical discussion of the subject.

RELIGION AND ART.

"Science, O man! thou sharest with higher spirits,
  But Art thou hast alone."

OD is revealed to all the faculties of the soul. He is truth; he is goodness; he is beauty. He is known; he is loved; he is adored. He is the first and final principle of all knowledge; he is the ideal of every art; he is the type of all' high and holy living.

Art is the expression of ideal beauty; the resplendence of mind in matter, of the archetype in nature. It does not copy, but creates; never rests in the seen, but is transcendental; looks beyond, through nature, up to God. Whatever it sees it despises, and whatever it does it straightway wishes undone; because the work is eternally below the thought. Like the soul, it is imprisoned in matter, which it half-loathes and half-adores; is drawn to earth by its form, to rise above which is the hope and despair of all its endeavor. Its aim is impossible, but the highest and most glorious. What God cannot do it would accomplish—give to the divine and infinite beauty a sensible form and local dwelling which will reveal and not obscure its immortal splendor. Hence the

' real never satisfies the artist; not even real art. In the presence of some work of creative power he shouts, he is rapt, he is borne upward into other worlds; thinks not of form or color or time : his soul has caught sight of the immortal and all-beautiful and is ecstatic.

Art disenchants; and this is a great merit. It teaches how little of what might be, is ; how far beneath our capabilities we ourselves are content to remain. It is a reproach and makes us feel our unworthiness ; it is a revelation from a higher world in whose presence we despise ourselves for resting satisfied with this. It is a gleam from the face of God seen through the veil of time and space—the eternal allurement and eternal disenchantment of the noblest souls. It elevates, purifies, and refines. It is the most perfect expression of the truest thoughts, the purest loves, the noblest virtues ; and when it is turned to base ends, it veils its face and hides its celestial beauty : the form remains, but the soul, like that of the virgin martyr, is borne away by the hands of angels. Even in nature it is art that is beautiful —the thought, the idea, symbolizing the unseen and uncreated, reflected from the blue heavens, the starry sky, from azure mountains or green isles.

When, in the spring, we seat ourselves on the border of a lake in whose pure waters the waving woods and laughing fields, with trees, plants, and flowers, are mirrored ; into whose bosom the rippling rills and rivulets are flowing, like joyous children that run to meet their quiet mother, while

the gentle zephyrs whisper to one another from
leaf to leaf, as if afraid to frighten the genius
of the place—the soul, free from all distracting
thoughts, escapes from earth and lifts itself on the
wings of contemplation to the throne of God.
Seated on the border of this· enchanted lake, we
grow sad and pensive ; a sweet melancholy takes
hold of us; we have caught a glimpse of home,
but are still exiles.

> Hence in a season of calm weather,
> Though inland far we be,
> Our souls have sight of that immortal sea
> Which brought us hither—
> Can in a moment travel hither,
> And see the children sport upon the shore,
> And hear the mighty waters rolling evermore.

There is a religious power, too, in the grand and
awful scenes of nature. The ocean, the desert,
high mountains and great rivers, storm and darkness, with the voice of thunder and the lurid
lightning—all speak of God. " He bowed the heavens, and came down: and darkness was under his
feet. And he did ride upon a cherub, and did fly :
yea, he did fly upon the wings of the wind. . . .
The everlasting mountains were scattered, the perpetual hills did bow. . . . The overflowing of the
waters passed by : the deep uttered his voice, and
lifted up his hands on high." The child of nature,
however rude and imperfect may be his idea of
God, is religious in his aspirations. Before he can
lose consciousness of the ever-abiding presence of
the Creator man must isolate himself, escape into

empty worlds of shadows and abstractions. So
long as he rests upon the solid earth the heavens surround him and God's presence is felt.
Art is man's effort to recreate nature, to bring out
the blurred image of the divine beauty. How unlimited is its range, how immense its power! Into the inner sanctuary of science few men enter, but
all feel the force and inspiration of art. Without
it there is no glory; it is the flower and fine odor
of heroic life; the idealization which gives to the
world its noblest characters; the soul's high struggle to transfigure the body and clothe it in celestial
light. Art is immortal; it is catholic; it survives
the ruin of empires and the decay of nations; is
held by no bonds of time or place. It is born of
use, but, breaking its shell, it leaves it there and
soars far away above all sordidness and all baseness.
It hears the music of the spheres, is bathed in the
light that never yet was seen on land or sea; higher
still and higher it is borne upwards by a love that
never knows love's sad satiety—the thirst of the
creature for the Creator, the groanings and longings
which make all nature plaintive and vocal. Banished
from heaven, and bearing with it the remembrance of
a better world, it wanders, in love which hopes and
despairs, through the universe, seeking the mysterious gift that opens the gates of light. It is the
love of the best, the spirit of unrest, the beauty
ever ancient and ever new, which tortures the heart
of man and fills it with a divine melancholy. All
high art is sad; it scorns enjoyment or whatever
else distracts from heavenly contemplation; and

when it is sought for pleasure, and not from religion and love, it degrades and is degraded. It mediates between man and nature; reconciles them; infuses human thoughts and passions into senseless elements, until, like St. Francis, we feel that the sun and stars and the very stones are our brothers, thrown out from the hand of God, and, like ourselves, with travailing and unutterable longings, seeking the place of eternal rest, the central heart of love that draws all things to itself. Nature's universal unfolding of herself in higher forms is her cry to God, her hunger of the infinite; the all-pervading tremor and vibration of matter, in heat, in light, in electricity, in the clinging of atom to atom, of body to body, of planet to planet, is the thrill and ecstasy of a world half-conscious of the divine presence.

The true philosopher, said Plato, longs for death; for the divine wisdom whose lover he is is given only to those who through death enter into life, who from the shadowy dreams of a slumbering existence pass into the clear vision of truth's splendor; and so nature struggles to transcend itself, until the new heavens and the new earth are reclothed under the eye of God, and the creature, no longer a wanderer, enters into its rest. And this is the aim and purpose of art. It seeks to transform the real; to strike from inert matter sounds of heavenly harmony. To its eye every common sight is apparelled in celestial light. It beholds that untravelled world whose margin fades for ever and for ever, and with voice, and motion,

and form, and color strives to reveal its hidden
glory as best it may to the coarser vision of the
uninspired. To make known the higher reality
which is concealed beneath the shell and surface of
things is the task at which it labors always. Like
religion, it appeals from time to eternity, from apparent to real, from man to God. In its light we
behold the transcendent beauty of heroic and noble life, which the logical faculty does not detect.
How common and unprofitable are man's proudest
deeds, if he is but an animal, stabled in this islet
of time, and feeding in the world's great trough of
matter! The heaven that lies about us in our infancy must break open higher and higher, else we
sink. Its finer and ethereal air must be the soul's
breath, or it dies. Hector and Achilles were but
bullies no better than a thousand Indian braves
who lacked the sacred bard and now lie buried,
unthought-of as the leaves that overshadowed
their fierce battles. Not her heroes, but art, made
Greece immortal. Shakspere is worth more to the
glory of England than all the victories which he
has sung; nay, not to England only is he of greater
worth, but to mankind. Dante, Raphael, and Michael Angelo, with many other names of highest
power, have made Italy the consecrated land of
poetry and of song, the home of beauty and of all
loveliness—the native country of the soul.

It is only when we look at art through the puri-
fying and chastening light of time that we fully
realize its influence in the history of the human
race. The present is always vulgar—loud, glaring,

and shameless ; too real to be beautiful. It is the slave of power and wealth, soiled by the idolatry of success, the hideous counterfeit of merit ; but this passes, and art remains for ever.

The movement which carried the European mind to its present state of enlightenment and refinement received its first impulse from art held in the hands of religion.

The study of the Grecian and Roman models of eloquence, poetry, sculpture, and architecture fired the Christian nations with a love of artistic perfection which the Hebraizing spirit of the Reformation weakened but could not destroy, and which has given to our civilization some of its most important elements. The historic power of art is greater than that of history, which, as a science, is known to few ; but, when made beautiful and sublime in poetry, in song, in eloquence, it moulds the national character by giving distinctness and form to noble and heroic lives which can in no other way be made manifest to the masses of mankind.

It has been maintained, indeed, that the influence of art upon character is evil ; that it develops the emotions to the injury of what is manly and earnest in our nature ; that it leads us to separate feeling from action, and tends to make us unnatural and insincere by causing us to seek effect rather than truth. This was a favorite theme of declamation with the Latin classics, who extol the rustic simplicity of the fathers and ascribe the downfall and ruin of their country to the introduction of Greek art and luxury. Sallust, the most sensual of men, would have us believe that a taste for painting is a vice no less than lewdness or drinking. But he declaims with equal vehemence against literature ; and, in fact, if his argument had any value, it would tell, not against art alone, but against all politeness and civilization. In spite of the corruptions of society, the civilized man is higher than the savage ; and in spite of the actual and possible perversions of art, its general effect is elevating and religious. The abuse proves the use. When it becomes sensual and immoral, it dies; its soul is fled, and the wings which had a seraph's power to bear us up, with no middle flight but to God's high heaven, are draggled in the mire and enfold a corpse. It should be an appeal to what is best, likest unto God in our nature; and if it seek to kindle desire or awaken passion, it has denied the soul and become material and atheistic. A low purpose ruins art, as superstition degrades and unbelief destroys religion. Nothing is more fatal to it than the realism of nature-worship with its sensual creed and desire. Nudity is not more beautiful in art than in nature, and only a low and degraded taste could find pleasure in lifting the sacred veil of shame with which the soul protects its heavenly modesty and shrinks from all coarseness. Art is symbolical, not realistic, and the grunting tribe that seek to clothe it in undisguised flesh and blood are animals.

2C

Chastity and beauty are sisters. Chastity is beautiful, and beauty is chaste. True beauty is never sensuous. It purifies and chastens. Hence art addresses itself less to sense than to soul. It seeks to awaken, not desire, but love, admiration, hope, faith, and all high sentiment. It is not form and color, but the expression of the ideal, the manifestation of the divine, the infinite peering through the finite, the heavenly reposing on an earthly bosom. Religion and art, then, are allies. Between them there is no antagonism, as there is none between theology and science. This truth the Catholic Church has ever proclaimed. "All religions," wrote Canova to Napoleon, "cherish art, but none so much as our own." In her universal life she embraces all the arts, gives to them harmony and special ends. Her sacred edifices are not alone the temples of the living God; they are also the sanctuaries of art which points heavenward. Her sublime conceptions of God and man have revealed a new world of thought and sentiment. She has clothed the highest truth in the most perfect beauty. Spiritual in all her teachings and aspirations, she understands that the visible is but the symbol of the unseen; that we must stand upon the solid earth before we can rise to higher worlds; and that this is not a sensuous but a reasonable creed which holds that God cannot be worshipped in spirit and in truth except through signs and symbols. For what else is thought, what else is language? Our truest conceptions of God and of the soul are but symbols. The very words which we use to express them are *equivocal*, as St. Thomas says, not *univocal*.

No human act can be wholly spiritual. We ascend, by a law of our nature, from the visible to the invisible, from the sensible to the supersensible. A purely spiritual religion would be to man an inaccessible and unreal religion. There can be no faith where there is no thought, nor thought without language; and language is addressed primarily to the senses. There can be no authoritative religious teaching without a church, and an invisible church is no church at all. The sectarian protest against the alliance of religion and art can be justified only by ignoring the most essential fact of Christian history, which is the manifestation of God's power and beauty and holiness in human form. To take from the church her symbolism is to deny the humanity of Christ. In an invisible society what becomes of his incarnation, miracles, and whole positive revelation? His religion is a system of things invisible visibly manifested—the symbolism of divine truth, love, wisdom, justice, in their relation to man immortal but sinful.

The union of the soul with God through faith, hope, and love is the first and highest aim of religion; but faith, hope, and love, like all the deep emotions of the human heart, tend irresistibly to incorporate and express themselves in symbols and acts. What purer or more spiritual love do we know than that of the mother for her child? And yet with itself is it never content, but rushes out and infuses itself into a thousand words, tendernesses, ceremonies, and observances; builds a temple, erects an altar, and becomes there the all-unselfish and ministering priestess of God to evoke from brutish apathy the heavenly thoughts and divine instincts of the heart of man; watches, prays, is patient, wearies not, stoops to all lowliness and is ennobled; fondles, caresses, speaks words of softest music, chides, threatens, rebukes; the truest, the deepest, the most ceremonial of all human devotions is this love which gives to the world its worthiest men.

A voiceless faith, a dumb hope, and a love without symbol sink back upon themselves and die. They are the religion of the infidel, " for the most part of the silent sort at the altar of the unknown and unknowable." *

When we believe in God we cry out to him; when we hope in him we lean upon him; when we love him we throw ourselves, like Magdalen, at the feet of his only-begotten Son; we hear his voice, we drink in his words, and are at rest. We stand beneath his cross; linger in sorrow and hope by his grave; are broken-hearted when he is no longer there, till his risen and immortal presence gives us life again; and then the desert, or the prison-walls of love, or any spot where we may forget the world wholly and live to him only, is our paradise. With him we keep fast and vigil and feast; hear the angel announce his birth; behold the immaculate maiden, Virgin and Mother; follow her into the

* Huxley, *Lay Sermons*, p. 16.

mountains, and with her we go up to Bethlehem. In the stable we adore our God, lying all-helpless between the ox and the ass, hear his first piteous cry of suffering and of love; for us the angels sing again the glad song the shepherds heard on the hills of Judea. The wise men come out of the East. Herod rages; the wail of mothers who cannot be consoled strikes upon our ear; and into Egypt we follow Mary and Joseph as they bear the divine Child. We are with him in the carpenter's shop, as he consecrates and ennobles labor; we are with him amid the doctors, as he shows that the folly of God is better than the science of men. By the banks of the river Jordan we hear the voice of John: "Behold the Lamb of God." The heavens are opened, the Holy Ghost descends, and with the Son of Man leads us into the desert, to fast, to pray, to dwell alone with sadness and with God, to be sorely tempted by the evil one, by the evil in ourselves, by the great world-picture of pleasure and of glory; and still, by the power of prayer and solitude, to conquer, " to rise on stepping-stones of our dead selves to higher things," until we feel and know and are certain that not on bread alone doth man live, but on every word which God's mouth speaketh.

Through the long centuries, year after year, with love's unerring instinct, the church leads her children along the sacred way the Blessed Christ did tread, lingers over each hallowed spot in joy, in thankfulness, in sorrow, or in triumph, nor feels the deadening weight of time nor the fatal curse of distance.

"For thou dost soothe the heart, thou Church of Rome,
    By thy unwearied watch and varied round
  Of service in thy Saviour's holy home."

Art's highest mission is to reveal to the world Jesus Christ in his birth, in his life, in his death, in his resurrection. He is the ideal of art—the most beautiful and perfect conception of the divine mind. He is God, the all-beautiful, made manifest. Purity and gentleness and grace, with power and majesty, combine to make him the fairest and the noblest figure in history, to whom the whole world bows in love and adoration. There is no other like unto him ; between him and all other men there is the distance that separates heaven from earth, the divine from the human. Every highest aspiration and worthiest love find in him at once their inspiration and their ideal.

There is a shadow on the countenance of Jesus which gives to it its artistic completeness. It is sorrow. In gayety and joy there is a trivial something which deprives them of the highest artistic effect. The cheek of beauty is not divine unless the tear of sorrow trickle down it. To preach Jesus Christ, and him crucified, is not to preach true religion only, but also the ideal of art. The first and noblest art is eloquence, which is in itself sculpture, painting, poetry, music—yea, and architecture; for what worthier temple of God do we know than the human body, all-conscious with soul, tremulous with generous passion, vocal with sublime thought and heroic sentiment? Christ Jesus blessed eloquence and bade it convert the world. " Go ye therefore," he said, " and teach all nations." The divine command was to preach the word, not to write it ; and this living word, spoken by lips touched with celestial fire, has infused life and warmth into the world, converted the nations, and changed the face of the earth. It was the first, and is always the sincerest and worthiest, free popular speech. Before Christ gave his great commission to the apostles philosophers had discoursed to their chosen disciples, and orators had declaimed to citizens on the interests of the state ; but no one had spoken to the people as moral beings with duties and responsibilities which lift them into the world of the infinite and eternal. There were priesthoods, but they were mute in presence of the people, intent upon hiding from them all knowledge of their mysteries. Religious eloquence did not exist ; it first received a voice on the shores of the Lake of Genesareth and on the hills of Judea, in the preaching of Jesus, who remains for ever its supreme exponent, speaking with God-like liberty, as one who had authority, on whatever most nearly touches the dearest interests of men ; speaking chiefly to the people, bringing back to their minds the long-forgotten truth which proves them the royal race of God. The preaching of God's word with the heavenly liberty which no earthly power might lessen became the great school of the human race ; it was the first popular eloquence, and like an electric thrill it ran through the earth. It belongs to the religion of Christ alone. Mahomet, who sought to

borrow it, was able to catch only its feeble echo.
This free Christian public speech is unlike all other
oratory; it possesses an incommunicable characteristic through which it has exercised the most beneficent influence upon the destinies of mankind.   It
is essentially spiritual; lifts the soul above the
flesh ; creates new ideals ; and, by inspiring contempt for whatever is low or ephemeral, begets
enthusiasm for the divine and eternal.   It is a
voice whose soul-thrill is love—the boundless love
of God and of men, who are the children of this
love, and therefore brothers.   This voice cannot be
bought ; it cannot be silenced.   *Currit verbum* said
St. Paul, and again from his prison-cell : "But the
word of God is not fettered."   On innumerable lips
it is born ever anew ; and always and everywhere
it is a protest against the brutality of power, an
appeal in the name of God, our Father in heaven,
in behalf of the poor, the oppressed, the disinherit-
ed of humanity.   Men may still be tyrants, may
still crush the weak, and sacrifice truth and justice
to their lustful appetites ; but the voice of God,
threatening, commanding, rebuking, shall be silent
never more.   Festus shall tremble before Paul :
at the bidding of Ambrose Theodosius shall re-
pent ; and before Hildebrand the brutal Henry
shall bow his head.   At the sound of this voice all
Europe shall rouse itself; shall rush, impelled as
by some divine instinct, into the heart of Asia to
strike the mighty power which threatened to blight
the budding hope of the world.   Who can estimate the priceless value and supreme force of this

free Christian speech, which, without asking leave
of king or people, but impelled by a divine necessity, made itself heard of the whole earth? Over
the portals of his Academy Plato wrote : " None
but geometers enter here." Over the ever-open
door of the church was the word of Christ : " Come
to me, all yè who labor and are heavy laden."

" All you," exclaimed St. Augustine, " who
labor, who dig the earth, who fish in the sea, who
carry burdens, or painfully and slowly construct
the barks in which your brothers will dare the
waves—all enter here, and I will explain to you
not only the $\gamma\nu\tilde{\omega}\theta\iota\ \sigma\epsilon\alpha\upsilon\tau\acute{o}\nu$ of Socrates, but the
most hidden of mysteries—the Trinity."

This new eloquence was as large as the human
race; it was for all, and first of all for the poor and
the oppressed. It was not artistic in the technical
meaning; it did not captivate the senses; it was
not polished. There was no showy marshalling of
words and phrases, no sweet and varied modulation
of voice, no graceful and commanding gesture.
Around the altar were gathered the slave, the beggar, the halt, and the blind—the oppressed and
suffering race of men. If among them were found
the rich and high-born, they were as brothers—their
wealth and noble birth entered not into the church
of Christ. Here was neither freeman nor slave—all
were one. Thus in every Christian assembly was
typed the humanity which was to be when all men
should be brothers and free. To these new-born
souls the apostle of Christ spoke : " My brothers,"
he said, or " My children "; and though all history

27

and all society shrieked against him, they who heard
knew and felt that his words were God's truth.
The heart is not deceived in love. " I seek not
yours," he said, " but you ; for God is my witness
how I long after you all in the heart of Jesus
Christ. . . . I could wish that myself were ac-
cursed if only my brethren be saved." And then,
with the liberty which love alone knows and gives,
he threatened, rebuked, implored, laid bare the
hidden wounds of the soul, nor feared to become
an enemy for speaking truth.

To the great and the rich he spoke right out,
reminding them of their duties, denouncing their
indifference, their cruelty, their injustice ; and then,
in accents sweet as a mother's voice, he breathed
hope and courage into the hearts of those who
suffer, showing them beyond this short and delu-
sive life the certain end and reward of their struggles and sorrows. He taught them that the soul is
the highest, that purity is the best, that only the
clean of heart see God ; that man's chief worth lies
in that which is common to all, derived from God
and for him created. Human life was perishing,
wastefully poured through the senses on every
carnal thing. No love of beauty or truth or justice was left. The mind was darkened, the heart
was paralyzed.

The great, strong passions that bore the people
of Rome in triumph through the earth were dead ;
everywhere, in religion, in art, in manners, was the
foul blight of materialism ; and a kind of delirium
drove men into animal indulgences, to soul and

body alike fatal. To a race thus glued to the earth by carnal appetites came the voice of the apostle preaching Christ, and him crucified; telling of the divine love that bowed the heavens and brought down God's own Son to suffer, to labor, to die for them. He was poor, he was meek, he was humble; he fasted, he prayed; he comforted the sorrowful, gave hope to the despairing; he offered up his life for men. Such as he was, those who believe in him must be. To be heartless, to be cruel, to be unjust, to serve the lusts of the flesh, is to have no part with him. This is the great work which Christian eloquence did for art; it turned the mind's eye from the contemplation of beauty of form to the inner life of the soul; from thoughts of power and success to principles of right and justice; from the narrowness of exaggerated patriotism to catholic sympathies; from the desire of enjoyment through indulgence to the idea of happiness through self-restraint. It brought home to man the fuller consciousness of his immortal and transcendental value; gave to him exalted aims and worthy ideals. It declared that man is more than the state, as God is more than the world, and in this way inspired those views of the paramount worth of the individual soul without which there could be no successful reaction against the sense-worship of paganism—a low and material creed without eternal verities upon which to rest. Power was its divinity, and it was therefore without pity or tenderness; success was its justification, and it consequently trampled upon right.

There can be no high art without great doctrines. If man is only an animal, Landseer is the noblest painter.

> ". . . . By the soul
> Only shall the nations be great and free."

As the Christian religion is the fullest revelation of the soul, it ought to produce the highest art. Since human nature has been transfigured and re-created by the immediate and personal union with it of God himself, art ought to be able to disclose the soul and permit us to gaze upon the divine possibilities which in it lie latent. It may no longer linger in form and color and motion, as if these were its abiding home. It is wedded to the soul and must soar or die. In the presence of men supremely great we cannot stop to notice how they are clothed. Homer was blind and a beggar, but who can remember this when in his adventurous flight he bears us upward, and we hear the great world-song to which all the nations have listened through a hundred generations? The inner life, if it be pure and high, elevates and ennobles the meanest forms. True art, like heroic souls, lifts itself above its embodiment, and, rising into the world of the eternal and the infinite, unwraps itself of the vesture woven in the roaring loom of Time. It leaves behind all passion and desire, all enjoyment of sense, and reposes supremely blest in that which, unchangeable, is yet never the same. It aims not merely at the beautiful, but seeks the true and the good ; knowing that

"Beauty, Good, and Knowledge are three sisters
  That dote upon each other, friends to man."

Without this union of virtue with beauty there can be no Christian art. All its purposes are holy. Its mission is not to multiply the pleasures of the fortunate, but to comfort the unhappy; to raise to heaven eyes weighed down by sorrow or blinded by the vulgar, garish world; to reveal to all who despair of this life the certain and immortal triumph of those who suffer in faith and hope and love.

There is no art for art's sake. It exists for man, and can be worthy only by being useful. The lordly palace grew out of the hut that sheltered from wind and rain some barbarous fisherman clothed in the skins of beasts; the sweetest and most celestial song caught its first faint echo from the tender lullaby with which some poor mother sang her babe to sleep. All art is born of man's craving for a higher and better life, and, though it cannot satisfy this desire, it ought to raise our thoughts to Him in whom alone the human heart can find repose.

Poetry is akin to eloquence, and, like it, has a religious mission. The orator and the poet are both born and both are made, despite the ancient proverb. The universe is God's poem, and art but a feeble attempt to interpret its mystic and infinite meaning. Poetry is the natural language of all worship, and the muse soars her loftiest flight only on the wings of religious inspiration. The most poetic word in language is the brief, immense word — God. It is the sublimest, the profoundest, the holiest word that human tongue can speak. It is the instinctive cry of the soul in moments of supreme trial. In the hour of victory, in the hour of death, in the ecstasy of joy, in the agony of woe, this sacred word bursts spontaneously from the human heart. It is the first word our mother taught our infant lips to lisp when, pointing to heaven, she told us of God, our Father, and bade us look above this base, contagious earth. When the mother for the first time feels her first-born's breath, in the overflowing tenderness of a boundless gratitude she pronounces the name of God; when, in the helplessness of misery, she bends over the grave of her only child, and her heart is breaking, she can find no relief to her agonizing soul, until, raising her tearful eyes to heaven, she breathes in prayer the name of God. When two young hearts that beat as one vow eternal love, it is in the name of God they do it; and the union of love loses all its sacredness and half its charm, unless it is sealed before God's altar and in his holy name. When the mother sends her son to do battle for his country, she puts God's benediction upon him: " God be with thee, my boy!" When nations are marshalled in deadly array of arms, and the alarming drum foretells the danger nigh, and the trumpet's clangor sounds the charge, and contending armies meet in the death-grapple amid fire and smoke and the cannon's awful roar, until victory crowns them that win, those banners that were borne proudly on till they floated in triumph on the field of glory are gathered together in some great temple of religion, and there an assembled people sing aloud: "We praise thee, O God! we glorify thee, O Lord!"

When we see clearly and feel deeply, prose no longer satisfies us. Poetry is truer than prose—expresses more nearly what all ought to feel in the presence of the glories of God's universe.

> "The meanest flower that blows can give
> Thoughts that do often lie too deep for tears."

We move about in worlds not realized; and to the poet's mind this thought is always present. He is lost in wonder, rapt in ecstasy; he laughs, weeps, exults, shouts, despairs, and hopes; and if he have but a common nature, the higher world that breaks open before his gaze dazzles and unsettles him. It is therefore genius is akin to madness, and they who have the highest thoughts may lead the lowest lives.

Poetry need not be wedded to verse, though noble sentiments and deep feeling will always find expression in rhythmical and harmonious words. The thoughts which are nearest and dearest to the soul it does not speak, but sings. The Bible is full of poetry. Sublimer or more touching lyrics than the Psalms of David have not been written. They are for ever the song of the soul craving, in the midst of darkness and of death, the light and the life. All true poetry springs from religious sentiment—from the longing for some higher symbol of the divine and uncreated. Never did child look out upon the glad earth or into the deep

heavens but he felt the need of poetry to speak
his reverence and gratitude. What sublimer poet
is there than Job? Like a Titan he girds his loins
to struggle with the eternal problem of human
destiny. Never has the radical misery of our present condition, as contrasted with the infinite aspirations of our being, given birth to more pathe-
tic or more heartrending lamentations. It is the
despairing cry of a boundless yearning, which heroic faith gradually subdues and changes into the
peace of tranquil hope.

What depth and spiritual force has not the
Christian religion given to poetry! Groves, flowers,
and running waters satisfied the poets of paganism; but not the boundless ocean, nor the starry
heavens, nor aught else can express the infinite
thoughts and emotions which fill the soul of a
Christian.

What chastening and ennobling influence has
not the veneration with which the church has surrounded the Blessed Virgin exercised upon the
spirit of poetry!

> " Mother! whose virgin bosom was uncrost
> With the least shade of thought to sin allied;
> Woman! above all women glorified,
> Our tainted nature's solitary boast;
> Purer than foam on central ocean tost;
> Brighter than eastern skies at daybreak strewn
> With fancied roses; than the unblemished moon
> Before her wane begins on heaven's blue coast;
> Thy image falls to earth."

The poet may now no more dream of woman, except as clothed in the sacred modesty and spot-

less purity of the Virgin-Mother of the God-born Child.

We cannot think of Mary but religion melts into poetry; and the thousand heavenly thoughts and heavenly sentiments which in Christian lands and Christian hearts centre in the hallowed names of mother, sister, wife—highest names of love, of beauty, of truth—owe their sweetness and their power to her influence. This devotion has purified and consecrated the passion of love, which no poet has left unsung; has lifted it out of matter and sense and wedded it to the soul; has crowned it with sacramental glory and immortal hope. Through the grave into life it issues forth again deathless. Such love is not possible where woman is common or coarse; and if she were forced into vulgar and noisy contact with the public ways and affairs of men, it would die as surely as in the mephitic air of an Eastern harem. To be divine, it needs a sanctuary and faith in God.

What poetry is like that which Christian faith has inspired? Dante, the sovereign poet, looms in colossal majesty above all who have followed him, and none is comparable to him. Through a trinity of transformations he rises to paint a three-fold world—sombre and terrible, sad and devout, rapt and ecstatic. There is no tenderness like Dante's; neither is there any intensity or seriousness like his. There are cries which drown the agonies of hell; silences which in a moment grow eternal; and then notes so sad and sweet that all our being melts to tears, and we would be content to weep for ever, were it not that the celestial light breaks upon us, and we hear the fountains of life like music flowing, and are borne upward into a world where we forget all time and place, and know and love God only. Man's spiritual nature has reconquered its supremacy, and, scorning matter, he enters into the realms where angels and demons contend in immortal warfare. From religious faith Milton, like a seraph strong, drew his high inspiration. "Of his moral sentiments," says Dr. Johnson, "it is hardly praise to affirm that they excel those of all other poets; for this superiority he was indebted to his acquaintance with the sacred writings."

Calderon, Lope de Vega, Camoëns, Tasso, are all witnesses to the poetic inspiration of religious faith. Lope de Vega, in saying his first Mass, fainted at the bare thought of the sublime and awful mystery of Christ's Real Presence. Most clearly seen, too, is the poetic power of the Christian spirit in Corneille and Racine, the greatest poets of France.

The modern drama, which embraces all other kinds of poetry, is not only based upon views of human life distinctively Christian, but grew out of the religious *Mysteries* of the middle ages which still survive in the Passion Play at Ober-Ammergau. This is true alike of the tragedies of Shakspere and of the *Autos Sacramentales* of Calderon.

Christ has lifted the pall which hung in dark and impenetrable folds around the life of man. He is no longer the plaything of fate, the helpless victim of inexorable destiny, who feels upon his heart the brutal foot of an unknown and pitiless power. He is free, and through the tangled web of good and ill walks with no uncertain step. He knows the divine efficacy that there is in suffering and sorrow, and that the uses of adversity are sweet. Above Necessity is Liberty, and Life is ever Lord of Death. In Christ he beholds the heroic and tragic ideal of the highest life. All-pure and gentle, he is trampled upon, crushed, nailed to the cross, and his tomb is walled in with ignominy and sealed with contempt. And still he triumphs—stands deathless over the grave and places his cross on the brows of crowned kings and on the summit of all earthly things. Here is the divinest drama. Suffering there is still, and still there is death ; but the heart that believes and is pure, is immortal and conquers fate. Compare the death-struggle of Laocoön with the agony of Christ on the cross. Laocoön, in terror and despair, struggles hopelessly with inexorable fate, which with cold and pitiless grip is crushing him ; Christ, in more intense and keener suffering, consents to death, but conquers agony ; is tranquil in the supreme sacrifice of infinite love, and through the shadows of the darkened sun the light of eternal day pierces ; or Niobe, turned to stone by hopeless grief, with the Mother of Sorrows, who stands beneath the cross of her divine Son with heart transfixed by the sword of anguish, and is calm because love like hers knows that God is love.

Poetry passes naturally into music ; for the poet

sings, and is tormented by his thought until it finds harmonious and rhythmic expression. The thought creates the rhythm, and when the rhyme seeks the thought there is no poetry. "The beginning of literature," says Emerson, "is the prayers of a people, and they are always hymns." Music is poetry in tones. It is the language of feeling, the universal language of man. The cry of joy and of sorrow, of triumph and of despair, of ecstasy and of agony, is understood by all because it is the voice of nature. The strong emotions of the heart all seek expression in modulation of sound; and religious sentiment is both awakened and calmed by music which lifts the soul out of the world of sense and elevates it towards the infinite and invisible. Nearer than anything else it expresses the inner relations and nature of beings; the universal order and harmony which is found even in seemingly discordant and jarring elements. It is the most spiritual of arts, and more than any other is degraded when perverted to low and sensuous uses.

"There is," says Cousin, "physically and morally a marvellous relation between a sound and the soul. It seems as though the soul were an echo in which the sound takes a new power."

Something of this kind Byron also felt:

> "Oh ! that I were
> The viewless spirit of a lovely sound,
> A living voice, a breathing harmony,
> A bodiless enjoyment, born and dying
> With the blest Tone that made me."

Music is the food of the soul in all its most
exalted moods. No other art has such power to
minister to the sublime dreams and limitless desires of the heart which aspires to God ; and therefore is it held that the man who has not music in
himself is fit only for base purposes and is but
sluggish earth. Without its softening and spiritual-
izing influence we grow wooden and coarse. At its
call the universal harmonies of nature stir within
us—" birds, voices, instruments, winds, waters, all
agree."

> " I was all ear,
> And took in strains that might create a soul
> Under the ribs of death."

He who cultivates music, said the ancients, imi-
tates the gods ; and therefore Plato wrote that " we
must not judge of music by the pleasure it gives,
nor prefer that whose only object is pleasure, but
that which in itself bears a resemblance to the
beautiful."

It was, St. Augustine says, sweet psalmody
which made the lives of the monks of old so harmonious ; and St. Columba, as in far-off Iona he
dreamed of Erin, thought nothing there so lovely
as the winds that sighed among the oak-groves,
and the songs of the birds, and the monks who
sang like the birds.

There is doubtless a music as vast as creation,
embracing all sounds, all noises in their numberless
combinations, and rising from the bosom of discord
in boundless and harmonious swell — the hymn
which the universe chants to God. From the dew-

drop that murmurs its inward delight as it kisses
the rose-leaf, to the deep and infinite voice of the
ocean, sounding like the heart-pant of creation for
rest; from the reed that sighs upon the river-bank,
to the sad and solemn wail of the primeval forest;
from the bee that sings upon the wing among the
flowers, to the lion who goeth forth into the desert
alone and awakens the sleeping echoes of the everlasting hills; from the nightingale who disburdens
his full throat of all its music, to man, whose very
soul rises on the palpitating bosom of song from
world to world up to God's own heaven—all nature
is vocal in a divine concert. " There is music in
all things, if men had ears."

As the numberless ideas which are the forms of
our knowledge are but the broken rays which in
the mind of God combine to create the pure white
light of truth and are one, so the infinite variety
of sounds rises up to him and is harmony.

> " From harmony, from heavenly harmony,
>   This universal frame began.
>   From harmony to harmony
>   Through all the compass of the notes it ran,
>   The diapason closing full in man."

The soul's most transparent veil is the human
voice, in whose true accent we best catch a man's
real self; since modulation of sound is the most
proper expression of all emotion.

Music gives repose like prayer or the presence
of friends, because it satisfies the heart. The mind
is prosaic; the soul poetic and musical. *Sympho-
nialis est anima.* " The soul," said Joubert, " sings

to itself of all beauty." Silence is golden only to
those who have power to hear divine melodies—
songs of angels and symphonies of heaven. Silence is the setting of music, its light and background ; and therefore melody is sweetest in solitude—in the night or in sacred convent walls that
shut in from the noisy, babbling world souls whose
hearts beat time to celestial strains and waft to
heaven sighs that are heard of whispering angels.
The Catholic Church loves to follow her divine
Founder into the desert, and to lift up her eyes to
the hills from whence cometh help. In solitude
she sings; her hymns rise in concert with the
winds that sigh through the oak-groves and faint
upon the desert's burning sands. She loves the
mysteriousness of nature, so silent and so musical,
resting and thrilling beneath God's brooding spirit.
Song is the voice of prayer, which is the breathing
of the soul in God's presence. Did not the angels
sing when Christ was born, and shall man be dumb
now that he lives and conquers and is adored?
God is essential harmony, the works of his hand
are harmonious, and his great precept is Love,
which is the source and soul and highest expression of harmony. The soul that loves sings for
joy and gratitude.

What divine and celestial accents has the church
not found to speak her love and sorrow, her faith
and hope!

What sound more heavenly does hill or vale
prolong or multiply than the voice of the bell, filling all the air, far and near, with benediction, until,

as the last peal dies away, heaven and earth grow
still and the Lord's day is sanctified? It has a
human sense and sympathy. Now it rings out
strong and clear like a shout from the heart of a
boy; and now its mellow notes dwell and linger
like sweet memories of childhood. In the solemn
night it seems God's warning voice; and then, pitiless as fate, it beats with iron stroke the hours that
make the little life of man.

The organ, the master-instrument, is the voice
of the Christian Church, "the seraph-haunted
queen of harmony," sounding like an echo from a
mystic and hidden world. How full and deep
and strong it rolls out its great volume of sound—
an ocean of melody! Now it bursts forth with
irresistible power like the hosts of stars when first
they wheeled into their orbits and shouted to God;
and now, with a veiled and mysterious harmony, it
wraps itself around the soul, shuts out all noise,
and composes it to sweet, heavenly contemplation.
It is tender as a mother's yearning, and fierce as
the deaf and raging sea; sad as angels' sighs for
souls that are lost; plaintive and pitiful as the cry
of those who in purgatorial fires cleanse their sins;
and then its notes faint and die, until we hear their
echoes from the eternal shore where they grow for
ever and for ever. With the falling day we enter
the great cathedral's sacred gloom, and at once
are in a vast solitude. The huge pillars rise in
giant strength, upholding the high vault already
shrouded in the gathering darkness, and silence
sits mute in the wide aisle. Suddenly we have

been carried into another world, peopled with other beings. We cease to note the passage of time, and earth, with its garish light and distracting noises, has become a dream. As the eye grows accustomed to the gloom we are able to observe the massive building. Its walls rise like the sides of a steep mountain, and in the aisles there is the loneliness and mystery of deep valleys into which the sunlight never falls. From these adamantine flancs countless beings start forth, until the whole edifice is peopled with fantastic forms, upon which falls the mystic light, reflected from the counte-nances of angels, patriarchs, apostles, virgins, mar-tyrs, who from celestial windows look down upon this new-born world. In the distance we see the glimmering taper that burns before God's presence, and then suddenly a great volume of sound, like the divine breath infusing life into these inanimate objects, rolls over us, and every stone from pave-ment to vaulted roof thrills and vibrates; each sculptured image and pictured saint is vocal; and from on high the angels lend their voices, until the soul, trembling on the wings of hope and love, is borne upward with this heavenly harmony, and, entranced in prayer, worships the Invisible alone.

In no art is the influence of the Christian religion more discernible than in painting; and here, as elsewhere, its dominant characteristic is spirituality —the placing the idea above the form. It gave to art the most exalted ideals—Christ and his immacu-late Mother; and the necessary effect of the con-templation of these models was the subordina-

28

tion of physical to moral beauty. It could no longer be the artist's aim to paint a comely and finely-formed body, but a body ennobled, purified, and spiritualized by a generous, unselfish, and sympathetic soul. A pure faith gave exalted aims, fixed purpose, and seriousness to art. It was no longer sufficient to be elegant and graceful; it was necessary, above all, to speak to the mind and the soul. All levity and frivolity were banished. A noble earnestness illumined the human countenance, softened only by a smile of loving tenderness such as is seen on the Virgin's face as she contemplates the divine Infant reposing in her arms. We cannot think of Christ as laughing or entering into gay or lively discourse ; nor can we so think of his Mother. There is self-satisfaction and egotism in all merriment. The love and pity of the God-man admit not the play of childish joy upon his sacred features—we catch there the expression of repose which comes of strength; of sweet, sad sympathy, of ineffable goodness, yet mingled with the awful earnestness of him who is Judge as well as Saviour, but whose justice is tempered with, mercy. In the Blessed Virgin there is a more human sweetness and light ; a grace that seems even more tender because her only office is that of love. Under this high influence art acquired new power and seemed to feel Christ's blessing—the peace which the world knows not. It learned the secret of repose, without which it has been said no work of art can be great, and which is the measure of all artistic excellence :

"The life where hope and memory are as one ;
Earth quiet and unchanged ; the human soul
Consistent in self rule ; and heaven revealed
To meditation, in that quietness."

Purity—the quality of soul most nearly akin to the spiritual and divine nature—became an essential requisite of human beauty and lifted Christian art into a world unknown to paganism. The material universe was looked upon as symbolical of a higher and nobler mode of existence, so that the body itself in the artist's contemplation was spiritualized—grew light and aerial, such as St. Paul describes it rising from death incorruptible and immortal. From this type the Christian artist derived the angelical form, as seen, for example, in Perugino's Michael, the Archangel—" with his triple crest of traceless plumes unshaken in heaven, his hand fallen on his crossleted sword, the truth girdle binding his undinted armor ; God has put his power upon him, resistless radiance is on his limbs, no lines are there of earthly strength, no traces on the divine features of earthly anger ; trustful and thoughtful, fearless but full of love, incapable except of the repose of eternal conquest, vessel and instrument of Omnipotence, filled like a cloud with the victor light, the dust of principalities and powers beneath his feet, the murmur of hell against him heard by his spiritual ear like the winding of a shell on the far-off sea-shore."

The body itself aspires to a spiritual state, and seeks to harmonize its gross elements with the soul, to bring back life's rosy dawn, when both

were one, like sweet music set to noble words.
The eye of faith sees more clearly the conditions and possibilities of the diviner life—catches
glimpses of things unutterable, too bright "to
hit the sense of human sight." The communion
of saints exists; angels watch over us; the loved
who have gone before us are not parted from
us; prayer rises like fragrant incense to heaven,
falls like dew upon souls who purge their guilt in
unknown worlds. This high companionship with
things unseen makes flesh and blood a wearisome
burden to the soul, and it cries out, "Who will free
me from this body of death?" The noblest natures, no longer able to endure contact with the
crowd sunk in sensuous indulgence, flee to the desert; in solitude find the untainted air of God's
presence; shake from the free Christian spirit all
manacles of deadly servitude; and, rebaptized in
silence and prayer, rise, like eagles new-bathed in
ocean, to purer worlds.

> " How beautiful your presence, how benign,
>   Servants of God ! who not a thought will share
>   With the vain world.
>
>   .   .   .   , ...
>   More sweet than odors caught by him who sails
>   Near spicy shores of Araby the blest,
>   A thousand times more exquisitely sweet
>   The freight of holy feeling which we meet
>   In thoughtful moments wafted by the gales
>   From fields where good men walk or bowers wherein
>   they rest."

This higher life created a higher art. This is
evident in the earliest records of Christian art. In

the paintings of the Catacombs there is a celestial purity, a translucence of soul, a predominance of spirit over matter, of faith over sense, which render these works, in spite of technical defects, infinitely superior to all art which draws its inspiration from less exalted ideals. Here art is pure and noble, because here is a sublime religious faith which gives to human life a transcendental and priceless dignity and worth. In the simplest and meekest face that looks upon us from those subterranean walls we behold the power of the faith which overcomes the world, which can give to a timid maiden a strength that conquers armies and empires, which makes death sweet as the breath of morning, and through defeat rises ever to diviner victories, triumphing in its martyrdom. It is truth and purity and love, habited in weakness and poverty, that rises up to strike dumb the loud and blatant world, with its shams and shows, carnal souls and hollow hearts.

On the walls of these hidden cities, in whose dark and silent streets we can almost feel the presence of the generations of martyrs, of whom the world was not worthy, and who in the narrow way walked towards the life and the light, there is the sublimest symbolical teaching. The Phœnix, rising from its ashes, proclaims the immortality of the soul, the triumph of spirit over matter, and the final resurrection ; the three youths in the fiery furnace declare that out of the jaws of hell God delivers those who put their trust in him ; and Pharao's army, swallowed up by the devouring sea,

shout from the mad turmoil that God only is great,
that it is vain to trust in princes, that they who
walk by faith securely tread where the mighty fall.
Here Abraham so believes in God against the
whole earth that he lifts the knife to slay his only
son ; from hard and flinty rock Moses strikes the
water of life ; and Isaias, with keen vision, piercing
the thick veil that hides the future from mortal
eyes, sees God's Virgin Mother rising like a fair
and lonely star upon the ebon brow of night, light-
ing a sin-darkened world; or the Good Shepherd,
on shoulders bruised by the cross of love, bears
home the sheep that had strayed from the fold and
was lost.

In all this there is high art, and greatness of
style, because the subjects of thought involve universal interests and profound passions.

Besides noble subjects and seriousness of purpose, the Christian religion gave to art exalted
aims.   It became holy and sought to sanctify men.
Artistic fraternities were religious associations.
" By the grace of God," said the Siennese painters
in 1355, " we are to rule men, who know not letters,
manifestors of the miraculous things worked by
virtue and in virtue of the holy faith; and our
faith is founded principally in adoring and believing one God in the Trinity—a God of infinite
power, infinite wisdom, infinite love and mercy."

" We aim," said Buffalmacco, " at naught else
than to make saints by our frescoes and pictures ;
and, in spite of the devils, to make men more devout
and holy."

All those early painters, so justly called the "great masters," worked in faith, with religious sincerity, without thought of gold or sordid motive, caring not to please the vicious taste of an ignorant public, but only to approve themselves to Him who is the great and eternal artist.

What delicacy, purity, and devotion are traceable in every line of Giotto's works!—the oldest, and in some sense the greatest, of the Italian masters.

Cennini, an artist of the early part of the fifteenth century, and widely known through his *Treatise on Painting*, insists especially in this work on the moral discipline required to form the Christian artist. He must abstain from all sinful indulgence, eat sparingly, remain often in solitude, learn self-restraint; and, since he is to be a teacher of holiness, he must himself be holy, and to this end must go regularly to confession and communion. Cennini declares that the use of good colors, especially in painting the Blessed Virgin, is a religious duty, and he adds that if the painter be underpaid, "God and Our Lady will reward him in body and soul."

Taddeo Gaddi, the godson and pupil of Giotto, who after the death of the master was appointed to complete the Campanile of Florence, when dying consigned his son to Casentino with the injunction to teach him the practice of art and the duties of a Christian.

Lippo Dalmasio, a Carmelite monk, never painted a religious subject without preparing himself by meditation, prayer, and fasting; and so wonderful was his success that Guido Reni could not contemplate his pictures of the Blessed Virgin without falling into a kind of ecstasy, and Pope Clement VIII. declared that he had never seen images more devout or that touched his heart nearer. He refused resolutely to touch money, but painted solely for the love of God and his blessed Mother.

Frà Angelico, the most religious and heavenly of all artists, painted Christ and Mary only on his knees; and when engaged on the Crucifixion a flood of tears burst from his eyes. He prayed constantly, smiled seldom, wept often, and never harbored an impure thought. His head rested on the heart of Jesus, and nothing had power to disturb him. All men have agreed to call him Angel and Blessed. In his Virgin we behold the very chastity and beauty of heaven incarnate, and of his angels Michael Angelo said that no man could paint them who had not seen them in some higher world. Only the pure of heart can depict the purest and sublimest sentiments, and they who paint Christ and his angels must be Christ-like and angelical: " Blessed are the pure of heart, for they shall see God."

No one, while looking upon the paintings of Beato Angelico, can harbor a revengeful or lustful thought. They influence us like the presence of holy and noble natures. They are the exponents of Spirit, and we cannot contemplate them without inwardly shrinking from whatever is sensual. There is in them a tenderness and repose, a love and peace, which, far above the storm-clouds and blinding dust of earth, breathe the air of heaven. Not less than in the tone and accent of a saintly man do we catch in these Madonnas and cherubs the hidden secret of the inward, diviner life. Faith and love inspired Angelico, and one who drank from fountains less pure or deep could not have unveiled to mortal eyes such celestial loveliness. The religious artist makes art religious. Never yet was there true poet who did not believe in his wildest dreams, nor can an artist paint what he believes not to exist. All art which is insincere is false; and deep, abiding sincerity can come only of religious inspiration. Without this the love of the beautiful, the pursuit of art for its own sake, degenerates into dilettanteism.

The great religious artists painted for the people, for believing souls, who were eager not to admire, but to worship, and who longed for symbols of their faith. Their masterpieces were never made to hang on the walls of the wealthy, to be gazed at as objects of curiosity or artistic skill. Demosthenes spoke not with more earnestness or deep conviction than they painted. They were able, because they believed.

To ask with Ruskin whether art has done good to religion is to put a meaningless question. If it has not served religion, it is condemned; for man's eternal and highest interests are religious. It is, moreover, impossible that a great and living faith should not symbolize itself in some great art. David sang and danced before the ark, and in all time the soul, feeling God's presence, will be tormented by a voiceless thought till art gives it relief. All true prayer is poetic and musical, and to whine and drawl when we supplicate God is as little proper as to stand bolt upright and speak to him as though he were some common mortal with official patronage to bestow.

Whosoever loves longs for poetry, music, song, pictures, flowers, or whatsoever else is beautiful, though the meanest object is ennobled if it be but associated with this passion. Religion is love, higher and diviner, more real and all-enduring than any other — a love which can make the desert bloom, people solitudes, light the dark-vaulted dungeon, make slavery sweet, disease a pleasant companion, and death a welcome guest. To him who feels this divine ardor kingdoms and principalities are but the dust he treads upon; fame, discordant babble; and all the ways and hopes of the world vain and purposeless as the rambles of a child. To him naught is but what is eternal; and in all corruptible things he sees an image of God's immortal glory. From basest matter his faith forms wings with which he would raise himself to companionship with Heaven. He longs for symbols which, by expressing, however poorly, his sense of God's presence, may strengthen and define his faith and hope and love. His strong desire creates, religion is clothed with beauty, and art is born.

Protestantism has produced no religious art, and no other argument is needed to prove that it is without deep religious faith. Its life is feverish

and artificial, not profound and interior. It's energy is drawn from strife and opposition, dissensions and controversies. It is tormented by the
spirit of unrest, it has no peace, and therefore can
have no art. It is critical, and therefore without
reverence ; it is self-conscious, and therefore without humility ; it is worldly, and therefore without
exalted ideals ; it is uncontemplative, and therefore without tenderness.

Having not within itself the deep fountains of
faith and love from which art draws its life, it by
instinct strove to shut religion within the soul.
It turned from all the Christian glories and hero-
isms of the past, virginities and martyrdoms, struggles and triumphs, defeats and victories, feeling it
had no part in them. It became censorious and
lost sympathy ; saw the evil, but passed by the
good with averted look. When it was ascetic it
was harsh and forbidding ; when it was self-indul-
gent it was vulgar and coarse ; when it was enthu-
siastic it was wild and fanatic. It has no ideals.
Its very founders refused to lend themselves to the
purposes of art. Luther was violent and gross ;
Henry, cruel and debauched ; Calvin, heartless and
vindictive ; Knox, coarse and barbarous. Its relations to womanhood were no better. It despised
virginity, and degraded marriage by destroying its
sacramental character and by admitting divorce.
Luther violated the sacredness of woman consecrated by chastity, and Henry alternated between lust
and murder. From the Virgin Mother it turned
away with horror, thinking to honor Jesus by scorn-

ing her who bore him. It never understood that imagination, not less than intellect, is the organ of the Godlike, or that the visible universe is the bodying forth of the invisible. By an instinct as shallow as it is opposed to art it shrank from mystery and entered on the fatal way that leads to scepticism and materialism. To man nothing is divine that is not clothed in mystery. Pluck away the fair, clustering flowers that over-wreath, protect, and sweeten man's life, filling it with charm and wonder, and there remains but a bare carcass fit for Darwinian experimentation. Our God is a hidden God— Christ is seen now no more, except in those who lead with him the silent, secret life which the animal eye perceiveth not. He comes to us not openly, as once he walked in Galilee, but veiled in sacramental rites and sacred symbols. In the Breaking of the Bread we know him, and in the silence of deep meditation, when the door is shut and the windows closed, he stands before us. God has symbolized himself in all the universe ; the heavens are his vesture, the earth is his footstool, and from sun and moon and star he speaks to man ; a gleam of his countenance is reflected from the circumambient eternity on this little islet of time.

And what does the church in all her worship but imitate, as best she may, God's own work? What is the pomp and splendor of her ceremonial compared with the glories of nature? Or how can it be wrong in her who knows not the guilty folly of Manicheism to seek to raise man to heaven by the chords that bind him to earth?

Then she is the mother of the people; comes nearer to their hearts than any other, as Jesus alone loves the poor; and for them criticism and science are not, but only faith and hope and love. They want no lecture-hall, with its bare walls and prosing teacher, but a temple of religion—the home of the multitude, where every art and noble gift of man bows in homage to God's presence. Therefore must she build for Christ and his poor, the temple of majesty and glory, the democratic palace of the people, where the beggar and the prince kneel side by side—a basilica prouder than that of kings, where all the arts are wedded and find a sanctuary in the divine harmony which religion alone can consecrate and make eternal.

> " This long-roofed vista penetrate—but see,
>   One after one, its tablets, that unfold
>   The whole design of Scripture history,
>   From the first tasting of the fatal tree
>   Till the bright star appeared in Eastern skies
>   Announcing One was born mankind to free;
>   His acts, his wrongs, his sacrifice:
>   Lessons for every heart, a Bible for all eyes."

Whether or not religion need the service of art, art certainly can never flourish except in her service; for of all things it requires the consecration of an exalted and unselfish purpose. He who works for money or praise may work cunningly and admirably, but never divinely. Between art and money or men's praise there is no equivalence, as there is none between mind and matter, beauty and use. Nor is there inspiration in art for art's sake. The phrase is meaningless; for, if art is not the symbol of a divine reality, it is frivolous and childish. To be great and worthy, it must be born on the holy mountain where God's law is given, and in the temple where he is worshipped. As soon as men stop to think whether it is dear, or what use there is in it, its soul is fled and materialism smothers all spiritual faith. It is of no avail to preach to those "who love the corn they grind, and the grapes they crush, better than the gardens of the angels upon the slopes of Eden." If man is only an animal, and the world his manger, let him eat the hay and the thistle and be blest. If there is no good in holy thoughts, in limitless desires, in unutterable longings for the highest and the best, in the faith that trusts that God is Love and is just, in the sweet hope that in a better world there is a more restful life, then indeed may men hold that God's temple is but a mill or bank, and should be taxed lest it be made beautiful.

If the people who work and suffer, begrimed with the dust and smoke and soil of earth, shut out from companionship with nature, are to have no home of the soul, no place of repose, no tabernacle of God's presence, no symbol of heaven, where every art conspires to raise the mind and heart to the invisible and higher world, then let the law make it impossible for them to retain the churches which they have built; and God pity them! He who made the heavens and the earth is not shut up in houses built by the hands of man. He dwells in his own immensity; the universe is

his temple; the sun the inextinguishable lamp
that burns before his presence; the stars the
lights that shine upon his altar; and in this vast
and divine temple all creatures adore him and
proclaim his glory; and the spheres, as they re-
volve, sing in his praise an immortal hymn. God
needs not the temples which we build to him; of
man and his works he is for ever independent.
But we who crave for God, and who, without him,
perish like the brute and have no hope, must have
sanctuaries, religious rites and symbols, to prevent
the heavenly spirit of faith and love from escaping
and losing itself in boundless and empty space.
From the crowd the thought of God is banished;
men dig into the earth and sail the seas for food
and raiment; they would make the sun and moon
pull their wagons; turn all nature to low uses, and
beneath the grinding wheels of mechanism crush
the soul.   Let us at least leave to man God's temple—the great soul-symbol, where he can still
breathe the air of heaven, and weep and pray.

> " The spirit of antiquity—enshrined
> In sumptuous buildings, vocal in sweet song,
> In picture, speaking with heroic tongue,
> And with devout solemnities entwined—
> Strikes to the seat of grace within the mind."

Did not He who is for ever the founder of the
religion of the soul, and only Saviour of man, fulfil all holy observances? He loved the beauty of
God's house, was often in the temple, kept fast
and feast, was circumcised, sent the lepers to the

priests for the sin-offering, paid the temple-tax, and performed all other offices of a ceremonial worship. He received the baptism of John; he breathed upon his apostles; he rubbed the mud-paste upon the eyes of the blind man; he commanded the anointing with oil. Of course, while the blessed Saviour walked among men, and for a long time after he had returned to the Father, Christian worship was of the simplest kind. No various ceremonies, no rich music, no high cathedrals, no mystic vestments, no solemn altars, no marbles or metals or jewels, or woods of cost, or fine linen, added splendor to the celebration of the divine mysteries. Christ instituted the most holy Sacrament of his real presence in an " upper room" of a hired house; in an " upper room " the Holy Ghost descended upon the Apostles, waiting and watching in silence and in prayer; in an " upper room " St. Paul preached in Troas; at Philippi he led the faithful outside the city to the river-bank where prayer was wont to be made; and with Silas he sang hymns in prison. St. Peter was praying on the house-top when he saw the vision, and Philip baptized the Ethiopian eunuch in the desert. Having no power or liberty to build churches to God, the apostolic Christians made the whole world his temple and offered to him everywhere the sacrifice of noble lives and heroic deaths. Their immediate successors were driven from the face of the earth into caverns, tombs, and subterranean galleries; but when from the darkness and the death of the Catacombs they issued forth like Christ from the grave, triumphant and immortal, God inspired them, as the Israelites of old who had passed through the parted waters and the desert into the Land of Promise, to build temples not unworthy of the faith which had conquered the world.

In nothing is the spirit of a religion more clearly seen than in the style of its sacred edifices. The character of the temple is determined by our conception of God and of the service which we owe him. The Greeks, plunged in mad delight in the enjoyments of this life and unconscious of a higher existence, thought their gods were stronger men, with greater passions and more ardent cravings for indulgence. Consequently their temples take the form of human dwellings, of wonderful grace and symmetry, harmony of lines and proportions; but without grandeur, mystery, or sublimity. In the dark mysteries of the religion of ancient Egypt death is the predominant thought; and its temple is a tomb, sad, solitary, motionless. This correspondence between architecture and religious faith is most discernible in the Christian temple, which is the highest symbol of the universe, as God's handiwork, ever created by human genius. It is the House of God not because it is consecrated to his worship, but because he dwells there really and truly under the sacramental veil; and it is his divine presence which gives to the whole edifice its form, its appropriateness, and its meaning, as the mind of God creates, moves, and harmonizes the universe. The vital principle in the Christian temple is the Real Presence. Take this away and it is a body without a soul. Therefore the whole edifice grows out of the tabernacle, and draws from it use and beauty, as from the heart the members are developed and by it are nourished. He is there—the mysterious and awful God, but the God of love, of beauty, of mercy. Banished, therefore, be all frivolity, all profane mirth, all trivial joy. Here are we in the presence of infinite mystery; the ground is holy, unseen spirits are adoring. How the great vault lifts itself to heaven, bending in mighty joy above the tabernacle! And the wide aisle opens out in limitless expanse, levelling the mountains and making straight the way of the Lord. The temple is a cross; its centre the tabernacle, and Christ is adored for ever in the divinest symbol of his love, which is borne upward on aërial spires far above all monuments of human pride, shedding benediction and gentler life through the world's waste. The whole edifice, and each separate part, rises secure and strong heavenward like the flight of angels. It is a universal temple, fit symbol of a catholic religion. All nature is here. Stones, and metals, and woods of cost, moss and lichen, and all kinds of grasses and plants cover its walls and entwine themselves around its columns. Reptiles, and monsters of the deep, birds of the air, and all animals that walk the earth, are gathered here, for God created them all. And last, as in the world's history, comes man to interpret the mystery and to be God's image and minister. He gives intelligence and a voice to this new creation.

At his touch the rock takes a human form ; saints and angels appear within the holy place ; the incense gives forth its fragrant breath ; the great organ, standing in lone royalty, utters its deep and mystic voice ; and stone, and moss, and plant, and living things of earth, air, and sea join the choir to chant to God the universal hymn of praise.

> "And, while the Host is raised, its elevation
> An awe and supernatural horror breeds,
> And all the people bow their heads like reeds
> To a soft breeze, in lowly adoration."

This is the temple of religion, type of the Church which God has reared.

THE LIFE

OF THE

Most Rev. M. J. Spalding, D.D.,

ARCHBISHOP OF BALTIMORE,

BY

RT. REV. J. L. SPALDING, D.D.,

Bishop of Peoria.

———————◄◆►———————

CONTENTS.

It is published in the best style possible, and makes a volume of nearly five hundred pages 8vo, with portrait on steel.

Bevelled Cloth..................................**$4 00**

Address

The Catholic Publication Society,

LAWRENCE KEHOE, Gen. Agent,

9 BARCLAY ST., NEW YORK.

www.ingramcontent.com/pod-product-compliance
Lightning Source LLC
Chambersburg PA
CBHW021111270326
41929CB00009B/823